P9-DHP-578

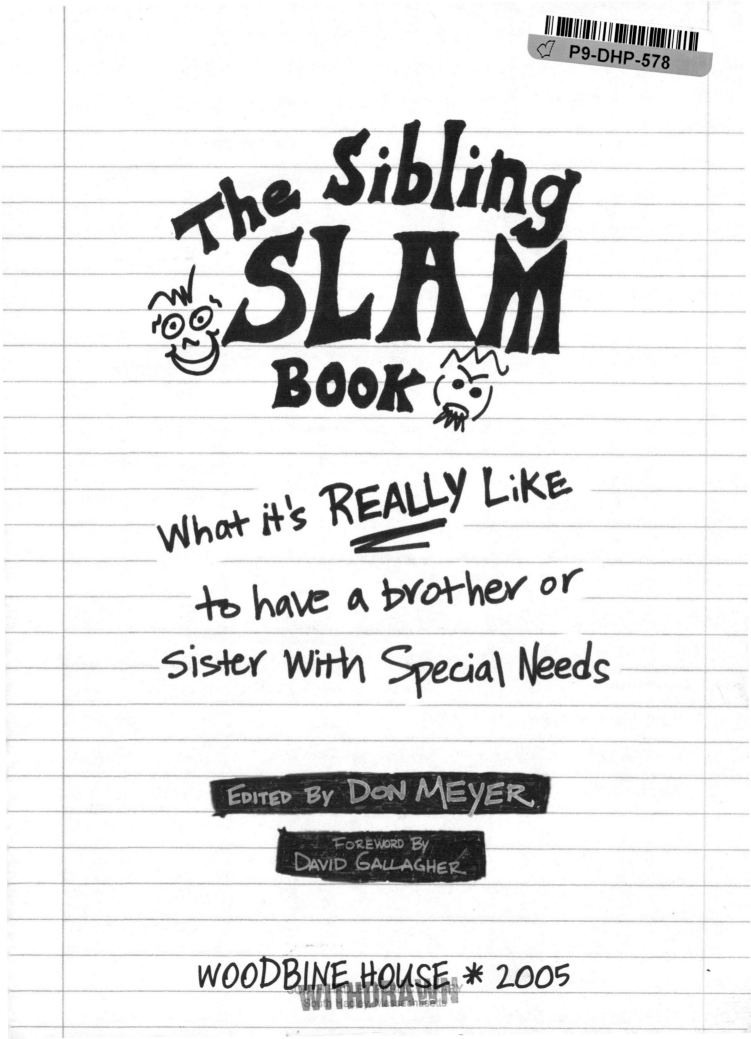

The Sibling SLAM Book

What it's REALLY Like to have a brother or sister With Special Needs

EDITED BY DON MEYER

FOREWORD BY DAVID GALLAGHER

WOODBINE HOUSE * 2005

WITHDRAWN
South Hadley, Massachusetts

For Terry

. SEP   2005

J 306.875

© 2005 Donald J. Meyer
All rights reserved.

Published in the United States of America by Woodbine House, Inc., 6510 Bells Mill Rd., Bethesda, MD 20817. 800-843-7323. www.woodbinehouse.com

Library of Congress Cataloging-in-Publication Data

The sibling slam book : what it's really like to have a brother or sister with special needs / edited by Donald Meyer.
   p. cm.
 ISBN 1-890627-52-6 (pbk.)
 1. Children with disabilities--Family relationships. 2. Children with disabilities--Home care. 3. Brothers and sisters. I. Meyer, Donald J. (Donald Joseph), 1951-
  HQ773.6.S58 2005
  306.875'3--dc22

2004022915

Manufactured in the United States of America

10   9   8   7   6   5   4   3   2   1

LIST OF QUESTIONS

FOREWORD

by David Gallagher

My little brother is the coolest kid. His name is Killian and he was diagnosed with autism when he was three. Between working on **7TH HEAVEN** and attending college, I'm not at home as much as I used to be. But when I am, it's the greatest thing—usually! Killian certainly lets me know that he's glad to see me. We play video games for hours and listen to music. Killian lip-syncs the words and makes funny faces and we spend most of the time laughing.

But life with Killian can be frustrating, too. Sometimes he acts like a baby when he doesn't get what he wants or tries to do something that might get him hurt or in trouble. He reverts to crying like an infant and that can be really annoying. I always try to be patient, and in a lot of ways, Killian has taught me patience—but it is still annoying.

Life with Killian is your basic mixed bag.

That's why I love **THE SIBLING SLAM BOOK**. It's great to read about sibs who are experiencing the same things I am and feeling what I often feel. It lets you know you're not alone!

As I read the questions and answers, it reminded me of the emotional rollercoaster my family has been on with Killian. It reminded me why my brother is so special to me and voiced the frustration I often feel about the things that aren't so special. In a lot of important ways, this book acknowledges the unsung heroes in the lives of kids with special needs: their siblings.

Many thanks to Don Meyer and all the authors for asking me to be a part of this wonderful project. It's a brilliant way to let brothers and sisters know there are other people out there just like them.

David Gallagher
Actor, 7TH HEAVEN, The WB Network
Youth Ambassador, CAN (Cure Autism Now)

INTRODUCTION

A million years ago—1965, in fact, I was in eighth grade. For us, one of the highlights of the secret world of eighth grade was slam books. Slam books were simply altered spiral notebooks. On the first page of the slam book would be a list of the contributors, usually a number, followed by just a name. On following pages, the creator of the slam book would post a question at the top of each page (for example, what is your favorite color?).

As the slam book was secretly passed around the classroom, each person would write his/her answers to the questions posed. (I still remember one classmate's response to the above question: frog-s--t green.) Usually, contributors ignored the page's ruled lines and instead of signing their opinions, they would simply underline their response and put their number below the line. (Slam books, as it turns out, are still around. There are even online versions.)

A million years later—2003, in fact, I found myself hosting SibKids, a listserv for young brothers and sisters of kids with various special needs. Besides writing about school, movies, books, politics, TV, and (oh yeah) their brothers and sisters, SibKids members would sometimes ask each other questions, often in the form of a survey. Because they are so wise and funny and have so much to say, **The Sibling Slam Book Project** was born.

With the help of the SibKids list, we generated almost 200 questions and pared them down to the 54 questions you see here. We included questions that have nothing to do with having a sib with special needs because, hey, that's only one part of their lives. We then put the word out about the project to sibs everywhere, with the results you'll find on these pages. In case you didn't hear about this project when we were writing it, don't worry! We've left space for you to add your own answers to each question.

I am in awe of the brothers and sisters who shared their lives, thoughts, opinions, and insights as we created this book. Their sibs, their friends, and their families are lucky to have them in their lives—and we're lucky to have their thoughts!

Don Meyer
Director, the Sibling Support Project
The Arc of the United States

What should we know about you?

(contributors listed alphabetically by their first name.)

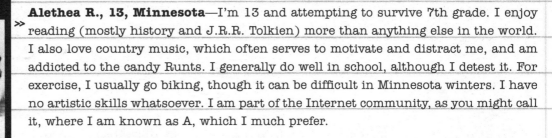

>> **Alethea R., 13, Minnesota**—I'm 13 and attempting to survive 7th grade. I enjoy reading (mostly history and J.R.R. Tolkien) more than anything else in the world. I also love country music, which often serves to motivate and distract me, and am addicted to the candy Runts. I generally do well in school, although I detest it. For exercise, I usually go biking, though it can be difficult in Minnesota winters. I have no artistic skills whatsoever. I am part of the Internet community, as you might call it, where I am known as A, which I much prefer.

>> **Ali N., 18, Massachusetts**—I live in a small city right near Salem, Massachusetts. I'm in my first year of college where I am studying liberal arts. I am the oldest of three; I have a sister, Becky, who is 13 and has Williams syndrome and a brother, Tommy, who is 10 and has severe autism. We also have Macauleigh, our 10-year-old cocker spaniel. I love body art and piercings. I have 3 tattoos—a Green Day one on my arm, because Green Day has been my favorite band and my savior since 4th grade, a peace sign on my right forearm, and a big green dancing monkey on my left leg I like to call "Al." I am a vegetarian and really do believe John Lennon was right when he said, "All you Need is Love."

>> **Alicia F., 17, Illinois**—I'm a senior at a high school outside of Chicago. I have a huge passion for working with people with disabilities and have coached Special Olympics for 8 years. I also have a huge passion for dolphins! I play on the girls' varsity golf team. I have experienced a lot in my life, but I've learned so much.

>> **Alisa A., 18, Oregon**—I am currently a freshman at Chemeketa Community College, studying dental hygiene. In high school, I was a cheerleader in the choir for all 4 years. Our choir received a Grammy, and won the 4A State champs my senior year and my cheerleading squad placed 2nd at State my junior year. I also love pottery and will hopefully be getting a wheel soon so I can make bowls, cups, and other things. I was a dancer for 10 years out of my life and greatly miss dancing; it was a relaxing way of getting away from everything in my life.

>> **Alli J., 15, Ohio**—I am in 10th grade at a public high school with about 2000 kids. Some of my favorite hobbies include acting and singing and I am actively involved in the Covenant Church. Although I am very open-minded about religion, I am very faithful to my religion. At school, I am a very outgoing person and try to get along with everyone, although my sarcastic sense of humor annoys my friends sometimes. At home, I tend to be more moody and sensitive, and much less open-minded, although I can usually be persuaded to be more flexible.

>> **Allison S., 17, Connecticut**—I'm a senior at a Catholic high school near New Haven, Connecticut. I'm best described as artsy and classic.

>> **Amanda M., 19, Washington State**—I live in Washington, near Seattle, but I am currently a sophomore at Mount Holyoke College in Massachusetts. I am a pre-med, Anthropology major. My main interest is in forensic science and I want to be a medical examiner. I play in the college hand bell choir and work in the college health center.

>> **Amber C., 13, California**—I'm in 8th grade. I love reading and sports, especially basketball and soccer. I also like hanging out with my friends. I love art, and I play the clarinet.

>> **Amelia C., 18, Minnesota**—I am a senior in high school, and very, very busy. I live in Minnesota, and am in the midst of applying to colleges. I have two younger sisters; the middle one, Lucy, has a disability. It used to deeply bother me that she was handicapped, but not so much any more. I just recently turned 18, and am in cheerleading and theater this year. I work at Barnes and Noble; in my free time, I like to hang out with my friends and my boyfriend. And one day I hope to become a successful broadcast journalist.

>> **Amy McK., 16, Tennessee**—I am a junior in high school. I play tennis for my school in the spring and love to do anything involving camping and the outdoors. My favorite activity is horseback riding. Every summer I go to a girl's camp where I meet girls from all over the country and form everlasting friendships. This past summer I was captain of one of the teams at camp and it was an amazing experience. My favorite TV shows are Gilmore Girls, 7th Heaven, One Tree Hill, and CSI. I am obsessed with the colors green and yellow. My favorite type of music is country. I am also a lifeguard.

>> **Amy S., 15, Washington State**—I'm 15 and in 10th grade. I like to listen to music, do latch hook, read, and play with my puppy.

>> **Anna H., 15, North Carolina**—I'm a sophomore. I play field hockey and I am a cheerleader during basketball season, play the piano, and take art classes. I like to hang with my friends, sleep, and shop.

>> **Ariella M., 16, N.S.W.**—I live in Sydney, Australia. I have a twin sister, Maia, who has cerebral palsy. We have a younger brother, Max, who is 8 years old. My family is Jewish. I am in Grade 10 at school and my favourite subjects are English and Visual Art. My favourite things to do are watercolour painting, writing stories and letters, seeing friends, reading, and going on the internet.

>> **Ashley S., 13, Minnesota**—I am 13 years old and in 8th grade. I have Juvenile Rheumatoid Arthritis. I like to participate in band and choir and also enjoyed playing volleyball on my school's team this year. (I'm on the right!)

>> **Britny G., 16, Missouri**—I live in central Missouri. I'm in the 11th grade, and have ADD and depression. I love to read, write poems, go to church, swim, ride horseback, baby-sit, and a whole lot of other stuff. I am the oldest of 3 kids.

>> **Brooke W., 13 , Virginia** —I'm 13 years old and my birthday is in November. I've lived in Virginia (near DC) my whole life. I'm in 7th grade. I like to draw (and I'm pretty good at it, if I do say so myself) and create stuff. I have a large imagination, too. I'm going out for track in the spring. My event is long jump. I also like to write. I wear glasses even though I REALLY don't like them.

>> **Caitlin M., 14, Maryland**—My name is Caitlin, but most people just call me KK. I love to write, hang out with friends, play soccer, and do volunteer work, especially in the disability community. I have really awesome friends; my best friend and I are practically cousins! My parents are divorced and I would say that I have a good relationship with them both. My mom and I are very close; I would consider her my other best friend. I love cats; I have an orange tabby named Shoes who I've had since I was three.

>> **Calen P., 14, Michigan**—My name is Calen but my friends call me Cal. I am a freshman in high school and I live in southern Michigan. I play tennis, piano, percussion (drums), trombone, and guitar.

>> **Carly H., 17, Georgia**—I will soon be attending the University of Georgia. I am actively involved in community service and sports, both in and out of school. I love to travel, speak many languages, and immerse myself in different cultures. But the people I love the most are my family—they are my friends, my mentors, and my foundation in life. Because of my love for my family and passion for helping others, I wrote a book, **My eXtra Special Brother: How to Love, Understand, and Celebrate Your Sibling with Special Needs**. I hope to help others see how awesome it can be to grow up with a sibling with special needs.

>> **Cassandra W., 15, Iowa**—I live in the eastern part of Iowa. I'm a junior and enjoy football cheerleading, basketball, 4-H, FFA, S.O.D.A., and choir.

>> **Cassey C., 15, Southland, N.Z.**—My name is Cassey and I'm almost 15 years old. I live in Invercargill, which is at the bottom of the South Island in New Zealand and in the province of Southland. I'm schooled at home—and I like my school! I am in year 10/11. My favourite sports are snowboarding and soccer. I enjoy learning the guitar and piano. I go to ATC (Air Training Corp) which I really enjoy. I have a 100cc motorbike that I ride on the beach and train for racing. My family and I like to do a lot of camping during school holidays.

>> **Cassie W., 13, Colorado**—I live in Colorado where I was born. I am in the 7th grade. I play competitive soccer for the U13 Nova girls gold team, and play basketball for the Colorado Wild. At school, I help with the Special Olympics programs (soccer, basketball.) I also like to sing and used to practice with a voice teacher.

>> **Catherine C., 13, California**—I am in 8th grade at a K-8 private school. I play volleyball, softball, soccer, lacrosse, and the piano. I really want to learn how to wind surf, too. My hobbies are reading and making jewelry. I like to sing and I do in public—but nothing can compare to the humiliation I felt when I messed up the first line of "The Hills Are Alive" in the school talent show.

>> **Christiana R., 13, Wisconsin**—I'll be in 8th grade next year. I live in eastern Wisconsin, have dark brown eyes and medium brown hair, and am about 5' 10" tall. My favorite sports are volleyball and tennis. I play cello and piano and sing a lot. I love theatre. When I'm not working on a show, I like to go shopping or travel. My most recent trip was to Germany for the second time. When I grow up, I want to either be a 1st grade teacher or be on Broadway.

>> **Daniel C., 17, Illinois**—I am from the great state of Illinois. I live with my mom, my dad, my little sister, and my little brother who has special needs. I enjoy video games, ultimate Frisbee, the guitar, reading, and hanging out with my friends. I get pretty good grades in school and I want to become a microbiologist and research treatments for new diseases. I am a member of our school's chess team, but that doesn't mean I am good at chess. I am also in J.E.T.S. and the Science Club along with the community service club. I am an Eagle Scout and I help out my troop whenever I can. Other than that, I am just a regular high school senior who wants to graduate and head on off to college as soon as possible. I have been to Space Camp and won the Outstanding Camper award there. I have also won several awards for my writing and I hope to use my talents to benefit the world.

>> **Dave S., 14, Michigan**—I live on an island 30 miles off the coast of Lake Michigan. I'm going into 9th grade and love to play soccer.

>> **Elizabeth T., 19, Oklahoma**—I'm 19 and a sophomore at a Christian university in Tulsa, Oklahoma, where I am a government major with an emphasis in pre-law and a double minor in technical writing and French. I've lived in Tulsa most of my life. I play many sports, but mainly tennis and fencing. I also play tenor saxophone and play in ensembles in school and in the band at my church. I work as a library assistant for a seminary where my father is a dean. My mother is a university instructor, but they're divorced.

>> Emily D., 18, Virginia —I'm a freshman at a university in Northern Virginia. I clock in at about 5'1" with brown hair and blue/green eyes. On campus, I am active with Campus Crusade for Christ and do a lot of charity work b/c it is my favorite thing in the world—helping others, that is. After college, I want to join the Peace Corps because I want to serve my country but am not cut out for the military. Oh yeah, I do not eat meat, been a veggie for two years.

>> Emily I., 15, Washington State—I am a sophomore in the International Baccalaureate program at a high school in southern Washington. I enjoy playing tennis and participating in school clubs. One of my great passions is young children. I have been babysitting and working with children at my church since I was 11. I also love being in leadership roles. I was very involved in student council in middle school and I am now activities coordinator for a community service club. I also enjoy reading, scrap booking, talking online, and hanging out with my friends.

>> Emily J., 14, Colorado—I'm in 8th grade and live near Denver. I really enjoy playing soccer, but I don't play competitively--just for fun. One of my favorite things to do is to play the oboe and I'm in my school's "Select Band" which I love. My older brother, Erik, has Down syndrome and he's 16 and my younger brother, George, is 12. I have a dog, Dustin, and 4 birds (a parakeet, a cockatiel, and 2 finches).

Emily N., 17, Oregon—I live in Oregon, not too far from Portland. Thankfully, I'm a >> senior in high school, so I only have one more year to go before I run off to college. My main activity in school (other than hours of homework) is band. I play the clarinet, and I have been playing since 6th grade. Grades are very important to me, so it has been my goal to get 4.0 throughout high school. So far, I am succeeding, but this last year is going to be a challenge. I'm deaf in my left ear, but I am so used to not hearing out of one ear that it doesn't affect me very much. I volunteer regularly with March of Dimes, Special Olympics, Camp Fire USA, and many other organizations. If I ever find any free time I love to hang out with my best friend, Lauren! We've been best friends since middle school.

>> Emily P., 13, Indiana—I live near Indianapolis and am in 8th grade. During the winter, I am on my middle school's swim team. I love to draw!!!!!!!!!!!! My favorite classes are Art and Science.

Emma F., 15, Michigan—I enjoy playing soccer and the trumpet. I am a freshman at Berkley High School in Michigan. After going to Sibshops for over 4 years, I now help run them in a couple of schools. I like running them because I get to hear what >> other kids think and I know I am not alone. I also love to travel; I have gone to Alaska, Europe, Israel, and Mexico. My most favorite thing to do is hang out with my friends, laughing, having a good time.

Erin G., 14, Alberta—I am in Grade Nine (school, grrrrr). I dance 15 hours a week, plus homework, plus time with friends and (gasp) family. So I'm a pretty stressed out kid. I don't understand why, but I love it. I moved to Calgary from Vancouver 2 years >> ago and hated it the first year and a half. Now I've met a group of the best friends ever and we hang out all the time. I like to be different, fight the conformity, as I like to say. I'm about the loudest, most obnoxious person you will ever meet. I like to sing at the top of my lungs, in the shower, on the bus, at school, you name it. The thing I hate most is ignorance, intolerance, and violence. I can't stand people who put others down and try my hardest not to myself (but you know how it goes...sometimes they deserve it).

>> **Jacob C., 13, Wisconsin**—I am in 8th grade. I live in Wisconsin and enjoy playing football and baseball.

>> **Jemma J., 18, Berkshire**—I live just outside London in England. I'm starting at university in October to study Computer Science, so therefore I like playing on the computer and the Internet, watching TV, and relaxing with my friends.

Jenna H., 17, N.S.W—I live in the sparkling harbour-side city of Sydney in New South Wales, Australia and love its vibrancy, energy, and diversity of people. When I have free time, I spend it with friends, enjoying a good novel while soaking up the
>> sun on the beach, playing soccer, writing, and playing music. I also enjoy eating at restaurants to hone my tasting skills so as to one day be a food critic for a major newspaper! There are always cultural, sporting, and artistic festivities happening in Sydney, and it's great to be part of them. One of my most memorable experiences was being in the choirs for the Olympic and Paralympic Games Opening Ceremonies of 2000, both spectacular events, the thrill of which I hope to enjoy again in the future.

>> **Jill B., 18, Florida**—I've lived in Florida all my life. I am preparing to be a freshman at Florida State University in the fall. I'm a certified scuba diver and I ride horses. I also love to sing and dance and I was on the dance team at my high school. I love sports. I recently went on a trip around the country with my family and I love hiking in the mountains.

>> **Kaleigh H., 16, New Hampshire**—I live in southern New Hampshire and am a junior in high school. I just got my license a month ago so I'm very excited about that. I like to hang out with my friends, shop, go to the movies, music, and go to my Sibs group twice a month.

>> **Kat F., 16, Washington State**—I'm a sophomore. I live in the western part of Washington State, which means that it always rains. I'm in band and play the cornet at football and basketball games and parades. I'm also on the swim team and do the 500. I don't really have a "classified" group of friends at school. I'm pretty short, have inky cerulean eyes, and natural blonde hair.

>> **Kate F., 13, Wisconsin**—I live in southern Wisconsin. I'm in 8th grade this year and am excited to graduate! I participate in volleyball, basketball, track and field, and lots of different kinds of dance. This year I'm thinking of becoming a member of the student council.

>> **Katelyn C., 16, Virginia**—I'm a junior in high school in Northern Virginia. I've been a cheerleader since age 6, and in 2002, I was nominated for All-American. One of my best friends has 3 therapy dogs and once a month we take the dogs to visit the special needs kids in our school. We work on their OT skills, and it's always a refreshing break from the normal routine of school to play with them.

>> **Kathryn C., 14, Illinois**—I live in the most boring town in Illinois--but that's just my opinion! I am a freshman in high school. I love to dance--ballet, Pointe, jazz, dance troupe. I have been dancing for 9 years. I love to read books and live to watch movies and go to plays. I like to travel, talk with my friends, and hang out at the movies or mall. I'm just another typical teenager, I guess.

>> **Katie J., 19, Illinois**—I go to Villanova University in Philadelphia, and live right outside of Chicago, IL. I play the flute in an Irish band called the Academy of Irish Music; in the summer of 2004, we will record our first CD! I am one of the coxswains on the Villanova crew team.

>> **Kayla L., 13, Arizona**—I live in Arizona with my bird, Kyle; my hairless rat, Cornelius; and my mouse, Dart. I don't play any sports but I play the oboe and like baseball.

>> **Kelsea R., 15, New Hampshire**—I have one sister, 17, who has autism and another sister who is 11. Although I am the middle child, in a way I am the oldest because of Robin's disability. I am a sophomore, and enjoy playing basketball and hanging out with my friends. I used to volunteer for the Nashua Special Olympics, and helped out in swim and golf.

>> **Kevin T., 14, Virginia**—I live in southern Virginia, near the beach. I am currently in ninth grade and love to play soccer, swim, skim board, surf, play guitar, and video games.

>> **Kristin S., 19, Virginia**—I'm a freshman at James Madison University majoring in Hospitality and Tourism Management. I love to listen to music and watch movies. I also love theater and singing in choir and doing photography. I played piano for 10 years and the clarinet for 8. I'm from Virginia (right outside of DC) and have lived there my whole life. I have two older sisters.

>> **Laura P., 15, Virginia**—I'm 15 years old, and I don't believe in cliques. I love adventures and meeting new, interesting people. I live eclectically and never stop dreaming.

>> **Lauren O., 16, Georgia**—I'm currently a junior and involved in Prom Committee, Beta Club, and Student Ambassadors. Outside of school, I enjoy going to church and spending time with my family and friends.

>> **Lauren V., 14, Connecticut**—I'm a 14 year old girl from Connecticut and a freshman in high school. My favorite sports are soccer, swimming, and ice skating. I love to hang out with my friends and I participate in a sibling group.

>> **Leah K., 13, Iowa**—I am in 9th grade except for math, which I'm in 10th. I'm not in any sports. I used to dance but am not really in any activities.

>> **Leslie C., 16, Washington State**—I live in the southern part of Washington State with my brother and my dad. I like to be with my friends and listen to music and be silly. Last year I was a teacher's assistant in my brother's Life Skills class. I am good at sports and I used to be on a soccer team. I like making friends, having fun, and making people laugh.

>> Reader, what should we know about you???

>> **Lindsay D., 17, North Carolina**—You might think that I'm Irish because of "Lindsay" and my last name, and you would be somewhat correct. My parents are in fact Irish and so is my sibling, but I was born in South Korea and look...well, pretty much South Korean. I was adopted at 4 months old and moved to the beautiful USA! I now live near Winston-Salem, North Carolina, where I enjoy practicing, teaching, and competing in martial arts, swimming, working out, gymnastics, dancing in my living room, acting, and of course having fun. I'm seventeen and a senior at West Forsyth High School.

Lindsay K., 15, California—I'm a high school sophomore and live in California's
>> Central Valley. I'm a pretty open-minded person, have an insane sense of humor, as
well as a fetish for classical music. I'm obsessed with the written word, don't like
spinach, love to laugh, am currently learning French (which somehow brings out my
silly idiosyncrasies) and also participate in cheerleading for an All-star squad based
in Modesto. I'm in the International Baccalaureate program, an intense college
preparatory program based on the European education system. This sucks away
much of my spare time, but when I do get free time, I enjoy creative writing. I'm
currently hoping to get one of my books published! In the future, I hope to attend
Stanford University and get my M.F.A and PhD in English and teach at a high school
or university. Otherwise, I consider myself to be a normal, though rather ambitious,
teen who likes to spend time with her friends and family.

>> **Lydia Q., 13, Massachusetts**—I am in the 8th grade and enjoy swim team, drama,
and lacrosse.

>> **Maggie W., 17, Wisconsin**—I live in south-central Wisconsin and am a junior
in high school. My passion is creative writing, although I don't plan to become a
professional author. I run for my cross-country team and I am a counselor at a day
camp. Overall, I am lucky to say that I have a pretty nice life. I play the violin in my
school orchestra and am a part of an a cappella group with a few of my friends. I
like organization, rhetorical questions, and Microsoft Word!

>> **Mandi D., 13, Wisconsin**—I'm 13 years old, in 7th grade, and live in Wisconsin
with my mom, dad, and brother.

>> **Margaret C., 14, Illinois**—I am a high school freshman in Chicago. I was on the
Cross Country team and I'm planning to try out for soccer! I absolutely love singing
and writing songs.

>> **Martha P., 13, Connecticut**—My name is Martha but my friends call me Loo,
PinkiLoo, or Keltha. I am 13 and a half and in eighth grade. I live in a small town
in the middle of nowhere known as Hebron, Connecticut. I have been taking dance
since age five. I do ballet, tap, hip hop, and jazz. I've been playing violin since I was
3 and drums since I was 9.

>> **Matt M., 15, Illinois**—I'm a sophomore in high school. I live in the suburbs of
Chicago. I'm a part of our marching band, which enjoys a national reputation. I
also play baseball whenever I can. Most of the time I'm doing my homework, with 2
honors classes and a college course.

>> **Matt M., 14, North Carolina**—I am 14 and live in North Carolina. I love to play soccer and basketball. Also, I am in middle school, in 8th grade.

>> **Megan D., 14, Michigan**—I'm a freshman at a Christian high school. I enjoy playing JV basketball and piano, although they both take up a ton of my time. I also like to read, hang out, and shop.

>> **Megan D., 18, Texas**—I am a freshman in college. I play on two soccer teams, I was on the swim team in high school, and I coach 2 youth soccer teams. My friends say that I am funny, and I love to listen to comedians.

Melisandre P., 14, Kansas—I am a ninth grader, a cheerleader, and secretary of
>> my class. I also dance. I like to hang out with my friends and go to movies. I get on the computer, cheer, talk on the phone, go to the movies, dance, and hang out with friends and family! I also am in LOVE with books and love to read. Some of my favorite authors are Marianne Curley, J.K. Rowling, Joan Lowery Nixon, and tons of others! When I get older, I would like to be a journalist for a magazine or newspaper and would like to write books. I am definitely going to go to college; I am just not sure which one yet. I have a dog, Jake—a Chihuahua—and I love to play with him.

>> **Michelle D., 16, New Jersey**—Hey everyone! I am a junior living in northern New Jersey. I am an active, fun-loving teenager. I play softball competitively year-round as a pitcher and outfielder, as well as field hockey and basketball. In my spare time I go to the beach, read, and sleep (according to my family, too much!), but I am always doing something. I live with my mom, my dad, older sister Theresa, 18 (a college freshman), and brother Erick, 8, who is in second grade.

>> **Michelle M., 15, New Jersey**—I am a sophomore at a magnet school, like photography, and am vice president of my school's photo club. I also like to write for my school's newspaper. I am part of my school's volunteer club and volunteer in my school and community. I play basketball and track for my school but like almost any sport. I am also a member of my church's youth group, the Godrockers.

>> **Michelle O., 14, Virginia**—I am in 9th grade and have lived in Virginia my whole life. During my free time, I baby-sit and sing in the church choir.

>> **Miri L., 16, Illinois**—I live in the suburbs of Chicago, IL. I am a sophomore in high school. I love art and working with people with special needs more than anything else in the world and hope to be either a production designer for movies or a special ed. teacher.

>> **Monica R., 15, Massachusetts**—I am a freshman in a public high school just outside of Boston, Massachusetts. I enjoy painting, kickboxing, good books, and great friends.

Nancy R., 13, California—I'm 13 and in 9th grade, and I like to play any sport. I live in Huntington Beach, California. My personality is nice, caring, understanding, and funny.

>> **Nicole P., 15, Pennsylvania**—I'm a sophomore in high school. I wear a uniform every day but out of school, I basically live in either jeans or sweatpants. I love my Converse sneakers and hooded sweatshirts. I listen to punk music and enjoy hanging out with my friends. My favorite sports are skiing, snowboarding, and I do the hurdles in track.

>> **Nora G., 13, Virginia**—I am in 7th grade. I don't really like sports very much so I ride horses a little and play the piano. I love listening to music, reading, and hanging with friends.

>> **Rebekah C., 17, California**—I live in the San Francisco Bay Area of California. I am a college freshman majoring in Nursing. I love talking with friends, going online, music, and reading. I love learning and work hard to get to where I want to be. I have 4 brothers and 2 sisters, which makes 7 of us, me being the 4th kid. I love writing about anything and everything and I enjoy spending time with my younger siblings (well, most of the time at least!).

>> **Sarah S., 18, Pennsylvania**—I'm 18 years old and grew up in western Pennsylvania. I graduated from high school with highest honors and am now a freshman pharmacy major at a university in Pittsburgh.

Stephanie B., 16, Maryland—I live in Maryland, right in between Washington, D.C. and Baltimore. I'm a senior in high school. I'm going off to college next year, which is hard to believe. Music is the bane of my existence. I want to be an opera singer or perhaps someday a conductor. I'm in a bunch of different choral groups both in and outside of school. I play piano, too, and I love music theory. My mom is a music teacher, and my dad likes to sing, too. I'm a vegetarian, Birkenstock-wearing hippie who fights for peace and the environment. I love animals, and I have two dogs. I live by my agenda book. I also love to write, read, knit, skate, kayak, sail, hike, volunteer, hug, and be with my family... and I try never to miss an opportunity to experience something incredible.

Stephie N., 15, Arizona—I live in Arizona with my parents and 4 younger sisters. I attend a local high school where I'm a freshman and I plan to become involved with Best Buddies and possibly run track there. I love to hang out with my friends, listen to music, watch movies, and participate in Life Teen--my church's youth group.

Teresa H., 13, Minnesota—I am in eighth grade, and I am a JV cheerleader. Also, I am in Band, Choir, Pep Band, Jazz Choir, and Dance! I LOVE IT ALL SO MUCH!!! I live in a family of seven, and we own a cat named PJ. My dad is a pastor and my mom is mostly a stay-at-home mom, but she has a part time job with a math program. I have two brothers, one 15 and the other 4. I also have two sisters, one's 9 and the other 7. I love to sing and act. I would love to be a professional singer/actor when I am older. I am a MAJOR fan of Hilary Duff, and I think Chad Michael Murray is pretty cool!

Ty H., 17, Washington State—I am a seventeen-year-old dude living in Washington State, in the great Pacific Northwest. I am a junior at a private high school called Wellspring Community High School. I am also a musician; I play cello and guitar, write my own songs, and compose music.

Tyler L., 15, Arizona—I like extreme sports and hot chicks.

What should we know about your sib?

Clinton is 18 and a senior in high school. He plays the drums in the school band and makes pizza in our school cafeteria. Last year he went to the prom with a T.A. from his class. He has fragile X syndrome. It's harder for him to read and do math, but he can work a calculator, count, and write. He's a funny guy, too. He makes people laugh all the time. He likes to be pretty loud, too. He can play sports and he's a fast runner. He likes to sing along with the radio. He's a really nice person to everyone. It's hard to believe he never gets mad and he's always happy.
—Leslie C., 16, Washington State

David is 21 and has Down syndrome. David does Special Olympics and plays bocce ball, basketball, runs track, and bowls. He also loves the Beatles and is a dancing machine! David is an RA (religious advisor) for our church's youth group, ACTION. He also has two jobs, one at Walgreen's pharmacy and another in a grocery store.　　—Katie J., 19, Illinois

Charlie is a very special kid. He loves trains, trucks, and animals. He touches and inspires everyone he meets. Charlie was born 3 months early and spent the first 6 months of his life in the NICU (neonatal intensive care unit). He came home to us as a foster child because his birth parents couldn't take care of him. He was not expected to reach his first birthday. He is 4 years old now and has exceeded everybody's expectations. He can walk on his own, but pretty slowly and somebody needs to be there with him in case he falls. His arms and hands don't work so he uses his feet for everything from coloring to stacking blocks to turning the pages of a book. He gets around by scooting on his bottom or in his wheelchair, which he pushes and steers with his feet. He can't swallow so he gets his nutrition from a special formula that goes straight into his stomach through a tube. The most difficult part of Charlie's condition is that he talks and talks but most of it is incomprehensible. He does some signs with his feet and is learning to communicate using a computer system. The names of the conditions he has are: cerebral palsy, arthrogryposis, congenital cervical spinal atrophy, chronic lung disease, short bowel syndrome, and a deep palate intubation groove. Still, Charlie is a very happy kid. He is developmentally on target for his age group and is very bright. We also always have one other foster child living in our house. Right now, that is "Juan." He is quadriplegic with some arm use due to a car accident. He's 3 years old. He's a really cool kid. He gets around in a wheelchair using his hands to push the wheels, and he has a tracheotomy to help him breathe and a feeding tube like Charlie's to feed him. He's eating more and more food on his own and will someday be able to get the tube removed.
—Rebekah C., 17, California

I have a brother, Matthew, who's 13 and LOVES his movies, toys, and his classmates. He enjoys dancing and being around a lot of people. He is mainstreamed in school and does fairly well. He's always improving and impressing people. My family would be lost without him. Oh, and he has Down syndrome.
—Nicole P., 15, Pennsylvania

I have a sister, Beatriz, who is 17 and going into 12th grade. She has arthritis. To me, Beatriz is like a regular person except she can't run like others because her knees and hips cause her pain. She also has pain in her wrists, which means she can't move them the way other people can.
—Nancy R., 13, California

I have a twin brother, Anthony. He has cerebral palsy and uses a wheel chair. He loves videos, the computer, and Play Station. Anthony is a very happy kid! He loves to laugh. He can do a lot of things, but sometimes he needs some help with things, like getting into bed, picking things up, using the restroom, etc.

—Emily P., 13, Indiana

I have two siblings with problems. My younger sister, Sylvia, is 14 and has Asperger's disorder and diabetes. She tends to act much younger than her age, although she is probably the smartest person in our family. Her diabetes can make life especially difficult at times because she will forget to check her blood sugar or do her insulin shots. My younger brother, Paul, is 12 and went through a time of serious clinical depression because of school and his severe ADHD. He was out of school for depression for about a month and was hospitalized last spring for a suicide attempt, which made things worse at school. He has been better lately because he's caught up in school and on different medication.

—Alli J., 15, Ohio

I have two sibs. My brother, J.L., is 14 and has full mutation fragile X syndrome, the leading cause of inherited mental retardation. I also have a cousin, Sammy, who came to live with us after our grandmother died. He is 12 and also has full mutation fragile X. Even though they have the same disorder, they have different traits, strengths, and weaknesses. J.L. is extremely intelligent and has the potential to be something great. His communication is pretty limited, though. Mostly he uses one or two word phrases and, for some reason, uses a high-pitched voice unless we tell him to "Say it like a man." He perseverates quite a bit and echoes what he hears on television or on films. His fine motor skills are almost nonexistent. He has no aggression at all. Sammy, on the other hand, has lots of aggression. He has great communication skills. He speaks in full sentences, but they make no sense for the most part. His entire vocabulary seems to be made up of phrases that he has heard others say. He has pretty great fine motor skills.

—Elizabeth T., 19, Oklahoma

I have two younger brothers. Cory is 14 and has learning disabilities, asthma, and ADHD. He is going into the 8th grade. Cory likes playing on the X-Box. Matthew is 10, has cerebral palsy, and is deaf. Matthew is in a non-graded classroom. He likes to play on computers, look at books, and ride horses.

—Britny G., 16, Missouri

My 11-year-old brother has Down syndrome. My mom named him after Harrison Ford! Anyways, Harry is amazing. He is in fifth grade. Harry can read, talks very well, and usually understands what is going on. Harry does have a hard time with writing and math. It's hard to explain my situation with Harry because there is so much to tell. Harry loves to be around other kids; however, sometimes he can get rough because he has a hard time with play skills.

—Alicia F., 17, Illinois

My 22-year-old brother, Travis, has Down syndrome. He reads at a third grade reading level and only made it to multiplication in math, but he is very social and loves to talk. His favorite activities are reading, watching TV or movies, and playing Nintendo. He also enjoys cross-country skiing with a group called SKIFORALL. He has worked as a grocery bagger and in a mailroom for a while, but is currently volunteering at a local food bank.

—Amanda M., 19, Washington State

My 8-year-old brother, Erick, has Down syndrome. Most people have 23 pairs of chromosomes. My brother has one extra chromosome in one of those pairs. He is mentally retarded and learns a little slower than typical kids. Although when he was a baby he had very weak muscles, he now enjoys baseball, basketball, golf, and swimming. He is a very happy little boy who has more energy than my whole family put together! He will be going into 2nd grade this year in a regular-ed classroom and has one in-class aide. He does have some difficulty talking, but his therapists have made huge strides particularly in this area.

—Michelle D., 16, New Jersey

My brother Ben has Attention Deficit Disorder, and recently completed chemotherapy for a brain tumor. During this time, it was impossible for him to be active; there were times when he could barely walk. My family is very thankful that he is doing well now.

—Lauren V., 14, Connecticut

My brother Daniel has Down syndrome, which means it's harder for him to learn. He plays baseball and soccer on teams for kids with disabilities. He's almost 9 and he is still having a hard time learning to talk. —Mandi D., 13, Wisconsin

My brother Clayton is 10, in the 5th grade, and has Down syndrome. He's in a class with the average kids but he does go to a special reading teacher and speech teacher. He takes extra speech classes at a private facility. He plays lots of sports including basketball, soccer, and baseball. He has many friends and they all love him to death. Recently one of his friends said, "I like him and he needs me." —Amy McK., 16, Tennessee

My brother David is 13 and in 7th grade. He loves to jump on the trampoline and go golf cart riding. He can watch movies all day and loves bonfires. I don't know what is so intriguing about them but he loves them. He has autism and he is very good at math. He can read but sometimes it can be hard for him. It's also hard to get him to respond to questions. But otherwise, he is just a kid--always wanting to have fun. —Kathryn C., 14, Illinois

My brother has Down syndrome, to start with. Due to severe blood loss and being born at 32 weeks, he suffered profound brain damage. He also has autistic-like behaviors and Pervasive Developmental Disorder (PDD). They believe that he suffered seizures very early in childhood (without diagnosis until a while later.) He is 50% deaf, non-verbal, and has severe food and medication allergies. Andrew also has hip dysplasia.

—Allison S., 17, Connecticut

My brother has high functioning autism. He is extremely good at math and computers. He is awful at interacting with his peers and so he has been bullied his whole life. His biggest problem is anxiety, which wreaks havoc on his behavior, speech, communication, and social skills. He is extremely honest and absolutely cannot lie, even when he should. —Miri L., 16, Illinois

My brother is Erik; he's 16 and has Down syndrome. He has an especially difficult time speaking/communicating. I don't particularly like talking about things he's challenged with; I'd rather talk about what he's good at. He goes to Cherry Creek High School and loves it. He's in 10th grade. He also loves to swim. He does Special Olympics Swimming and I'm a Unified Partner, which I think helps him because I understand him better and know how to work with him. He also plays soccer and he loves that too. This year he went to the high school homecoming, which I thought was awesome because no one thinks that someone like Erik could do that. Like any teen boy, Erik loves movies and video games. He also loves pretzels and spaghetti—probably his favorite foods. Erik's a really cool brother.

—Emily J., 14, Colorado

My brother John is 20 and attends high school. He is mentally retarded with a learning disability. He enjoys playing Nintendo, watching TV and playing sports. He plays baseball and basketball for a Challenger League in my town. He also is training for swimming for Special Olympics. —Michelle M., 15, New Jersey

My brother Micah is 19 and has some cognitive impairment. Micah loves surfing the web, talking about politics, and running. Some things that are difficult for Micah are reading, writing, and doing math. Sometimes he stutters. Right now, he is taking some classes at a local university. Micah is one of the first students with a cognitive impairment in Michigan to be going to a university after high school. He wrote a rap called, "I Wanna Be a College Boy."

—Emma F., 15, Michigan

My brother Steven is 19 (16 months older than me) and has autism. He is my whole life! He is a high school senior and participates in a basketball and bowling league called the Dynamites for kids with disabilities. He loves swimming and boating. He also likes going to the video arcade.

—Jill B., 18, Florida

My brother Will is 9 and going into 3rd grade. He has Translocation Down syndrome, the second rarest form. He can't talk well, but uses some signs. He started swimming around the same time that I did, very little. He loves Pokémon, playing video games, and going to the park. His other favorite past time is doing what I do. (Like if I balance on the curb, he has to too.) Both he and I love to read, and he inherited my old books and VHS tapes. He also uses a computer very well.

—Kat F., 16, Washington State

My brother, Adam, is 15 years old and has been diagnosed with autism. He does have verbal communication skills, but can get easily frustrated and starts making grunting noises and screams. Adam likes his structured routine, and you can almost set your watch by the times he changes from watching Cartoon Network and Nickelodeon Junior in the lounge to playing on his PlayStation in his room—as well as demanding his lunch and dinner.

—Jemma J., 18, Berkshire

My brother, Chad, is 22 and has P.D.D. (pervasive developmental disorder). Instead of going to college, he goes to a workshop place called Hope Village, where he makes small things like patches. Chad likes birds, big trucks, comedians, and watching T.V. There really isn't much that he can't do except for play contact sports because of the two metal rods that he has next to his spine to correct his scoliosis.

—Megan D., 18, Texas

My brother, Ian, has fragile X syndrome and is 15. He is in the 10th grade and can do regular tasks, but he needs just a little help. He participates in Special Olympics, and pretty much does every activity in it. My brother has also joined a new program in Boulder called Sky's the Limit, which was created by one of his teachers. He really enjoys basketball.
—Cassie W., 13, Colorado

My brother, Phillip, is 10 and in 5th grade. He is about 4' 11" tall, has sandy brown hair and light brown eyes. He loves to go swimming and go for walks. His favorite sport is football and he loves to watch it on TV. His disability doesn't really have a name because only 10 other people have been diagnosed with it, but not all of the cases have the same problems. Phillip is just learning to walk and is unable to talk. He also has Agenesis of the Corpus Callosum (ACC).
—Christiana R., 13, Wisconsin

My brother, Scott, is 22 and is an awesome brother, a close friend, and simply a happy person. Scott has fragile X syndrome, the world's leading inherited cause of mental impairment, and he is proud of it! Scott and I both share similar values such as family and community service. Although he may not be able to read or drive, he is still a very accomplished man. He has won 13 gold medals in Special Olympics Georgia in weightlifting, golf, and basketball. Scott has many interests; right now, he loves NASCAR, WWE, and soap operas.
—Carly H., 17, Georgia

My brother's name is Alex, and he has autism. He's 22 years old. He graduated from the same high school that I'm attending, and is now looking for a job where he can use his well-developed skills and learn some new ones. He's very high functioning and is an awesome guy. He's also involved in lots of sports through Special Olympics —he plays hockey, softball, volleyball, soccer, bowling, and basketball!
—Stephanie B., 16, Maryland

My brother's name is Clinton--he is 12, in his 7th year of school and has autism. Clint bowls and skates with Special Olympics and at school. At school, he does everything everyone else does, but with a special helper. He loves to play games on the computer and watch movies a lot! He likes to find favorite scenes in the movies, rewind the tape and watch them again and again. He is REALLY good at video games and plays them all: Game Boy, GameCube, PlayStation, etc. He likes to play with Jake, our 3-year-old Chihuahua. Jake gives him someone to always play with and have as a best friend. Clint likes to go swimming in our pool—he's a "water bug." He can do all sorts of tricks in the water (somersaults, jumping off the edge into the pool, or anything else you can do!). My brother is one of the sweetest and nicest people you will ever meet!
—Melisandre P., 14, Kansas

My brother's name is Eric. He has Asperger's syndrome, which is a mild form of autism. I'm still trying to learn all about it. He has a beautiful heart and loves animals. He has a few friends who visit him often, and I'm glad he has them around because they keep him happy.
—Laura P., 15, Virginia

My brother's name is Jeff. He is 11 and in 5th grade. Jeff has Williams syndrome and is probably the most outgoing, people-person I know. He loves anything that has to do with

>>

music. He takes drum and trumpet lessons and is in a school band. Jeff also plays football and baseball. In the past, he has done karate, soccer, and been in several children's plays. Jeff is pretty high functioning but has a hard time with his fine motor skills and school is very tough for him. He also has some major behavior issues. Overall, Jeff is a great kid and if you just met him on the street, you probably wouldn't even be able to tell he has a disability.
—Emily I., 15, Washington State

My brother's name is Jeremy. He has blue eyes, freckles, blond hair, and a charismatic smile that can always make you feel better. Jeremy is 18 (which he would say is almost 19) and would be very upset if you called him a boy; he prefers "big man." And he reminds me constantly that whenever dad is out of the house he is "the big man of the house." He is forever trying to protect me from anything that could be threatening (boys in particular). Jeremy has Down syndrome. (Excuse me-- "Up" syndrome, as he would put it) Jeremy's disability never stops him from reaching the limelight. He's a junior and enjoys performing karate (as long as there is a crowd), acting, swimming, and dancing. He's also addicted to his Game Cube and DVD player. The most frustrating thing for Jeremy is communication. He uses sign language, objects, and anything else that help us understand. Even with his difficulties communicating, he remains a lovable and caring older brother that my family deeply treasures.
—Lindsay D., 17, North Carolina

My brother's name is Joshua; he's almost 15 and has epilepsy, which is a seizure disorder. He really likes landscaping and taking care of lawns. He and my dad work together cleaning lawns and gathering leaves.
—Kaleigh H., 16, New Hampshire

My little brother has autism and basically, he is classified as being nonverbal, as he cannot talk. He is about 12 years old, very active, and, all in all, very energetic about life.
—Daniel C., 17, Illinois

My little brother Stephen is 12 years old and has Down syndrome. Stephen has a hard time doing strenuous physical activity, and learns slower than the rest of us. He is currently in 7th grade at a local middle school. He is deeply involved in Special Olympics, swims, plays baseball and basketball, and loves music. He is also a very good reader.
—Kevin T., 14, Virginia

My little brother's name is Dylan. He has C.H.A.R.G.E syndrome. He is 7 and in a pre-elementary classroom. He has two undeveloped parts in his ear so he has trouble with balance and he can't hear. He also has undeveloped eyes so he can't see well. He can't eat because when he does the food goes into his lungs instead of his stomach.
—Kayla L., 13, Arizona

My older brother's name is Charlie and he is 20 years old. He is an amazing artist (mostly paints and stamps), loves good music, and once had a fetish with Harley Davidson motorcycles. He was born with cerebral palsy, which was caused by a large percentage of his motor nerve cells being damaged or killed when he lost oxygen. This makes it possible for Charlie to send messages to his brain (which works perfectly fine, thank you very much), but not from his brain to other parts of his body. As a result, he does not have speech, nor can he walk or eat as the rest of my family does.
—Maggie W., 17, Wisconsin

My sib's name is Dennis; at 17, he's older than I am. Dennis likes to be on the computer, play Nintendo, and play with the puppy. His disability is Asperger's syndrome.
—Amy S., 15, Washington State

My sib's name is Riley; he is almost 13. At 9, Riley was diagnosed with Williams syndrome. He is a little cute-faced squirt and is only the size of a 7-year-old. He has a pixie face and is really active. He has a colostomy, which means a part of his intestines that lead down to his bowels is pulled out of his side, and a special bag is then stuck over it and that is where he does poos. He can swim, ride a bike and loves running around. He loves music and dancing but is not very good at writing and maths. He can be a pain, breaks a lot of my stuff, and can get right in my face sometimes. —Cassey C., 15, Southland, N.Z.

My sibling, Arianna, is 3, which means there's a 12-year age gap between us. She has epilepsy, cerebral palsy, and developmental delays. She still can't talk besides babbling but she's a generally happy and joyful child. I love her very much and feel almost like I'm her second "mommy." I call her "Mini-Me" like Mini-me in Austin Powers because if you compare my picture at three years to her, we look like twins. It's so uncanny it's scary. —Lindsay R., 15, California.

My siblings are 10 years old and going into 3rd grade. Liz has a visual disability. It is difficult for her to go downstairs or see what is in front of her. She basically just memorizes a room. If something is in a room where it is not supposed to be, she won't see it. Emily has cerebral palsy. For her it is difficult to walk around or keep up with her friends, so she gets left out a lot. But she's trying to walk with a little help of walker and is not swimming with wings anymore so she's getting more independent. —Kate F., 13, Wisconsin.

My sibling's name is Matthew, and he has Down syndrome. He is 10 and plays baseball on a special needs team (Go Orioles!!), which I help out with. He also enjoys football, basketball, swimming, and running. His favorite activities are probably watching Sponge Bob, chasing around the dog and cats, and playing with his favorite sister!! —Katelyn C., 16, Virginia

My sib's name is Asenath and she has a disorder called mitochondrial neurogastrointestinal encephalomyopathy or MNGIE. She is 3 years old and her only activities (if that's what you want to call it) are physical, occupational, and speech therapy! She has dysautonomia (erratic heart rates and apnea) at night. It makes her have irregular breath patterns and problems with her temperature. She has seizures, migraines, and strokes. Asenath has lots of medications for her seizures and other reasons. She has heat and exercise intolerance and a low immune system. She uses a G-tube at night to drink three cans of PediaSure because she doesn't eat a lot. She has 4 narrow arteries in her brain, which causes her strokes. The two disorders are so rare doctors can't believe she has BOTH the brain vasculitis and the Mitochondrial Disorder. This is a life and death situation and the doctors are currently trying to find out how to help her. —Leah R., 13, Iowa

My sib's name is Keaton; he is 12 and has epilepsy. To control his seizures, he's on the ketogenic diet and will be getting a Vagus Nerve Stimulator (VNS) put in soon. He is very active and his favorite thing to do is play basketball. He loves going to Camp Courageous and riding the city bus. He also likes playing outside and in the water. —Cassandra W., 15, Iowa

My sister Adrienne is 14 and an 8th grader at the school where my dad is the principal! She enjoys school and loves hanging out with her friends. Adrienne has Benign Congenital Hypotonia, which is a form of cerebral palsy. Regardless of her disability, she is the most beautiful girl with the biggest heart.   —Lauren O., 16, Georgia

My sister Becky is a 13-year-old 6th grader. She loves Aaron Carter, The Backstreet Boys, Nsync, Hanson, and is just now getting into my old Ace of Bass tapes. She is very friendly and loves to be around people. She is very smart, can read sentences out loud, and tells me memories that I had forgotten over the years. She is a mega girly-girl and she also happens to have Williams syndrome. She knows that she has it and has told me before that she wished she didn't so "she could have more friends." My brother Tommy is a nonverbal autistic who lives at a residential facility a couple cities away. He comes home every weekend. I get emotional thinking about my brother because he was normal up to 12 months and then the brother I knew disappeared. It's not happy.
          —Ali N., 18, Massachusetts

My sister Caroline has cerebral palsy and mental retardation. She cannot walk or talk without help. She uses a wheelchair to get around and a computer to be her voice. I know she has a lot to say and I think she notices a lot of things that we don't, simply because she has the time to— she's not rushing around or self-absorbed. She has a sweet, outgoing, loveable personality and a beautiful smile. I try to connect with her and include her in conversation as much as possible. I think that with the right supports and people who believe in her she can succeed in life because she's a truly good person and she's very smart. It really bothers me when people can't see past Caroline's disability, when they treat her like she IS a disability and not a person, or when they say the word retard in a derogatory way. I want people to get to know Caro they way I do, because otherwise they're missing out on a lot.   —Caitlin M., 14, Maryland

My sister Catherine has fetal alcohol syndrome. She is adopted. Her birth mom used to drink when she was pregnant with her, so her brain didn't develop all the way. She can walk, but she couldn't talk until I taught her to say a few things. She is 18 but is only 4'2".
          —Margaret C., 14, Illinois

My sister Debbie was diagnosed with autism when she was 6.   —Sarah S., 18, Pennsylvania

My sister Emily has hyperlexia, a disorder on the autism spectrum. Emily taught herself to read before she was 4; however, she has verbal communication issues. Like many other 13-year-olds, Emily loves pop music, tv, and junk food.   —Monica R., 15, Massachusetts

My sister has Williams syndrome. She lives with our family in Salem, Wisconsin, and is 11 years old. She can't play many sports or many activities because of her disability.   —Jacob C., 13, Wisconsin

My sister Heather has partial Trisomy 2q 13-23. She has very limited verbal skills, and some physical limitations.   —Ashley S., 13, Minnesota

My sister is 14 and has Down syndrome. She is very high functioning, and speaks and reads well. She has difficulty with math and team sports, although she loves basketball and swimming.
                                                                —Lydia Q., 13, Massachusetts

My sister is 15 and we have a fairly typical teen-sibling relationship. She likes a good book, knows all the words to the top 40 songs on the radio, enjoys doing crafts and her favourite school subjects are Food Technology, Science and Silver Jewelry making. She has spina bifida and gets around in a snazzy manual wheelchair. Her fine motor skills are not crash-hot (Aussie slang for "fantastic") and she can't walk, but she does have an alternative sense of humour and can more than hold her own in a debate!   —Jenna H., 17, N.S.W

My sister is Lise and she is 11 years old. She has Williams syndrome (it's sorta like Down syndrome only...not). So basically, she has an incredibly short attention span and trouble with speech, writing, and math (but don't we all?). She is actually very smart in some ways. Example: She is the most amazing reader; she can read a book like a million times over really fast. One other thing about Lise, she watches brain-mushing amounts of TV. Oh, and she likes to yell, and scream, and get her way. But she's a good kid and we all love her energy.
                                                                —Erin G., 14, Alberta

My sister Jackie is 5 years older than me, and my only sibling. She has mild-to-moderate mental retardation. We graduated from the same high school and she now attends the Rappahannock Adult Day Center. Jackie eats meat, likes music, and can sense a sketchy person when she meets them. Oh yeah--every time we drive somewhere we have to listen to "Puff the Magic Dragon" by Peter, Paul, and Mary.   —Emily D., 18, Virginia

My sister Janae is 22 and has Down syndrome. She moved into her own apartment with support services 2 years ago. Sometimes I go to her apartment and she makes me dinner. She has a hard time with changes. She also has a hard time determining what is real and not real.
                                                                —Ty H., 17, Washington State

My sister Jessica is 9, in 3rd grade, and was adopted from Guatemala. She has a combination of a few things like: sensory integration problems, ADHD, speech delay (this is MUCH better), and fine and gross motor skills delay. She is fun and adores people. She absolutely loves music, singing, and dancing. She likes to write and type. She has a TON of energy. She always wants to comfort you when you are sad, and loves to give compliments. She is very appreciative of anything you give her and loves making things for others. One thing that is tough is she gets into trouble a lot. She will do something and you will tell her not to do that and then a few days later she might do it again. It is like she doesn't understand. I would NEVER trade her for anyone else. I LOVE HER SO MUCH!!!
                                                                —Teresa H., 13, Minnesota

My sister Lauren has Down syndrome. She has a difficult time remembering basic math skills and tying her shoes and she has to have a routine for everything. She has to have the same thing for breakfast every day, in the same order. She has to get ready for work in the same order and she has a movie she has to watch for every day of the week. But she is very good at memorizing things.
                                                                >>

She knows every song by the Beatles and the Monkees, plus music from tons of musicals. For her job, she delivers mail and she remembers where every person's office is.   —Kristin S., 19, Virginia

My sister Lucy was born with arthrogryposis, a neuromuscular disorder. This disease does not allow her to feed herself, walk, talk, or really do much of anything except smile, which she does a lot. Growing up was hard, but I love her now, and I am proud that she is my sister.   —Amelia C., 18, Minnesota

My sister Sally has a seizure disorder and a metabolic disorder (mitochondrial myopathy), which makes it difficult for her to talk, feed herself, stuff like that. Because of this, she develops a lot slower than other people. She loves to play in water and with toys that light up and make noise. She is 11 and she is a lot like a 2 year old.
                                                                                —Calen P., 14, Michigan

My sister, Mallory, is 13 and has Down syndrome and autism. She spends most of her time in school or watching videos. Mallory can't do many things by herself and even needs to be changed by my parents. She can't speak clearly to us, which makes it impossible to communicate with her. It is not easy living with her.
                                                                                —Matt M., 15, Illinois

My sister, Monica, has cerebral palsy, is legally blind, has deformities, and is severely retarded. She can brush her hair, turn on lights, suck through straws, feed herself, walk with only a little assistance, and is learning how to draw. Recently, she got glasses and has been looking around at what she is doing; for example, looking at her food when she eats. Like me, Monica has red hair and is in 8th grade, though she is 15. My sister enjoys having her hair done, scooting on her scooter board, and lying in her pink beanbag.
                                                                                —Martha P., 13, Connecticut

My sister, Naomi, is 10 years old, and supposedly has Rett syndrome, although now some doctors aren't so sure. Anyway, whatever she has, she can't walk, talk, or eat on her own, but she uses switches and stuff to help communicate. She also communicates by waving her arms and legs, and with her eyes and by making sounds. She really enjoys swimming and being read to. She eats with a g-tube, which means her food is a special formula that goes through a tube directly into her stomach.   —Amber C., 13, California

My sister, Robin, is 17 and has autism. She knows a lot about birds, plants, and Pokémon—her three favorite things. She has a little bit of a harder time in school, but if she puts her mind to it, she is capable of pretty much anything.   —Kelsea R., 15, New Hampshire

Reader, what should we know about your sib?

My sister's name is Julie, and she has been diagnosed with autism and mental retardation. Though she is 15, she functions at the level of a 3- or 4-year-old. She can't read or write very well, but she is fairly verbal. Some people like to say that she inherited my lost hearing because she can hear almost anything! She has severe behavioral problems and cannot calm herself down once ≫

she gets angry. If she is lashing out at my family or me, we have to hug her or apply some sort of pressure on her body to calm her down. Her sensory needs are very high, so she likes to make strange noises and eat non-food items. This is called pica, and it is something that anyone working with my sister has to constantly watch for. I asked Julie what she likes to do and she said that she likes to eat. If Julie were given unlimited amounts of food, she would eat, and eat, and eat, and eat...until she made herself sick. Julie likes to twirl strings and beads, cut paper into small pieces, and look at pictures of our family. Julie also likes to swim and play with our cat, Daisy Mae.

—Emily N., 17, Oregon

My sister's name is Kristin. She was born prematurely with a heart defect. She was fine and VERY smart, but small and slow physically. When she was 8, she had a surgery to correct the heart defect. The actual surgery went fine but afterwards she went into cardiac arrest and her heart stopped. They resuscitated her but during that time she lost blood flow to her brain and many of her brain cells died. Now she has very little control over her body. She can't talk so to communicate she cries.

—Catherine C., 13, California

My sister's name is Morgan. She is 16 and has Aicardi's syndrome. Morgan likes to play baseball, soccer, basketball, and go bowling. Morgan is a very smart girl but is a slow learner. She is at about a kindergarten learning level.

—Matt M., 14, North Carolina.

My sister's name is Vickie. She's 17 years old, autistic, and going into her junior year in high school. In her free time, she likes to cook for our church's Community Meal. Vickie hasn't been autistic her whole life. When she was about 3 years old, she stopped talking and my parents thought she was going deaf. They took her to the doctor for her to get tested and they discovered she has autism.

—Michelle O., 14, Virginia

My sister's name is Caroline. She is 14, in 7th grade, and has Down syndrome. She's very bossy, but really funny too. She loves to sing.   —Anna H., 15, North Carolina

My twin sister, Maia, has cerebral palsy. Cerebral palsy can affect people in different ways, but for my sister it means that she uses a wheelchair because she cannot walk, she has little use of her arms and hands, and her speech is unclear, although you get used to it pretty quickly. She understands everything that is going on around her and has the best, most cheeky sense of humour.   —Ariella M., 16, N.S.W.

My younger brother, Grant, is a high-functioning autistic child. He is 11 and in 6th grade. He's a little short and a bit chubby and loves GameCube. He gets really hooked on it sometimes. While watching tapes, he rewinds all the "silly" parts and has broken 3 VCRs doing that. He is also a very good reader and my family thinks he taught himself to read. When talking to family, he has no trouble blabbing away, but he has trouble talking to other people—eye contact, picking up on conversations, etc. He is improving. Grant also has really sensitive ears and he plugs his ears when he watches movies. He repeats questions often, which might be annoying to some people, but I love him anyway.

—Brooke W., 13, Virginia.

My sister, Sarah, is almost 18 years old. She has CDG (Carbohydrate Deficient Glycoprotein Syndrome or Congenital Disorders of Glycosylation) which is a very rare genetic disease. It affects all of her muscles so she can't walk and has other physical and mental difficulties. She can't read or do real schoolwork and some people have trouble understanding her when she talks. She loves people—especially boys—and talking on the phone. She has a great sense of humor and is very social. She is almost always smiling and gives great hugs.
—Megan D., 14, Michigan

My youngest sister, Sarah, is 4 and has Down syndrome, dysphasia, apraxia, and problems with her thyroid. We have to put something in her water to thicken it so she won't aspirate it into her lungs and she has to take a pill every morning to help regulate her thyroid. She can make oral-motor noises, but she can't always get the words out. So, Sarah does say a few words, but she mainly uses sign language to communicate. In addition to the physical, speech, occupational, music, and hippo (horse) therapies Sarah receives each week, she still goes to preschool, plays with friends, and leads a fairly "normal" life.   —Stephie N., 15, Arizona

Nathaniel is a moderately high-functioning autistic 8-year-old. He can verbally communicate, but he's difficult to understand. He enjoys messing around on the family computer, listening to music, being tickled, and trying to figure out how to get into my padlocked room. He does have behavioral problems and has problems restraining his affection, which he displays in the form of near-suffocating hugs. Sophia is a much lower-functioning autistic 6-year-old. She can verbally communicate sometimes when necessary. She can't seem to stop eating or destroying things (which Nathaniel helps in). She enjoys watching her videos, snuggling, and escaping from the house. She can't understand things as well as Nathaniel, but speaks much more clearly and has a knack for using phrases she picks up from videos and other people at just the right moment, although I think it is mostly echolalia (repeating without understanding).   —Alethea R., 13, Minnesota

Well, my brother is Dylan; he is 21 and lives in Salem, Oregon. Dylan has schizophrenia and intermittent explosive disorder, among other things. Despite this, he is a fun-loving guy who likes to crack jokes, even if they aren't always funny, and his infectious laugh will get you laughing right along with him. He's been involved with special needs baseball teams for as along as I can remember and Special Olympics—basketball and track—and got a few medals in the process. He always does it with a smile. He really loves to play video games and it seems like that's all he ever does. I don't see how he could love it so much.   —Alisa A., 18, Oregon

Well, my sister is 3 and has Down syndrome. She tries to talk but communicates better in sign language. She has great motor skills and is just learning to walk.   —Dave S., 14, Michigan

How many kids are in your family?

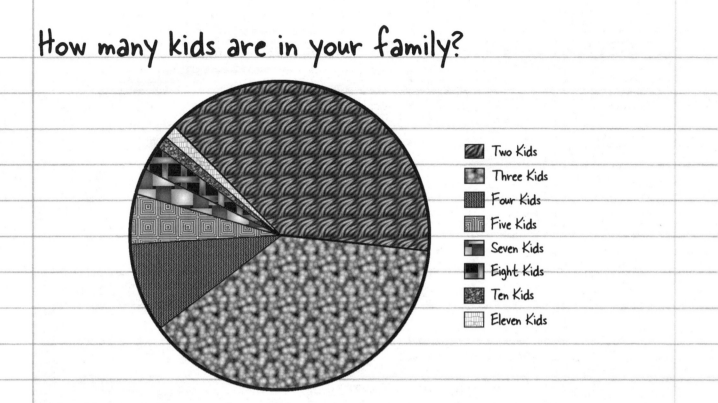

Legend:
- Two Kids
- Three Kids
- Four Kids
- Five Kids
- Seven Kids
- Eight Kids
- Ten Kids
- Eleven Kids

Two kids (29): Calen P., 14, Michigan; Amy McK., 16, Tennessee; Leslie C., 16, Washington State; Cassey C., 15, Southland, N.Z.; Amanda M., 19, Washington State; Amber C., 13, California; Ty H., 17, Washington State; Erin G., 14, Alberta; Caitlin M., 14, Maryland; Mandi D., 13, Wisconsin; Monica R., 15, Massachusetts; Katie J., 19, Illinois; Nicole P., 15, Pennsylvania; Nancy R., 13, California; Stephanie B., 16, Maryland; Lauren V., 14, Connecticut; Emily I., 15, Washington State; Nora G., 13, Virginia; Amy S., 15, Washington State; Emily N., 17, Oregon; Lauren O., 16, Georgia; Christiana R., 13, Wisconsin; Kaleigh H., 16, New Hampshire; Catherine C., 13, California; Martha P., 13, Connecticut; Kat F., 16, Washington State; Jenna H., 17, N.S.W; Brooke W., 13, Virginia; Cassie W., 13, Colorado

Three kids (28): Alicia F., 17, Illinois; Anna H., 15, North Carolina; Emily J., 14, Colorado; Kevin T., 14, Virginia; Kayla L., 13, Arizona; Lindsay D., 17, North Carolina; Lydia Q., 13, Massachusetts; Melisandre P., 14, Kansas; Michelle D., 16, New Jersey; Emily P., 13, Indiana; Britny G., 16, Missouri; Ariella M., 16, N.S.W.; Miri L., 16, Illinois; Daniel C., 17, Illinois; Elizabeth T., 19, Oklahoma; Megan D., 14, Michigan; Kate F., 13, Wisconsin; Michelle M., 15, New Jersey; Lindsay K., 15, California; Laura P., 15, Virginia; Carly H., 17, Georgia; Kristin S., 19, Virginia; Maggie W., 17, Wisconsin; Kathryn C., 14, Illinois; Alethea R., 13, Minnesota; Tyler L., 15, Arizona; Dave S., 14, Michigan

Four kids (7): Katelyn C., 16, Virginia; Megan D., 18, Texas; Matt M., 14, North Carolina; Michelle O., 14, Virginia; Ashley S., 13, Minnesota; Cassandra W., 15, Iowa; Allison S., 17, Connecticut

Five kids (4): Matt M., 15, Illinois; Teresa H., 13, Minnesota; Stephie N., 15, Arizona; Alli J., 15, Ohio

Seven kids (2): Emily D., 18, Virginia; Rebekah C., 17, California

Eight kids (2): Leah K., 13, Iowa; Margaret C., 14, Illinois

Ten kids (1): Kelsea R., 15, New Hampshire

Eleven kids: (1): Alisa A., 18, Oregon

Tall, husky guy with blond hair. —Jacob C., 13, Wisconsin

Describe yourself to someone who can't see you.

I have reddish blonde hair and pale skin dotted with freckles. My hair is almost halfway down my arms and is very thick. My eyes are constantly changing color. Sometimes they are blue, green, or even gray. I usually keep my nails well manicured and I have dancer feet: not a good thing. I weigh somewhere around 110 pounds and I am 5ft 3 inches tall. —Martha P., 13, Connecticut

Most of my friends say I am short. But actually, I am 5'5", which I don't consider very short at all. I have shoulder-length brown hair that doesn't always do what it is suppose to. It likes to be half-curly and half-straight, which can make for an interesting look when it won't cooperate. I have yellow eyes, which everyone comments on. (Everyone thinks they are pretty now but when I was little, kids called me an alien.) I have two ears, two eyes, a nose, and a mouth. I think my nose is crooked but no one else seems to notice it. I have 3 piercings in each ear, and a bellybutton pierced as well. I like to wear clothing that is from American Eagle Outfitters, Abercrombie and Fitch, and those kinds of stores. So I guess some would say I am preppy. —Alisa A., 18, Oregon

5 foot, 7 inches tall, short dirty blonde hair, blue eyes, slightly tan, and always a smile. —Megan D., 18, Texas

Long brown hair, brown eyes, olive skin, 5 ft. Most people say I am skinny. —Teresa H., 13, Minnesota

Height: 5'1. Weight: a girl never tells. Hair: short and brunette. Eyes: blue/green (depends on my mood). Small hands and feet (size 6½). —Emily D., 18, Virginia

I'm just above 5 feet, which is extremely short for my age! Because of my small stature, my big personality surprises a lot of people. —Lauren O., 16, Georgia

I have short brown hair. Someone could run their hand on the back of my neck and would feel little prickles in their hand. I have big brown eyes and lots of freckles—even more in the summer. I am very tall (5'7"), especially for my family. I am the second tallest, taller than my mom and brother. —Emma F., 15, Michigan

I am first-generation Australian and my family originates from Sri Lanka, Burma, and England, with Dutch and Middle Eastern ancestry. This genetic melting pot of nationalities has produced a young woman with a slender build, light olive skin, dark hair, and hazel eyes. —Jenna H., 17, N.S.W

I reach 5'4" and am pretty svelte. I have China pale skin and large blue eyes, with a mop of wavy, dark brown hair. Cut Marilyn Monroe style. I have a light sprinkling of freckles, full lips, and straight teeth (thanks to orthodontia). —Allison S., 17, Connecticut

I have short, red hair, blue eyes, freckles, and am 5'1". Very short! I have pierced ears (only one hole in each and in the regular spot; at least I'm hoping it's the regular spot but anymore, who knows?!). —Leah K., 13, Iowa

I'm assuming you mean my outside shell. I am short, 5' to be exact—a wider girl. I have shaggy brown hair, my lip pierced and my nose pierced. I have 3 tattoos and I'm always wearing a Green Day shirt. —Ali N., 18, Massachusetts

I am about 6 feet tall with auburn hair that is dyed blond. I could stand to lose some weight and I am working on that now. I have green eyes and easily-burnt white skin. Still single (for any good-looking ladies needing a guy who is witty, gentle, cooks, and is good with his hands and around the house). —Daniel C., 17, Illinois

I am about 5'8" tall. I have long, straight, dark brown hair. I have brown eyes, chubby cheeks, and people say that I smile often. —Jill B., 18, Florida

I'm tall; I have long dirty blonde hair, and green eyes. It's really hard to describe yourself to someone! I can't describe my face or style or anything else that really makes me me. —Caitlin M., 14, Maryland

I am Kinda on the small side. I am 5'2", have long thick brown hair, and have hazel eyes. I wear my hair in a ponytail most of the time. I have a dimple in my right cheek when I smile. I also wear contacts. —Britny G., 16, Missouri

I have very brown skin with light brown hair that goes just below my shoulders. I am 4 foot 9 ½ inches tall and weigh about 70 lbs. I have a square-ish face with dark brown eyes. —Kayla L., 13, Arizona

I am short – only 4'11" – and I have thick brown hair, which is currently shoulder length. My eyes are brown as well and I like to wear jeans and t-shirts, skirts in summer, and other comfortable and nice clothes. —Ariella M., 16, N.S.W.

I wouldn't try to, because they wouldn't know what I meant. I'd only tell them to make up their own picture of me, and that way, they could never make fun of me for any physical trait, be jealous, or anything that goes along with that. —Laura P., 15, Virginia

Well, I have brown hair, brown eyes, tan skin, and people say that I look like I am in high school. I am sort of a goodie-goodie, I don't do bad things, I don't use bad words, and I don't smoke or anything. I love to be with friends and draw. —Emily P., 13, Indiana.

I am Korean so think Asian when I say black hair and brown eyes. I have dark olive skin in the summer and stand at a proud height of 5 feet 4 inches. I know I'm not tall, but I like to think that considering I'm a girl and Asian that I am plenty tall. My mom tells me that my best feature is my smile (which is good because I do it often). So if you saw me I would probably be smiling. —Lindsay D., 17, North Carolina

I am about 5 feet 4 inches tall and I'm pretty muscular. I have medium length brown hair and hazel eyes. You can usually find me wearing jeans or shorts and t-shirts, or pajamas (my favorite type of clothing besides maybe socks). —Alli J., 15, Ohio

I'm medium height with dark, long, straight hair, big eyes, a pleasant smile, and I'm funny. I talk a lot. I'm nice but I'm cranky when I'm tired. —Lydia Q., 13, Massachusetts

28 ★ Describe yourself to someone who can't see you.

I'm a 5'3" female. I have light long brown hair, green eyes, and lots of freckles. —Kate F., 13, Wisconsin.

I am 5'7". I have brown eyes and brown hair. My hair just barely touches my shoulders. My favorite things to wear are jeans and a t-shirt.
—Amy McK., 16, Tennessee

I would have to say I'm kind and polite, very friendly. Hopefully they would understand that my personality is who I am and not my looks.
—Kathryn C., 14, Illinois

I have fairly long neutral-brown hair that thinks it's funny when it doesn't stay in place, so it rarely does. My eyes change color periodically; lately they've been green. My skin is a shade under olive. In the summer, the sun gives me freckles, highlights my hair, and burns my skin because I'm careless when it comes to sunscreen. I'm 5 feet, 2 inches and just taller than my mother. I hardly ever wear makeup.
—Maggie W., 17, Wisconsin

I am a female, 5'5", 125lbs. I am Caucasian with short brown hair. I have blue eyes and freckles. And right now I have braces :-P
—Rebekah C., 17, California

I'm about 5'3" with hazel-green eyes and black hair. —Leslie C., 16, Washington State

I have blue eyes, long, light brown hair and I am 5 feet 7 inches tall. —Emily I., 15, Washington state

Tall - 6 feet tall, thin, long straight brown hair, blue eyes, braces, and usually a smile.
—Megan D., 14, Michigan

I am 6'2" tall with shoulder-length brown curly hair.
—Ty H., 17, Washington State

I'm about 5 ft. 3 in., brown hair, brown eyes, freckles, slightly overweight, and usually wearing jeans and a t-shirt. —Amy S., 15, Washington state

I have brown hair, and hazel eyes. I am about 5 foot 7 and medium weight. I am not perfect but who is?
—Michelle M., 15, New Jersey

I wouldn't. Someone who can't see me should be able to see who I really am through my personality. —Katelyn C., 16, Virginia

I'm 5'10" with brown hair and brown eyes; I wear dark rectangular framed glasses.
—Sarah S., 18, Pennsylvania

I'm 5'3", with long, very blonde hair and about average weight. Can't say I'm entirely awful looking except on Saturday mornings at 8 am when I have to get up for dance class. —Erin G., 14, Alberta

I'm tall with blond curly hair and blue eyes. I have really big feet and am usually wearing jeans and a t-shirt.
—Kristin S., 19, Virginia

Tall (6'1"), brown hair, brown eyes, skinny (140 lbs), funny, good at math but not so good in the rest of the stuff.
—Tyler L., 15, Arizona

I am 5' 4". I have bright blue eyes and a lot of freckles! I also have long brown hair and I am always wearing a smile!
—Michelle O., 14, Virginia

A friendly, brown-haired, brown-eyed female that is about 5' 10" tall. —Christiana R., 13, Wisconsin

There's isn't much to tell. I wear glasses. I always have my hair in a ponytail, hoop earrings in my ears, and my Etnies on my feet. Nothing too terribly special here!
—Stephie N., 15, Arizona

One eye is green, the other is brown; they're kinda freaky. —Miri L., 16, Illinois

I am not skinny, or the exact picture of popularity, at all! I have big eyes and dark eyelashes. I have curly dark brown hair, which I always wear straight.

Well, I'm 5ft and a 1/2 in. tall, brown hair, blue eyes, quite strong (can lift 100 lbs.), fair-skinned and skinny. —Dave S, 14, Michigan

Blond/red/brown hair, 5'8", and blue eyes.
—Calen P., 14, Michigan

I'm short, that's what everyone says, but I don't really care. I'm probably around 4'11" (rounding up). I have long light brown hair a little past my shoulders. My ears are pierced. I'm not very good at this, so that's about all I can tell you! It'd be better to send a picture.
—Emily J., 14, Colorado

I am a 5' 3" male with brown hair and pale blue eyes. I am medium built with fair skin. I have a good smile thanks to the braces that were just removed. —Kevin T., 14, Virginia

A person who loves to have fun! A person who loves to laugh and enjoy life to the fullest! Smart, nice, and is very caring.
—Melisandre P., 14, Kansas

Well, I have brownish hair, which has very grown-out bleached streaks. I am fairly tall and thin, and I have brown eyes (some people say they are gold, though). —Emily N., 17, Oregon

Blonde curls and almond eyes. I love to laugh.
—Monica R., 15, Massachusetts

I have blonde hair that is shoulder length, bluish green eyes; I usually have a smile on my face.
—Mandi D., 13, Wisconsin

Medium height, chin-length brown hair with natural blonde highlights. Blue/green eyes. Slender and medium skin tone. —Cassandra W., 15, Iowa

Think "superstar." Just kidding! I am about 5 foot 3 with shoulder-length blonde hair and dark hazel eyes. Pretty much just like any other person you'd see walking down the street. —Michelle D., 16, New Jersey

Physically, I am 5'3" with short brown hair and big brown eyes. I weigh 110ish and love to paint my nails and doodle on myself when class gets boring so I might look kind of funny with pen marks. I don't really wear make-up because too many girls I know look so fake with it on—so what you see is what you get! —Nicole P., 15, Pennsylvania

I'm 5'3"; I have brown eyes, and brown, really curly hair. I'm sort of tan. I'm a normal-sized person and I try to stay in shape. —Anna H., 15, North Carolina

I'm 5'5" to 5'6". I have brown hair and brown eyes. I'm funny, caring, helpful, understanding, and nice. —Nancy R., 13, California

Young, happy, and healthy. —Carly H., 17, Georgia

One may feel my bright smile. One may hear my peaceful and intelligent voice. —Elizabeth T., 19, Oklahoma

I am about 5 feet 7 inches, average, blue-green eyes, brown hair, funny, fun, understanding, and always up for a great time! —Kelsea R., 15, New Hampshire

I'm about 5'6", with crazy, curly brown hair. My cheeks are perfect for grandmothers to pinch, and I have really long eyelashes. My fingernails are always bitten away (especially when I've been nervous) and I always wear comfortable clothes. —Stephanie B., 16, Maryland

Reader, this space is for you.

I'm 5'6". I have light brown hair and blue eyes. I have pretty straight teeth. —Margaret C., 14, Illinois

I'm about 5'7" inches with short ash blonde hair and light blue eyes. I'm about 67 kilograms (hey, I'm from New Zealand!). I have a scattering of freckles on my face. I am a solid build. Cassey C., 15, Southland, N.Z.

5 feet, 5 inches, 130 pounds, green eyes and long, light brown hair. I am sweet and generous. —Alicia F., 17, Illinois.

—Lindsay K., 15, California

sickly thin, but healthy. I have a long torso, short legs, and broad shoulders.

I'm about five four with brown, extremely curly hair and blue-green eyes. I'm not

Fair to good. It depends if she's "Happy Lise" or "Angry Lise"! —Erin G., 14, Alberta

How would you describe your relationship with your sib?

Close. Being my only sibling, we have become really close. We like to be in each other's company and goof off. It is a lot like "normal" sibling relationships. —Emily D., 18, Virginia

I think to them, I'm more of a playmate than anything else. It's like that for me too, but I also enjoy their company more than anyone else's sometimes. They never judge me, and being with them, it's like staring into innocence. And other times, it's like looking straight at mischief. Either way, it's never boring.
—Alethea R., 13, Minnesota

Adrienne is one of my best friends. I love being around her! We hang out together as much as we can, but sometimes our busy schedules get in the way. However, I love coming home from a night with my friends to a sister with her arms open wide, waiting for a hug. —Lauren O., 16, Georgia

My relationships have their ups and downs. Sometimes my younger sis and I get along great, and sometimes she and I completely hate each other. But I guess she really looks up to me, as I found out when I read a letter she wrote. She said something about how much I mean to her and that I'm her role model, which almost made me cry because I'm not a very good role model. My younger brother and I seem to have a typical sibling relationship, except that when we physically fight he likes to talk about it afterwards and make sure that we make up, which is really sweet.
—Alli J., 15, Ohio

We have a very typical brother-sister relationship. However, since he is much younger, I help him out and even act like a mother figure when he needs it! —Michelle D., 16, New Jersey

It's good. I love her, she loves me, and we're a great big happy family (OK, I'll stop!). We get along really well. My relationship with her is the best I have with anyone in my family. But we do still fight and get on each other's nerves; we're sisters, what do you expect?
—Stephie N., 15, Arizona

I would say that my brother and I are close. It is really hard now that I am away at college all the way across the country. I really miss him.
—Amanda M., 19, Washington State

I would describe it as very, very close. My sib and I have always had that special bond. I love being with my sib and I love that I am so close with him. —Cassandra W., 15, Iowa

Not very close, actually. I don't know how he feels and what he thinks about.
—Cassie W., 13, Colorado

I used to really resent my sister when I was a young teenager. Now that I am 17 and she lives in her own place, I think she is OK.
—Ty H., 17, Washington State

We're close, but he doesn't really know the meaning of love. —Kayla L., 13, Arizona

I would describe my sister's and my relationship as a love-hate relationship, just like most siblings have. We fight over things that are not important to fight over, and then we tell each other we love each other.
—Emily N., 17, Oregon

Strong. Even though he can't talk, I can tell what he is trying to say. He can tell when I'm having a bad day or when I'm in the mood to go outside. I love him and he loves me. It's that simple. —Christiana R., 13, Wisconsin

I would describe it as OK. Most of the time I just watch her when my parents can't. We don't interact too much.
—Matt M., 15, Illinois

32 ★ How would you describe your relationship with your sib?

Wonderful--almost indescribable. We do so many things together. No matter what we do, we end up having a blast! —Michelle O., 14, Virginia

It has its ups and downs just like everything else. There are times where we get into fights but usually not that often because I know when to back off and give her space—and she knows when to do the same for me. —Kelsea R., 15, New Hampshire

Like sisters. We get along most of the time but sometimes make each other nuts. —Megan D., 14, Michigan

We fight a lot. Both of us can be pretty nasty. But I love my brother with all my heart and sometimes I let it out. —Nora G., 13, Virginia

We fight a lot. I think that if my brother didn't aren't many things we can do together.

Reader, this space is for you:

We miss each other when we are apart and can fight like cats and dogs when we are together. We do have our good times. —Cassey C., 15, Southland.

We are always joking around, laughing, and having fun. We don't have deep conversations, but we enjoy each other's company and that's all we need. —Michelle M., 15, New Jersey

Very close; we know each other from our moods to our eating habits. Most importantly, we love, respect and trust each other. —Carly H., 17, Georgia

Tense at best. It's hard to reach my brother and he and I are mutually frustrated with each other. When it is important, I am very supportive of him and I try really hard to help him feel safe and happy in the world. —Miri L., 16, Illinois

Very good; one of the best brother/sister relationships you could ask for. I think that if my brother didn't have special needs that we would probably be fighting all the time—I like it how it is. —Melisandre P., 14, Kansas

Probably not that close. It's often very hard for us to relate to the other and there aren't many things we can do together. However, when we have done things together, we've had a great time. I wish that we were closer than we are. —Ariella M., 16, N.S.W.

Like any other kid with a younger brother. He gets into my stuff, aggravates me to the point that I get in trouble, gets all the attention. I also have to baby-sit him. —Kat F., 16, Washington State

Pretty much like any other sibling relationship. I find myself sticking up for him in public but he knows how to push my buttons at home. —Emily P., 13, Indiana.

Unique—communication isn't a part of it, because he doesn't communicate. He recognizes me, and I know I would do anything for his sake, despite my temporary aggravations. —Allison S., 17, Connecticut

My relationship with my sister is a loving one—even if she automatically says, "Go to your room!" when she sees me! I know that Emily loves me and misses me when we are apart, just as I do her. —Monica R., 15, Massachusetts

My brother and I are usually each other's best friends. We seem to understand each other better than other family members. However, we are still sibs so we fight, but it's mostly me becoming angry with him. —Elizabeth T., 19, Oklahoma

Do you like hanging out with your sib? What do you do?

I love hanging out with my sib. Like any sibling, sometimes you love your brother one day and hate him the next. That is how it is with me. One day we will watch a movie, go on the internet, and wrestle. The next day he may embarrass me. I have come to the realization that not all sibs, not just sibs with disabilities, like their sib every day. This was very important for me to learn. I hang out with my brother when I feel comfortable and I am in the mood, not because I feel obligated. —Emma F., 15, Michigan

As much as I don't like hanging out with my little brother, we still watch movies and play video games together. —Daniel C., 17, Illinois

I don't often hang out with my sib. But when I do, it is not really fun. Usually it's my best friend, my sib, and me. We just hang out and chat. Well, my sib can't talk so we do the talking. —Catherine C., 13, California

I like hanging out with my brother, David. He tells me about work and news about people we both know. —Katie J., 19, Illinois

I do like hanging out with my brother, Matt, because he enjoys being with me so much that it makes me happy to see him having such a great time. He really looks up to me. We play "Sorry" almost every night—he usually wins. I baby-sit him sometimes and we have fun by blasting the music in the house and dancing all around like fools. —Nicole P., 15, Pennsylvania

I actually don't mind hanging out with my sib. We love to listen to music and watch movies and play bingo. —Matt M., 14, North Carolina.

I like to hang out with my brother... but he doesn't always like to hang out with me! When I was little I used to always try to get him to play his video games with me, and sometimes we play game shows together. —Stephanie B., 16, Maryland

I love hanging with Caro. I really enjoy it when Caroline, my mom, and I hang out. Usually we just go to the mall or out to eat or something little, but I think it's really important that parents not only make sure that their typically developing child gets to know their child with a disability, but that the whole family is close. My mom has done an amazing job of that. —Caitlin M., 14, Maryland

I wish I could hang out with my sib. I try all the time to get him to come out with me and my friends, or just me. He won't leave his computer long enough. Sometimes he talks to me about some random thing and I try to talk to him about it. This is as good as it gets. —Miri L., 16, Illinois

Hanging with Scott is one of life's greatest pleasures! We like shooting hoops, watching TV, and especially singing in the car together. Scott is great company and allows me to be my silliest self. —Carly H., 17, Georgia

For the most part, my sib would not be my first choice as someone to hang with. However, sometimes it is tolerable. We watch movies together, play outside, and just act silly. —Elizabeth T., 19, Oklahoma

I love doing things with my sibs but I especially like doing things with Matthew because we get along better. I like to take Matthew for a walk in his wheelchair to the park behind our house. —Britny G., 16, Missouri

Yes, I love watching TV, playing games, or being crazy with my sister. One of our other favorite things to do is shop together. —Megan D., 14, Michigan

Sometimes I don't always have the patience to be understanding and I get frustrated, but most of the time I enjoy hanging out with my sister. We like to go to the movies or to the mall to shop. Sometimes we just sit at home and play Nintendo 64 and Game Cube. —Kelsea R., 15, New Hampshire

Well, sometimes I try--but Lise really isn't the motivated type. Occasionally we'll go to the park but that's about it. When we do hang out I love it and we have lots of fun. I swear Lise's got a split personality. —Erin G., 14, Alberta

Sure do. We just goof around. We like to go to the movies, Wal-Mart, Target, or wherever the wind takes us. Plus, we like to listen to music and dance around the house. —Emily D., 18, Virginia

Yes, of course, he is funny, we sometimes go to see a movie, and when he rides in my car with me, we listen to music really loud and he likes that. He thinks it's funny, and I love it when he laughs. —Megan D., 18, Texas

Not really but sometimes I do. My sister can act pretty stupid sometimes, but that is to be expected. —Tyler L., 15, Arizona

When we aren't fighting--we play foosball or bake something. Sometimes we even go on bike rides. —Emily I., 15, Washington State

The truth is that he likes to be independent and doesn't want his little sister parading around with him all the time. We probably would hang out more if he didn't think of me as family. The best times we have together are in the car on the way to school. We listen to the radio as loud as we please while Jeremy dances as much as he possibly can while staying in his seat. This usually results in memorable moments—especially when we get strange looks from other drivers. —Lindsay D., 17, North Carolina

Sometimes I like to hang out with Phillip, but just like most other siblings, you eventually get bored. But when we do hang out, we go swimming, take a walk, play with pasta, make cookies, or watch TV. —Christiana R., 13, Wisconsin

Hanging out with Andrew becomes harder every day. —Allison S., 17, Connecticut

My sister loves music and she likes to dance not like actual dancing but just hopping around. She also likes if you make noises so I do that with her. She was never into dolls or anything but just likes to be around people having fun.
—Margaret C., 14, Illinois

We goof off, usually. I don't mind doing stuff with him, as long as I'm not forced to. (I had to go to his third grade party without being asked.) But I like hanging out with him. —Kat F., 16, Washington State

I love taking my sister to the movies; we can just sit in the dark and laugh. It's almost like a "normal" sister relationship at the cinema. —Ali N., 18, Massachusetts

Yes, although Stephen embarrasses me at times. He has to overcome so much that it is sometimes stressful to do things with him, but in the end, he makes me proud. We go to church together, we go to the beach together, and we play sports together. My favorite thing to do with Stephen is probably to be his "buddy" in the sports he does. As a buddy, I help him get the balls in baseball, run with him, and help to teach him the rules. That way we both get to have fun together. But there is a lot of pressure on me because Stephen loves to be with me.
—Kevin T., 14, Virginia

My brother and I don't have many of the same interests. He only wants to hang out with me if it's on his terms. I sometimes play Playmobile or Harry Potter with him. He has friends, but they don't come over.
—Nora G., 13, Virginia

It's hard for me to hang out with my sib, since she can't do much. I would like to hang out, but that would be very hard.
—Matt M., 15, Illinois

Sylvia and I hang out sometimes. I'll take her to a movie with my mom or we'll play with the dog together, but mostly I try to avoid her (she gets on my nerves a lot of the time). Paul and I will play games when we're not getting in fights and arguing about who gets the computer. —Alli J., 15, Ohio

Yeah, most of the time. She is a little younger than I am so we don't do things like my friends and I do. We usually just do activities around the house together like make things, play computer, or go outside. —Teresa H., 13, Minnesota

Reader, this space is for you:

My favorite thing to do with my sister is to sing the blues. We will get together as a family to eat a meal. When we are done, I grab my guitar. While I play a blues tune, Janae sings to it. She sings with all her heart. She will sing, "I've got the blues, my mom and dad got married. I've got the blues, I love my brother Ty. I've got the blues, my birthday is coming up." She is really funny.
—Ty H., 17, Washington State

Loud, crazy, fun, Erin, happy...it all fits.
—Erin G., 14, Alberta

Cute. —Tyler L., 15, Arizona

How do your friends describe you?

My friends describe me as being very feminine. I wear pink every day and am into the whole "stop the violence" thing. However, I am also a partygoer and the one who likes to do crazy things such as see how many times I can go on the same roller coaster until I vomit! —Martha P., 13, Connecticut

Funny, outgoing, laid back, caring, respectful, and a good friend. —Megan D., 18, Texas

Most of them think I'm goofy and a bit carefree. But that's just how I act most of the time. I sometimes say whatever is on my mind. —Brooke W., 13, Virginia

A person who is loyal, understanding, and responsible. And someone who is funny and they can talk to about anything. —Kristin S., 19, Virginia

A listener. Fun/funny. Compassionate. Interesting. Unique. Silly. Cute. Clever. Creative. —Emily D., 18, Virginia

I had no idea so I went ahead and asked a few of my friends. Carlo said, "um... sincere, loyal, friendly, and loving." Jamie said, "simply amazing, a real beautiful person." Manda said, "nice, kind, caring, loving, good person to talk to, understanding, polite, and a good friend" and Neftali said, "sweet gal, a good good friend, and she's good with kids". I found out that their answers were very different than I'd say they'd describe me. Pretty cool to hear what they had to say.
—Rebekah C., 17, California

Loud. I tend to have a lot to say and I don't go about saying it quietly. They also describe me as optimistic, outgoing, friendly, authoritative, a good people-person, and caring. —Emily I., 15, Washington State

My friends would describe me as being: optimistic, open-minded, musical, unique and "poodle-icious."
—Emily N., 17, Oregon

— Kathryn C., 14, Illinois

I like to be open and honest, and that I

Funny, happy, nice.
—Lydia Q., 13, Massachusetts

Responsible, trustworthy, and helpful. They say I help out in my community a lot. —Emily J., 14, Colorado

That I am friendly, sarcastic, and free-spirited. That I love to dance, and

Probably smart, short, kind, a good friend, and sometime kind of weird. —Teresa H., 13, Minnesota

As a realistic intellectual. I enjoy reading and learning new things, but there is no way I will try to learn the concepts of astrophysics. —Daniel C., 17, Illinois

They say that I'm a really nice person, I make them laugh, and I'm hyper. —Leslie C., 16, Washington State

I am described as motherly, disciplined, smart, nice, funny, crazy, and mediating. My parents are the strictest parents ever. They worry about me constantly. My dad is a college administrator and my mother is a nurse. So I am always being protected from "becoming one of those college kids" or "the latest medical tragedy." My parents' constant worrying rubs off on me and I start to be the mediator amongst my friends. I'm also addicted to karate competition. —Lindsay D., 17, North Carolina

They think I am shy, smart, mature, funny, and a great listener. —Britny G., 16, Missouri

Also a very caring person, especially towards my brother, as well as being a mad woman who likes Buffy. —Jemma J., 18, Berkshire

Shy at first, but once you get to know me—watch out! I am very excited about everything, not an outgoing person, but someone who will have fun no matter what. That I am someone who is always there when they need me. —Alisa A., 18, Oregon

Relaxed, quiet and a good listener. Also a very caring person, especially towards my brother, as well as being a mad woman who likes Buffy.

Not that I'm crazy or anything... —Elizabeth T., 19, Oklahoma

Impulsive, curious, hyper, out-of-it, graceless, insane, bitch (can I write that?). oh, yeah, they think I'm BLONDE! —Kat F., 16, Washington state

A person who is funny, you can have fun with, nice, and cares a lot for people. Loves to read, because every time they see me I am reading. Someone you can have a lot of fun with and laugh a lot with. —Melisandre P., 14, Kansas

...or going to change personalities. You never know when I'm going to change personalities.

I'm pretty unpredictable. You never know when I'm going to change personalities.

Cheerful, fun to be around, smiley, and always there for them. One of my friends (who lives far away) says that I "have this sweet little voice that I can still hear because it isn't like anyone else's," that really made me smile knowing that I left that kind of impression on someone. —Cassandra W., 15, Iowa

A really outgoing person who's not afraid to speak her mind. They would also say that sometimes I can be a bit bossy but mostly I just try to make people happy, and usually I'm pretty happy myself. A lot of my friends would also say that I'm a good listener. —Alli J., 15, Ohio

Most people who don't know me well would probably say that I am shy and really quiet. Once I get to know people, I am usually really loud and talkative, though. —Amy Mck., 16, Tennessee

As a calm, mellow person—but one who surprises you.

Reader, write in any space you can find!

Funny, strange, fun, etc... —Calen P., 14, Michigan

They say I'm quiet and I'm always serving others. And that I always put a smile on their face. —Leah K., 13, Iowa

I have no idea, ask them! ☺ Kate F., 13, Wisconsin.

I think people see me as being a sensitive-yet-confident musician with an easy-yet-funny personality. I usually have a guitar in my hands. My friends would describe me as the guy who writes and sings really great stuff. —Ty H., 17, Washington State

Smart, cynical, and thoughtful. However, those words would probably not be my first choices for describing myself. —Monica R., 15, Massachusetts

As feeble, because I'm skinny and little. Also, wacky and crazy around them, but shy around people I don't know. They made up a word to describe me, squabbly. I like it; it fits me well. I don't like confrontations, so if there are ever fights I always try to make peace. —Katie J., 19, Illinois

They say that I'm "really cool." I've heard them say artistic, talented, optimistic, intelligent, revolutionary. I guess the best way is just to say Bohemian. They say I belong in the '50s Hollywood era instead of now. —Allison S., 17, Connecticut

My friends describe me as a caring, trustworthy person who is fun to be around. —Lauren O., 16, Georgia

Words that come to mind include analytical, responsible, loyal, fun-loving, outspoken, at times serious, contemplative, sensitive, considerate and 'jen'erous. What an ego trip! To balance that I admit that I can also be quite cutting and cynical. Hopefully, they don't say too many wicked things behind my back. —Jenna H. 17, N.S.W

My friends say that I am talkative, outgoing, and sometimes moody. —Emily P., 13, Indiana

one of the loudest quiet people they know. Someone who likes to have fun but is a good listener. —Megan D., 14, Michigan

I think they think I'm trustworthy, because I never tell any of their secrets. Some of them have described me as small, neat, smart, and creative. —Nora G., 13, Virginia

As serious, intelligent, and aloof. I can't really relate to many of my classmates because most of them have never had things not go their way. —Catherine C., 13, California

My friends would describe me as high energy, talkative, hypersensitive about issues of bullying and compassion, and kinda smart. They would probably say that I am easy to trust and talk to. —Miri L., 16, Illinois

Logical, hard-core, and bossy. Yeah, definitely bossy. —Maggie W., 17, Wisconsin

Probably quite easygoing and not a problem. —Cassey C., 15, Southland, N.Z.

Kind, crazy, funny, hyper, and a good friend. My friends always come to me when they have a problem and that makes me feel like a very good friend knowing that they can come to me with their problems and trust me. —Michelle O., 14, Virginia

As a fun-loving, cool kid. —Dave S., 14, Michigan

Outgoing and funny. I love making people laugh. That is one of the best things. —Margaret C., 14, Illinois

Loud and outgoing, but also sweet and kind and fun to be around. They know that I'm loyal and caring. They always come to me whenever they have a problem or need someone to talk to. My closest friends always say that they envy my strength and courage to deal with my brother. —Jill B., 18, Florida

Friendly, too smart, "Lauren-ish." —Lauren V., 14, Connecticut

They say I'm funny, nice, helpful, caring, and understanding. Also, they say I give really good advice. —Nancy R., 13, California

Crazy, loud, weird, optimistic, energetic and nice... but in my opinion, nice is the most dreadful word in the world. It's in between good and okay... so nondescript and boring! —Stephanie B., 16, Maryland

Sweet, caring, cute, silly. —Katelyn C., 16, Virginia

Fun to hang with, willing to try anything, loves to meet new people, loveable, and high-spirited. —Kelsea R., 15, New Hampshire

Happy, healthy, optimistic, intelligent, generous, intuitive, and genuine. —Carly H., 17, Georgia

I think they'd describe me as responsible, caring, mature, and fun. —Kaleigh H., 16, New Hampshire

Loud, outgoing, outspoken, and funny. —Caitlin M., 14, Maryland

Bizarre, "sweetheart," funny, but sometimes spacey, haha. —Laura P., 15, Virginia

Short, crazy, smart, *mostly* funny, and a terrible artist. That about does it. —Alethea R., 13, Minnesota

As a very funny and outgoing person. I go up to people I don't know and start talking to them. —Ashley S., 13, Minnesota

Generous, funny, compassionate, insightful, and patient. —Alicia F., 17, Illinois.

Most of my friends would say that I am shy and quiet but funny—and that I am patient and always willing to help. —Amanda M., 19, Washington State

I think as sensible, generous, happy, friendly, quiet, organised, and highly motivated. —Ariella M., 16, N.S.W.

Crazy, funny, smart, and a drama queen. —Anna H., 15, North Carolina

Friendly, smart, loyal, a great advice-giver, funny, and always there when they need me. —Kevin T., 14, Virginia

I'm so busy that I'm never home when they want me to be. They'll tell you that I'm ambitious and determined. All of them say that I'm lovable, honest, and sweet. —Christiana R., 13, Wisconsin

Happy, funny, loud, bold, and weird. —Lindsay K., 15, California.

They would say I'm too much of a singer. —Mandi D., 13, Wisconsin

That once you get to know him, you may see that he's a little different, but he's still a person and it hurts him when other kids reject him. —Amy S., 15, Washington State

What do you want people to know about your sib?

He is human too, he can hear, he has feelings—and he is a kid too. —Kathryn C., 14, Illinois

Just because my sister has a severe disability, doesn't mean that people should ignore her, or judge her before they know her. Just like everyone else, my sister has feelings and her own personality, and people can't know what she is like unless they take the time to get to know her. I sometimes think that people forget this and all they see is her disability. —Ariella M., 16, N.S.W.

It can't get any better than him. Even though I might want to throw him out the window, I don't think having a "normal" brother would be different. He's just like all his friends. He gets into my stuff, loves my room, and tries to get me in trouble, like any younger sibling. —Kat F., 16, Washington State

That he isn't scary. He has behavioral issues, and he can seem scary when he's in a "mood," but that's it. He's special in every single way and is so loving and caring. —Katelyn C., 16, Virginia

She is the most amazing person in the world and I wish everyone could meet her because I'm sure she would do so much for the spirits of anyone she meets. —Lauren O., 16, Georgia

I want people to know that she is capable. Adults at her school take one look at her and say "she can't." I want them to know that she can. People try to teach her things I taught her when she was three or four. Most of all, they talk about her when she's in the room as if she can't hear them. I want them to know she can. —Caitlin M., 14, Maryland

Just because she has a disability that doesn't make her any less of a person. So what if she's not "normal"? Who really is? Yes, sarah is different ... just like everybody else. —stephie N., 15, Arizona

She can't control herself when she hits people. In the store, I think people misunderstand, so when she accidentally hits someone they get mad. I just wish that people would understand what my family deals with every day. —Emily N., 17, Oregon

He's not stupid, so don't treat him like a baby. He is also a human being with real feelings! If you mess with him, you'll have to answer to me! —Jill B., 18, Florida

That he is a great kid, and his disability is not who he is. He is a person just like anyone else. He is a very happy kid and loves to laugh! —Emily P., 13, Indiana

He is a very dramatic kid who is full of energy! He loves music, people, and sports. He can play the trumpet pretty well and is getting good at the drums. When he grows up, he wants to be a firefighter, in a marching band, or a band conductor. —Mandi D., 13, Wisconsin

I want them to know that you cannot catch Down syndrome!! —Emily I., 15, Washington State

People often wonder if I treat him differently because he has a disability. I answer no. I am not especially careful around him or think that because he has Down syndrome I should do this or that. I mean, there are certain differences like the fact that I act older when he's really a year-and-a-half older. But I never really take into account that he has Down syndrome. I mean we still kid around and annoy each other as best we can (after all, he is my brother). —Lindsay D., 17, North Carolina

That although he may express his skills differently, he is very talented, and although he may not be able to carry on a philosophical conversation, he ain't stupid. —Carly H., 17, Georgia

That he has a mental disability that is irreversible and may do weird stuff but is a good guy at heart. —Brooke W., 13, Virginia

Reader, write in any space you can find!

Deep down at the core, Arianna is human. She's not some robot strapped to machines, she's a lovable child. —Lindsay K., 15, California.

That there is more to him than not being able to talk or walk perfectly. His disability is not the story of his life. —Nora G., 13, Virginia

That Heather isn't dumb. She knows the rules just like everyone else. And that they should treat her with the same respect that they want in return. If they have questions, then ask, don't just stare. It's rude! —Ashley S., 13, Minnesota

Stephen is a person too more than anything else. The way people look at Stephen sometimes, it's as if they were looking at some kind of animal, and it really bothers me. Even though Stephen is different in some ways, he deserves the same respect all people do. Kevin T., 14, Virginia

David is extremely happy and people don't have to pity him. He's pretty independent and doesn't need someone to watch him every second of every day. —Katie J., 19, Illinois

I want them to know that he has a lot more spirit then a lot of kids have. —Tyler L., 15, Arizona

When Monica was young, she tried desperately to walk. Every day, for 6 years, she tried and tried. Finally, when she was 6 years old, Monica walked. —Martha P., 13, Connecticut

Everyone can see how my sib is different—but what's just as important is to see how he's the same. He does so many things that normal kids do and I wish people could see that. —Emily J., 14, Colorado

He's a great guy. Living with him can be frustrating (and I'm sure he feels the same way about me!), but I'm really lucky to have him, and he's a great friend. —Stephanie B., 16, Maryland

That she's a strong-minded, cool, bubbly, clever kid with a quick wit and a sense of humour. —Jenna H., 17, N.S.W

That if you give him the chance to surprise you, he turns out to be sweet and smart. He gets nervous when he feels rejected, so if you want to meet the greatest kid in the world, all you have to do is be kind to him and he'll come out of his shell. —Miri L., 16, Illinois

Matthew is a very smart and intelligent boy even through he is deaf. —Britny G., 16, Missouri

Do you think your sib knows he/she has a disability? (If so, what does that mean to him/her?)

I don't think she knows that she has a disability. I think that she thinks she is a normal person. —Matt M., 15, Illinois

I believe that the both of them realize that something is not right about them. They see me going out with friends and probably wonder why they do not have them. They see that I can communicate effectively with others and they cannot. I think it frustrates them a lot —Elizabeth T., 19, Oklahoma

Charlie has no idea that he's any different than other kids his age. That will come in a few years. Juan thinks that when he grows up he'll be able to walk like Daddy. He thinks it's just a part of growing up and it makes me sad. He doesn't realize he's any different than his peers either--well, he knows he has a trach, and they don't; he has a wheelchair and they don't, but it doesn't seem to mean anything to him. —Rebekah C., 17, California

Andrew resides in a world very much apart from my (or anyone's) reality. He knows of nothing but his personal wants and needs. His world is in his mind—but God knows what that mind might hold. —Allison S., 17, Connecticut

I think he knows something is different with him. Inside he wants to talk to us but he just can't explain it. —Daniel C., 17, Illinois

I really doubt it, because my brother hardly has any language for us to let him know. —Tyler L., 15, Arizona

David knows he has Down syndrome. He knows he's different, but it sits in the back of his mind because, for the most part, people don't treat him any differently. He doesn't realize exactly how he's different, though. —Katie J., 19, Illinois

I don't think my sister has any idea that she has a disability. She is not "with it" enough to figure that out. I think that she doesn't even understand what is going on with her body, let alone the social label of being disabled. —Emily N., 17, Oregon

In a way, yes. I can tell that my brother senses that he is different than other kids. He doesn't have friends (except me) and he keeps asking if he can invite someone over like I do. He wants to have friends but doesn't know how. My family hasn't told him that he has a disability yet. —Brooke W., 13, Virginia

I think my sib does know that he has a disability and it makes me sad to think that he knows it. —Amy S., 15, Washington State

Jeremy often says that he has "Up syndrome" (known to you and me as Down syndrome) when he is frustrated. Sometimes he says this when he can't think of the exact words to express himself or when he thinks things are too hard to do by himself. He tells me this as if I don't know and I try to explain to him that he can do it if he's patient. I am not sure how much of it Jeremy understands. I am not sure how much of it I understand for that matter. He knows that he is different from most other kids his age but I don't think he knows exactly why. —Lindsay D., 17, North Carolina

I don't think my brother knows he has a disability. I think about that a lot--wondering how he would act differently, if at all, if he knew. —Laura P., 15, Virginia

My brother is very aware of the fact that he is different. It makes him very angry and sad. But, he doesn't give a lot of thought to his label, autism, because he knows he is more than just a diagnosis. —Miri L., 16, Illinois

My sister literally knows she has a disability - she could tell you that she has cerebral palsy - but I'm not sure that she fully understands the limitations that c.p. places on her. She knows the basic ones like that she obviously can't walk - but I don't think she has ever really thought about what her life would be like if she didn't have a disability and I honestly don't think she cares about that either. She has her own priorities. —Ariella M., 16, N.S.W.

Janae loves to tell people she is a "damn mushroom." Sorry... that is my joke about what it sounds like when she is trying to tell people that she has Down syndrome. You have to keep a sense of humor. When Janae sees a young child with Down syndrome she is very proud to tell the parents that the baby is "special" just like her. She is proud to be "special." —Ty H., 17, Washington State

My brother does know he has a disability, but I am not sure if he quite understands what that means. Sometimes when he gets mad or frustrated because he can't do something he will say, "I can't do this because of my Williams syndrome," then we explain to him that having a disability may make some things harder but it doesn't mean he can't do them. —Emily I., 15, Washington State

My sister and brother both know that they have problems. My bro wants to deny it most of the time, but my sister tries to use hers to her advantage. I guess she doesn't really know how different it really makes her, which is probably a good thing since she gets made fun of a lot. —Alli J., 15, Ohio

Sometimes Lise will say something or show disappointment, frustration, or anger at what she can't do. It's almost a "why me?" kind of reaction. I think for Lise, these are things that she has to figure out, or learn to ignore. She knows her diagnosis and I think she understands better than we suspect. —Erin G., 14, Alberta

No, Debbie doesn't really know. She doesn't need to know. She's happy how she is right now. Even if we told her, I don't think she'd understand it. Truthfully, I don't even understand it. I don't see her as having a disability. She's not a disability, she's a person. —Sarah S., 18, Pennsylvania

Yes, I think she knows she can't do what everyone else does, but a lot of things don't bother her. She is pretty content with herself. She does a lot of things she enjoys and people like and reach out to her. —Lydia Q., 13, Massachusetts

My brother knows he has a disability. Like some people,

though, he gets so upset. —Nora G., 13, Virginia

he can't tell how he doesn't sound normal, or can't move as quickly as everyone else can. If he sees or hears a tape of himself,

No, I don't think she does. She has a lot of pain but I think she just thinks we have it too. —Leah K., 13, Iowa

I know for a fact that my older sister knows that she has a disability. To her, it means that she is a little bit different, but I think she is truly OK with that. She still has everything else everyone she knows has. She has a family, sisters, friends, and those little things that make a big difference. What helps is that she knows we all love her and we understand. —Kelsea R., 15, New Hampshire

If Adrienne knows, she doesn't seem to care. She is the happiest and least selfish person I know. If everyone was like Adrienne, world peace would be a much more realistic goal! —Lauren O., 16, Georgia

Reader, this space for you!

Sometimes I think so; he probably doesn't care. He probably enjoys it sometimes 'cause he gets hugs and cool, different gifts. But other times, I think he's frustrated 'cause we don't understand what he wants. —Kathryn C., 14, Illinois

When I was in 2nd grade and just learning about my brother's disability, I asked him at the dinner table if he knew he had a disability. He said "yes" and that was the end of the discussion. Now, my brother's disability means a lot to him. He participates in a lot of self-advocacy for people with disabilities and has a presentation about being someone with disabilities. He will be going to the first national "Disabled and Proud" march in July in Chicago. —Emma F., 15, Michigan

Yeah, my brother realizes that he has a disability. He didn't realize it until just recently, though. He gets frustrated when he can't do things as easily as others can. When he was little, being the way he is didn't faze him at all and now that he is older, it seems almost like he is trying not to stand out as much because he is different. —Alisa A., 18, Oregon

Yes, I think they know. Sometimes one will feel helpless because she can't do things by herself. And the other will feel like she can't do a lot or that what she does is dumb because it takes her a little while to get something. —Kate F., 13, Wisconsin.

I think she is aware that she is different but I don't know if she knows how she is different I think she just knows she isn't like most other people she knows. —Kristin S., 19, Virginia

Actually, I remember when Alex was told that he had a disability. At first, he used it as an excuse, saying that he was having trouble doing things "because of the autism," but I'm pretty sure that he realizes that he is different from other people. —Stephanie B., 16, Maryland

I do. I think it is very frustrating for her that she no longer can do the things she used to be able to do, like go to the movies or the beach. Instead, she has to stay behind and wait while my parents and I go. —Catherine C., 13, California

Yes, whenever someone in my family suggests that Sarah do something she doesn't want to do, she says "I not can do that, I handicapped." She always laughs about it. It doesn't seem like it bothers her, though. However, she can't understand why my mom and dad won't let her drive the car! —Megan D., 14, Michigan

Got any good stories about your sib?

Charlie slept in a crib until about 3 months ago when he got a "big boy" bed. He was soo excited to get this bed. One evening soon afterwards, my mom and I were watching TV when Charlie comes scooting through the kitchen in his pajamas! He had discovered he could get out of bed on his own. Some people would say, oh no, what a bother. But my mom and I were really excited because it's another developmental milestone. He was doing something that other 4 year-olds do: sneak out of bed when they're supposed to be sleeping. My mom tucked him in and he went back to sleep. I could see how happy my mom was. —Rebekah C., 17, California

Matthew loves the book "Green Eggs and Ham." One day, he became upset and to make him feel better, my older brother decided to make him some Green Eggs and Ham. They made scrambled eggs together with green food dye and ate ham. It was so cute! —Katelyn C., 16, Virginia

Once, at a public pool, Clint suddenly handed my mom his swimming trunks! I thought I was going to die! It was so funny! We had him put them back on in the water, and luckily no one noticed. —Melisandre P., 14, Kansas

Once, when my mom and I were watching TV, my sister announced there was a scorpion in her room. This was strange because we live in Virginia and it's not really known for scorpions. It turns out it was a spider about the size of a grain of rice. —Kristin S., 19, Virginia

My brother's random vocalizations once prompted 4 different families to leave their restaurant tables during a 40-minute period! —Allison S., 17, Connecticut

My sister picks up all sorts of phrases and once told a teacher at school to "Talk to the hand." The teacher didn't think it was very funny but I did! —Megan D., 14, Michigan

Jeremy has moments of sincere kindness that few people witness. I am fortunate to have experienced many of them. A few years ago, our neighbor's father died. Jeremy often played basketball and Nintendo with him so he knew him better than I ever did. I wasn't sure if Jeremy understood death but he surprised all of us. Jeremy gave our neighbor a miniature bible. While this might be astonishing to some, those of us with siblings like Jeremy know that they are full of surprises. —Lindsay D., 17, North Carolina

My parents were in the market for a new car and one day drove to a city dealership, parking our vehicle amongst the shiny new ones on the shop floor. They left me (then aged 8) and my sister (then 5) in the car to play, and wandered off to look at the new models. As soon as my parents were out of sight, a man jumped into the driver's seat and began to reverse out of the place. Shocked and desperately calculating the logistics of escaping the moving vehicle, I ventured a tentative, "Excuse me..." My sister was much more direct, reprimanding the hijacker with a strong and indignant, "We're not for sale!" My parents were highly amused when the car salesman "thief" (who needed to reach the car in front of ours) relayed the incident to them. —Jenna H., 17, N.S.W

My brother was a senior in high school last year and was on the homecoming court. He was nominated by a friend and selected by his entire class to be the only male in his grade to represent his class. I love this because he was considered "cool enough" to be selected. I was proud of my brother and told all of my friends. The best part was that my parents had nothing to do with the nomination. It was a complete surprise for us all. My parents pushed for a lot of things in high school for my brother, but they had nothing to do with this. —Emma F., 15, Michigan

As I left for school one morning, I went to my brother's room and said "bye." He called me over; I expected he would punch me and I tightened up to prepare for the impact. Instead, he reached up and gave me a big hug. It meant so much to me because he hates hugging so I knew he really meant it. —Miri L., 16, Illinois

My sister drools so she wears a bib to catch the drool. We always have to say "Catherine, wipe your mouth." Then, she does. This one time I was watching TV on the couch and she comes up and drools all over my leg. "Ewww, Cath, wipe your mouth." So she takes her bib, wipes my leg, and then wipes her mouth. It was so cute because I didn't have to ask her to. —Margaret C., 14, Illinois

During her last Special Olympics T-Ball game, my sister hit the ball all by herself. She looked at me and said, "It's all in the wrist!!" I thought that was pretty cool! —Michelle O., 14, Virginia

My sister only learnt to talk in sentences at age 6. One of her first sentences came about one night when my mother was feeding her dinner and watching the news at the same time. My sister—who felt that my mother was concentrating too much on the news and not enough on her—said "Mummy, meatloaf in my eye." There wasn't actually any meatloaf in her eye, but her fabulous sentence certainly caught my mother's attention. This was only her second sentence ever and already she was joking with people—which really shows my sister's personality!!! —Ariella M., 16, N.S.W.

My mom, who was rushing back from a dance class we took, ran a red light and was stopped by a policeman. Before the policeman could say anything, Allison (who has Down syndrome) yelled out, "Hi, I'm Allison, I'm 5 and this is my sister Lydia. She's 4!" The policeman was so surprised he just told my Mom to drive more slowly. —Lydia Q., 13, Massachusetts

Once my sister was talking to one of my friends about boys and my friend asked my sister if she thought anyone in our gym class was cute. My sister said, "Not exactly because I'm just getting into the 'boy phase' although I'm not quite there yet. But I probably will be soon." —Alli J., 15, Ohio

Several years ago, we were in the car, and Jared was asking my parents about fragile X. He had just learned that fragile X is a genetic disorder, carried in the genes. Curious to know if Scott had picked up on this concept, Jared asked, "Scott, what's in your genes?" Scott looked down, thought for a moment, and then proudly responded, "Underwear!"
—Carly H., 17, Georgia

One year, Monica had to have a spinal fusion during the Christmas season. The doctors told us that she would not be able to leave the hospital for Christmas. I was disappointed and decided I would wait until Monica was out of the hospital to open my presents. Well, on Christmas Eve day my family and I were informed that Monica would go home! That was the best Christmas ever! —Martha P., 13, Connecticut

Reader, this space for you!

Once, my family went to a restaurant that had a crane machine in the back. My brother stuck his arm up the slot where the toys come down. He got his arm stuck and it took about a half-hour to get it out. My mom thought she was going to have to call the fire department. —Laura P., 15, Virginia

Once when we were at the dinner table, my brother asked, "How many people get hurt by salamis?" We were all confused because nobody gets hurt by salamis. Then we realized he was talking about tsunamis—you know, tidal waves. —Brooke W., 13, Virginia

One day Harry was late for school and told his teacher he was late because "my sister forgot her damn medication." The teacher said, "Harry we don't talk like that!" Harry replied, "My mom does!" Honest, this really happened! The teacher had to go outside to laugh! —Alicia F., 17, Illinois.

We were teaching my brother John the first four books of the New Testament, the synoptic gospels: Matthew, Mark, Luke, and John. He would say, "Matthew, Mark, Luke, and...ME!" That just shows you how smart he is. —Elizabeth T., 19, Oklahoma

When Jackie received her diploma at her graduation, she ran down the back of the auditorium, towards the exit where her teachers were. The resource officer— one of Jackie's favorite people—had to literally stop her by throwing himself in her race for freedom. —Emily D., 18, Virginia

48

Is your outlook on life different from your friends' outlook on life? How?

I feel I am more serious than some of my friends, and have been jokingly accused of being a "granny"—apparently very conscious of their well-being. It sometimes angers me to see my peers at parties completely taking their health for granted. As I watch them, I can almost see the problem-free years of their lives dissipating with each clumsily formed smoke ring. I value my own health, and though I might not have the hair, the eyes, or the precise shape of fingernail that I most desire, I appreciate my working body for what it is. As a result, I have a slightly more contemplative and perhaps cautious approach to life, if only for the fact that I value my own so much.
—Jenna H., 17, N.S.W

Most of my friends have lived very sheltered lives— and I admit I have as well. But because they have never suffered a loss, they don't appreciate the little things. They seem to look at life as a game, and never realize the seriousness that goes along with it. I will admit, however, that I do take life a bit too seriously.
—Catherine C., 13, California

My friends may see that life is not fair, but I get a daily example of that with my sibs. Sometimes I just have to say, "God, it's just not fair for these kids to not have a normal childhood."
—Elizabeth T., 19, Oklahoma

I think it's the way I see people. If I see someone with a disability walking down the street, I don't think AHHHHH, or eww, I think wow, that person is out, taking care of herself, being independent. I feel proud of them, even though I don't know them because I understand, a little, some of the things they have had to overcome.
Erin G., 14, Alberta

My outlook is different because of the way I was brought up. I am a very optimistic person, and it sometimes scares my friends when I make the best out of a horrible situation. Also, school and getting a good education is more important to me than it is to most of my friends. Another outlook on life, to me, is being against doing drugs. Many of my friends either do drugs or are not as against drugs as I am.
—Emily N., 17, Oregon

My friends can move through the world without being upset by every incident of cruelty to complete strangers. But I can't see people who are different as strangers, because I see my brother in all of them. —Miri L., 16, Illinois

Different—Early in my life, I realized that some things are just not as important as they seem when you are caught up in a moment. Joy and contentment is not all about possessions but in personal milestones that can be tackled without material objects. —Monica R., 15, Massachusetts

Definitely different. I tend to see things that are different or strange as just "normal" and I know that there is no real definition for "normal"—it's just what you think. My friends notice people's differences and think of them as being weird, rather than just being unique.
—Alli J., 15, Ohio

Most of my friends are Christians so they have an outlook on life that is probably like mine—except I probably understand more that we could die any time. —Leah K., 13, Iowa

In my life, I try to find happiness in little things, not in accomplishing big goals. Most of my friends are worried about what they're going to do once they get out of school, but I like to take classes that interest me and do things that are fun. —Katie J., 19, Illinois

Nope, I tend to surround myself with people with similar values. However, my outlook is perhaps more optimistic than most. —Carly H., 17, Georgia

I think we are similar. We think about what we can do in life to make the world better. We are aware of how our actions affect others. We care about the environment. We are not materialistic. My friends are authentic. Maybe life with my sister made me more aware of what is worthwhile or not. But I am not superficial and neither are my friends.
—Ty H., 17, Washington State

I'm more positive than my friends because I know how lucky I am. I look at my brother and how he struggles at almost everything he does—and then I look at how so much comes easy to me. I bet a lot of my friends would have a more positive outlook on life if they had a sib with a disability. —Nicole P., 15, Pennsylvania

Not much different, except I tend to think about my future more than my friends do. I often think about how my brother's future will be like and the things I might be able do that he probably won't get to. —Emily P., 13, Indiana.

Reader, write in any space you can find!

My friends want to grow up, have families, and have fun, and--even though I want that too--I want more. There are so many people who need my help and I don't think my friends see that. I'm not trying to sound rude by saying this, but a lot of my friends are shallow because they haven't experienced what I have. —Margaret C., 14, Illinois

Yes, my friends don't have to deal with behavior problems every day, and their families can just decide to go somewhere—but my family can't. We have to plan it out because we always have to take meals for my sib (he is on a special diet) and we always have to make sure it is something he can be a part of. Also, just being around my sib makes me realize that we need to treat everyone we meet with as much respect as possible, and never question that amount of respect. —Cassandra W., 15, Iowa

Not really, but I do think that I have been blessed with the ability to easily accept people for who they are, which will help me in the future. —Lauren O., 16, Georgia

My outlook is most certainly different than my friends'. They care more about irrelevant matters that are totally futile, whereas I think I have become a bit more levelheaded than they are. —Daniel C., 17, Illinois

Yes, because I know that not everything is perfect—and that has made me a stronger person. I think I can deal well when things don't always go right because I deal with that a lot with my sister. —Lydia Q., 13, Massachusetts

I think my friends see life the same way I do, because my friends are also my brothers' friends. They understand him and his problems just as I do. I think my friends and I both see our lives as privileged, and people like my brother are blessings. —Megan D., 18, Texas

My friends look at life like a roller coaster—you don't care how scary it is, you just hop on and go and things turn out all right in the end. But when I think about my brother and myself I must think about the future because you never know what is going to happen that could change your life forever. —Christiana R., 13, Wisconsin

Yes, I do. I appreciate the little things in life, and I embrace imperfections. I know that life is a winding road and you never know what's lurking around the next corner, but regardless of what it is, you just need to make a quick stop, stick it in the back seat, and keep going. —Michelle D., 16, New Jersey

Being a sib has made me grow up twice as fast. As a result, I tend to expect other people to be as mature as I am. —Elizabeth T., 19, Oklahoma

Do you think being a sib has affected your personality? How?

It has. Unlike others, I am accomplished in the art of going with the flow—which is just about all you can do when your autistic sister is having a meltdown in public. —Monica R., 15, Massachusetts

Absolutely!! Having Alex as a brother has shaped who I am in so many ways. I worry a lot about things that I don't have to or shouldn't, like what is going to happen to Alex after my parents retire and don't have as much money to support him, and I'm very responsible, in ways that some of my friends who are only siblings aren't. I feel like I am the older sibling, because developmentally, I basically am. . . Being Alex's sister has also made me appreciate life SO much, and understand how lucky I am to have the opportunities that I do. Also, if Alex wasn't my sibling, I would have never joined SibKids (which has definitely affected my personality)!
—Stephanie B., 16, Maryland

Growing up with Janae has helped me think about others' needs before my own. I don't look at people and judge them for the way they might appear. I also learned to take life not so seriously. I have learned to be flexible; life is full of changes. A person's value is not based on their intelligence. Janae has helped me to understand that people with disabilities are often freer and honest in a spiritual sense. When I meet people, I am more intuitive to their genuineness.
—Ty H., 17, Washington State

Definitely. If we go to the store and Catherine is making noises, people look at her weird and it bugs me. But then I think if I didn't have Cath, then I might be that person who's staring. I'm also sensitive on a lot of topics—like if someone calls someone a "retard" as a joke or something. It makes me so mad and I take it personally.
—Margaret C., 14, Illinois

Because I had to comprehend my sister's limitations and be considerate of her differences and needs, I subconsciously played the role of carer when we were at the same primary school. I made sure she was okay, worried when she didn't have friends to play with, and checked to see she had taken her medicines. I preferred listening to adults talk rather than frolicking with kids my own age, and was (and still am) very discerning of who I am friends with. Like me, my friends tend to be fairly adult, self-motivated, and independent people. Perhaps due to my role as an older sister I have high expectations of myself—although I may have been this way regardless.
—Jenna H., 17, N.S.W.

It's taught me that no matter what, I'm going to have to share. —Kathryn C., 14, Illinois

I think I'm a stronger person for having a sister with special needs. I've had to stand up for more things—for both my sister and myself—than I would have if she wasn't in my life. —Sarah S., 18, Pennsylvania

I can't really separate what's just me and what's been part of my experience as a sib. I am mature for my age, and I have learned a lot about the world. I like to think that knowing Caroline has made me less of an "oblivious teenager." —Caitlin M., 14, Maryland

Definitely--My brother has taught me a lot about being a good sister. I know when he wants my help and when he wants to be left alone. I have learned to advocate for all kinds of people, not just those with disabilities. When I hear kids being teased about anything, I am comfortable sticking up for them or afterwards just asking them "how they are feeling." —Emma F., 15, Michigan

It has had a dramatic effect. I am quieter and more serious because I am a sib, and I have such a reputation for being a "sensible girl" among people I know that it has become a standing joke within my family. I think I am more aware and tolerant of others who are different because I am a sib. Although I am sure that my personality is different because I have a sibling with a disability, it is still not easy to put my finger on something and say "I am like this because I am a sib"—it's just who I am. —Ariella M., 16, N.S.W.

Because of my younger sibs, I think that I am more flexible and outgoing. There are so many chaotic things going on in my life all at once that I've developed a great sense of humor—although my friends don't always take what I say as a joke. —Alli J., 15, Ohio

I think being a sib is also the reason why I love taking care of children. —Emily L., 15, Washington State

Yes, a lot. It changed the way I thought about my life and how people suffer. I appreciate how lucky I am to be very healthy. —Nancy R., 13, California

I am extremely compassionate, sometimes too much. I am always the one everybody comes to with their problems and I always stand up for kids who need me to. I would never be this person if I hadn't had to face the bullying my brother experienced. —Miri L., 16, Illinois

It has made me open to all types of people.

Reader, how about you?

Being a sib has made me more patient. Sometimes it takes David a while to tell a story, but in the end, it's worth the wait. —Katie J., 19, Illinois

Yes, my sib influenced my morals, the way I think and make decisions, and the way I treat people. He has such a love for life and family that it makes me want to show others that I really do care, too. —Cassandra W., 15, Iowa

Most definitely. Although I was young when Erick was born, I had looked at people with disabilities as being different from the rest of us. Now I realize that although they may have some trouble doing things we take for granted, they are not very different from the rest of us. My brother has also helped me to be more forgiving. —Michelle D., 16, New Jersey

Andrew's entrance into my life shaped my personality, for better and for worse. His presence has allowed me to be less egocentric, and more accepting and tranquil. Because of Andrew, I have made my life a never-ending quest to realize my dreams. Andrew gave me rebellion, motivation and an exquisitely painful yearning for something, and to be someone more than I am. I realize special gifts, and take nothing for granted. For worse? I am more cynical, many times resentful, and constantly tired. While I can be mature and understanding, in many ways I am also like a small child. I crave the attention that Andrew absorbs and I often feel needy and almost always feel alone. I can be extremely sensitive, and feel misunderstood, and I worry far too much.
—Allison S., 17, Connecticut

Yes. I am shy because when I was little, people treated me differently because of my brother. Parents wouldn't let their kids come play with me because of him. It's like people were scared that his disabilities were going to rub off on their children. I wouldn't let people into my life until I really got to know them. Only then would they see the real rambunctious person I can be! Only a few people have gotten to know the real me. —Alisa A., 18, Oregon

I am quieter and more cautious because of my brother. —Lauren V., 14, Connecticut

Yes. I think I'm a much more relaxed person; I can calm a situation down before it gets out of control. I also think I'm a more emotional person than I would be otherwise. Jemma J., 18, Berkshire

Clinton's personality has rubbed off on me. I'm an outgoing and joking person like he is. —Leslie C., 16, Washington State

Because I have a brother who is different, I see things in ways some people just don't understand. If I see an opportunity, I take it because you never know if it's still going to be there in the future. Also, I'm very motherly. My friends come to me for advice and know they can talk to me about anything. —Christiana R., 13, Wisconsin

I think my little brother has made me much more grateful for what I already have and has made me more responsible than others my age. —Daniel C., 17, Illinois

Yes, it has affected me. We were in crisis when Sharon almost died and now I am happy we're all alive! —Dave S., 14, Michigan

When I was 6 years old, Harry came into my life and changed who I was and what I was going to become. I learned so much, so fast. Before Harry was born, I looked at people with disabilities with such pity. I did not know why they were different. I felt bad. Today, I see Harry as a gift from God. He fills my life with new ideas and challenges every day. Today I see people with disabilities as someone just like me. —Alicia F., 17, Illinois.

Yes, I do! It has showed me how much I love my sibs and that I should spend as much time with them as possible because we don't know when something could happen. It showed me that something like this could happen to any family even though a lot of times we think we are invulnerable! —Leah K., 13, Iowa

Her high spirits and how she is always smiling. —Kelsea R., 15, New Hampshire

What makes you proud of your sib?

The fact that he got through the treatments for his cancer without always asking "Why me?" —Lauren V., 14, Connecticut

Everything makes me so proud of him. He plays t-ball, rides horses, goes to camp, plays basketball, and it always seems like he is enjoying life so much. He just lives every day to the fullest, even if he doesn't know it, and that is so great. He always tries to do things on his own and he always makes people laugh.
—Cassandra W., 15, Iowa

His strength, courage, and innocence.
—Jemma J., 18, Berkshire

I am really proud of my sister when she does stuff that she needs to do without being asked—everyday tasks: practicing her horn, checking her blood sugars, getting her insulin on time, things like that.
—Alli J., 15, Ohio

I feel proud of Stephen when he overcomes the odds, and accomplishes something most people think he couldn't have done.
—Kevin T., 14, Virginia

Everything! I wouldn't trade him for the world!
—Jill B., 18, Florida

I take pride in my sister's achievements, especially when she has had to overcome obstacles that are the result of her disability in order to accomplish them. For example, her fine motor skills are not fantastic, yet this year she managed to make a number of intricate rings in her silver jewelry class. Also, she gave a speech to a senior class at her school on disability issues and what it was like being in a wheelchair. She got "such a thrill" from doing it, and I was so proud of her for having the confidence and stage presence to pull it off well. A couple of her friends even skipped their own classes to attend and support her. This to me demonstrated a social achievement, and a unique skill I didn't know she had.
—Jenna H., 17, N.S.W.

His loving abilities. He loves everybody and everything! It is so amazing to see him relate to different people. I am so proud that he's my brother because of the sense of radiance he gives off.
—Lindsay D., 17, North Carolina

He has dreams, and goes after them. Some people sit around just thinking about what they want to do with their life, and Alex makes an effort to make his dreams become reality. Alex is also an incredible bowler, and he's a great friend. —Stephanie B., 16, Maryland

His artwork—Charlie is an amazingly good artist. His musical tastes—all very cool, with Dave Mathews, Red Hot Chili Peppers, Greenday and good music like that. It's also good because then I can burn his CDs. —Maggie W., 17, Wisconsin

Everyone loves my sister and I get to say, "That's right, she's MY sister!" —Lauren O., 16, Georgia

That he is developing his vocabulary better every day. He works very hard every day. He is learning a lot more with each day and he is one of the nicest, funniest people you will ever meet. I am proud of him for just being him.
—Melisandre P., 14, Kansas

That he is so animated in his personality, and although it might not be the best thing to do, he looks up to me and tries to copy me.
—Kathryn C., 14, Illinois

All the things he's accomplished. It's amazing. No one would have ever guessed he could've done so much. —Emily J., 14, Colorado

When he accomplishes something—from the littlest thing such as getting a homework problem right to big things, like winning a medal at Special Olympics. —Michelle M., 15, New Jersey

He's the strongest purest person I have ever known. He is the closest to an angel this damned earth can get. —Allison S., 17, Connecticut

That she can deal with what has happened to her. If it happened to me, I would just want to die. —Catherine C., 13, California

Reader, write where you can!

I am proud of how nice and kind she is. —Calen P., 14, Michigan

The fact that she doesn't let people get her down. She refuses to see the negative things and is a role model in that aspect for me. —Emily D., 18, Virginia

His positive attitude and the fact that he keeps trying and working hard no matter what. He's an amazing role model. —Rebekah C., 17, California

My sib seems to have no fear. Of course, that's not always a good thing, but fear has kept me from enjoying much of life. So, his fearlessness makes me proud of him. —Elizabeth T., 19, Oklahoma

Monica's life proves that disabilities do not affect how loving you can be. That no matter how disabled you may be. —Martha P., 13, Connecticut

I am proud of my sister not because of how far she has to go, but how far she has come in such a short period of time. —Monica R., 15, Massachusetts

I am proud that my brother doesn't care what other people think of him and that he can just be himself despite all the bad things that have happened to him. —Alisa, 18

In his freshman year in high school he made honor roll—all A's and B's. He had never achieved this before and even though I don't think he understood, my parents and I were very proud. —Kaleigh H., 16, New Hampshire

I am proud that she doesn't even notice how she's different than everyone else. —Margaret C., 14, Illinois

That she is learning to walk with my help. —Dave S., 14, Michigan

When I think of how far Nathaniel and Sophia have come in school, sometimes with lots of help—but sometimes not—I can't help but be proud of them, especially Nathaniel, who had to go 4 years in school without the help he needed. I'm also proud when Nathaniel solves a difficult homework problem and when Sophia says the right word to ask for something. A few years ago, this would have almost been impossible. When I think about how hard they've worked, how far they've come, how much they've struggled, I wonder if I would have accomplished as much in their place, and I'm more proud of them than I can say. —Alethea R., 13, Minnesota

I was so proud of Janae (my sister with Down syndrome) when she went to the Special Olympic World Games in North Carolina. It took a lot of courage for her to play tennis in front of all those people.
   —Ty H., 17, Washington State

Well... I used to want to break a bone. —Nora G., 13, Virginia

When you were younger, did you ever wish you had a disability so your parents would pay more attention to you?

Even though I don't want to admit it, I know there were times when I wished it was me with the disability, and I was the one who got to go see those fun people (physical therapists) and play with the fun toys. —Emily I., 15, Washington State

I never had attention problems. —Calen P., 14, Michigan

Absolutely! I broke my arm 3 times, and I used to sprain my wrists and ankles and such all the time. I seriously don't think I was that accident-prone--I was probably just seeking attention. —Stephanie B., 16, Maryland

I never wished I had a disability, but I did feel left out and unloved so I gave my parents a hard time by changing my attitude and becoming a little brat. But we finally talked it out and they explained to me that although he may get more attention, I get more money, which settled the issue! —Jemma J., 18, Berkshire

No, I get a lot of attention as it is. I don't think I can handle more. ☺ —Michelle O., 14, Virginia

I think rather than wishing that I had a disability so that my parents would pay more attention to me, I tried to succeed in things I was good at so they would pay attention. However, my mum says that when I was 2 years old, I used to pretend to have muscle spasms like my sister did. My mum ignored me whilst I was doing this and I soon stopped. —Ariella M., 16, N.S.W.

Never, I just wanted them to ignore Lise. —Erin G., 14, Alberta

Reader, what about you?

I have always had my own problems to deal with so, no, I have never wanted to be disabled just for the attention of my parents. To get out of doing work...well, that's another matter... —Daniel C., 17, Illinois

I never wished I had a disability, but I wished that my parents would make a bigger deal about the little accomplishments I made, just like they did for my brother. —Katie J., 19, Illinois

No. I was only 5 at the time, and quite the ham, but my parents were gracious and respectful enough to tell me about my brother—all they knew of him at the time. Therefore, I understood fully his need for attention when he came into this world. I was not jealous. —Allison S., 17, Connecticut

Yes, I often wished I had something wrong with me so I could get attention, even before I really understood that that's why my brother seemed to steal it all. —Miri L., 16, Illinois

I did wish that sometimes when I was younger, and once in a while I still do, but then I realize that I'm so blessed to have a normal life, and a family that loves me, that I can spare some of my parents' attention. —Alethea R., 13, Minnesota

No way! I didn't want to be like my brother. In fact, I used to be glad I wasn't like him. —Brooke W., 13, Virginia

56 ★ When you were younger, did you ever wish you had a disability so your parents would pay more attention to you?

No, not really. I'd find other ways for them to notice me, mostly positive ways. I have had times, though, when I feel like any problem I have they unconsciously compare to Charlie's problems and downsize my problems. —Rebekah C., 17, California

Sometimes I did, but then I realized that my life would be even more complicated than it is now. —Kathryn C., 14, Illinois

No, I had my attention days for 6 years before Matthew was born. I was perfectly fine sharing the limelight with him. —Katelyn C., 16, Virginia

I was always jealous of my brother being able to ride in his wheelchair. Whenever he wasn't looking, I would zoom around the house in it and if we went on a walk or to a store, I would sit on his feet in the chair until he got mad and made me get off. —Maggie W., 17, Wisconsin

No, my dad paid pretty equal attention to us. If I wanted more attention, I'd act silly or something. —Leslie C., 16, Washington State

No, my parents always tried to give us the same attention. Sometimes I do wish I had a disability for a day so that I would know what it's like for my brother. —Nicole P., 15, Pennsylvania

No, I never even thought about it. —Cassie W., 13, Colorado

Yes. I often was jealous of the attention that Stephen got I wondered if I would get more attention if I had a disability. Now I realize he needed that attention, and that I should be glad that I have what I have. —Kevin T., 14, Virginia

No. I do not believe I have ever had issues regarding a lack of parental attention, which is a positive reflection on my family. —Jenna H., 17, N.S.W.

I have occasionally thought that, but I have learned to catch myself because I don't want to have a disability. —Catherine C., 13, California

Absolutely not! I don't think my parents paid more attention to my brother. Maybe I was so independent that I didn't want the attention. —Elizabeth T., 19, Oklahoma

No. My parents always did stuff with all of us as a family. It was never a problem for me and I never felt like my parents were doing stuff with her and leaving me out. —Kristin S., 19, Virginia

Yes. I remember refusing to get up off the floor and walk because I wanted to be "like Caroline." —Caitlin M., 14, Maryland

No. My parents went out of their way to give me significant attention. I understood that sometimes my mom needed to take care of my sister's problems. My parents would take turns taking me out to eat or to the park. I would get time alone with them away from my sister. I also went to Sibshops. —Ty H., 17, Washington State

Nope, never did. My parents pay a lot of attention to both of us. I have never felt left out. —Lindsay D., 17, North Carolina

yes, it happened a lot, but then I started thinking my parents are already suffering and worrying about one of their children. If I did have a disability, it would just make it worse for them. —Nancy R., 13, California

I don't choose my friends by how they get along with my family. They all are nice to my sister but we don't hang out with her that much. —Amber C., 13, California

Do your friends get along with your sibs?
Do you tend to pick friends who are likely to get along with your sib?

All of my friends think my sister is really sweet and that my brother is really annoying (funny how that works) even though I think they're both annoying. They usually understand about my siblings' problems and don't have too much trouble getting along even if they don't always understand my sister. —Alli J., 15, Ohio

Reader, what about you?

Oh yes! When my friends come over, my brother greets them at the door and says, "Welcome home!" He even has pictures of some of them. —Jill B., 18, Florida

My friends absolutely love Scott! Sometimes they call just to talk with him. My love for Scott is obvious, so my friends usually create their own special bond with him. —Carly H., 17, Georgia

My friends are so kind to my brother. They might be uncomfortable, but they don't show it. They're the best. —Nora G., 13, Virginia

My sister wants to marry most of my friends. She always wants to talk to them on the phone when she calls from her apartment. She will say things like, "Aaron, I love you!" Fortunately, Aaron has an aunt with Down syndrome so he is pretty cool about Janae. He doesn't seem bothered at all. In fact, he seems to like it. I pick my friends not on whether or not they are tolerant of my sister. They just end up being that way.

Maybe, as a sib, you end up having friends who aren't influenced by trends or peer pressure. —Ty H., 17, Washington State

I don't actively pick friends that would get along with my sister, but it usually turns out that way anyway because I don't like people with negative attitudes towards people who are somehow different. A lot of my friends don't really know my sister very well, but the ones who have met her have always been polite and friendly towards her. —Ariella, 16, N.S.W.

All of my friends are very good and they put up with Catherine. I said, "put up" because they don't understand her. Even though I've been living with her since I was born, even I don't understand her. —Margaret C., 14, Illinois

All my friends are awesome to my sib. They are always so nice. However, I don't pick friends to get along with my sib. After all, they are my friends. —Emily J., 14, Colorado

My best friend, I think, works with my sister better than anyone does. My parents even hired her to work with my sister at camp. —Emily N., Oregon

All my friends are also friends with my brother. Anyone who does not respect my brother is not welcome where I am. My friends stick up for him when someone is making fun of him. —Megan D., 18, Texas

58 ★ Do your friends get along with your sibs? Do you tend to pick friends who are likely to get along with your sib?

I make sure all my friends are OK with my sister. If they make fun of her or anyone in my family, then they can't be my friend. I will always choose my family over friends.
—Teresa H., 13, Minnesota

ALL of my friends have gone through the embarrassing (for them) question of "what happened to your brother?" and have gotten my full explanation of cerebral palsy. From then on, they always speak to him. One friend and I have a tradition (dating back to second grade) of always performing a haphazard can-can for Charlie, which he loves. —Maggie W., 17, Wisconsin

I make sure all my friends know about Adam before they meet him, so they're not shocked and don't upset him. I don't think I really pick out friends who will get on with him, but I believe that my personality attracts relaxed people who won't have any problem with him. —Jemma J., 18, Berkshire

Yeah, my friends like my sib. They jump on the trampoline or shoot hoops with him. Most live close and I've known them a long time so they know what's going on. However, I don't specifically look for that kind of understanding in a person. When I make a new friend, usually I tell them right away about my brother and usually they are very understanding. If they weren't though, I probably wouldn't be friends with them anymore.
—Cassandra W., 15, Iowa

My friends like David; they're happy to see him when they come over. I don't pick my friends by whether or not I think they'll get along with David, but I don't think I could be friends with someone who didn't like him. —Katie J. 19, Illinois

Doesn't matter. If they don't like Andrew, it is their problem to deal with. I don't like him sometimes either.
—Allison S., 17, Connecticut

My two very best friends get along great with Matthew. I have a lot of other friends who are great to him as well. Then, I have some friends who treat him like dog poop. But what can I say? That's the way the world turns.—Katelyn C., 16, Virginia.

Yes, I think I do tend to pick friends who are likely to get along with Nathaniel and Sophia, because it's easier that way. And besides, my take on it is if they're not going to try to get along with Nathaniel and Sophia, they're not really my friends. —Alethea R., 13, Minnesota

Occasionally, my friends have gotten the idea that they can insult my brother just because I did. However, there is a world of difference between what I say and what other people say. I demand that my friends treat my brother with respect or they are out of the picture. —Miri L., 16, Illinois

My friends and Stephen get along very well. But I don't pick friends specifically because they will get along with Stephen. Rather, I pick friends who are compassionate and understanding, and as a result, they get along with Stephen. —Kevin T., 14, Virginia

My friends love Sarah. They all get along very well. And it seems like I do tend to pick friends that would treat my sister with respect. The way I see it is if my friends can't accept my sister, then they can't accept me. She's a part of me, and she comes with me. —Stephie N., 15, Arizona

My friends usually ignore my sib. She tends to scream a lot especially during dinner and that annoys, to say the least, my friends, and me too. Catherine C., 13, California

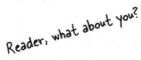

What do you tell your friends about your sib's disability? Do they ever ask questions?

I have a wonderful speech explaining how my brother acqired cerebral palsy. It's very scientific, and in my opinion extremely flattering towards my brother. Most people just ask really obvious qestions that are easy to answer and go along the lines of "but his brain?" —Maggie W., 17, Wisconsin

I tell my friends that my sib was born with cerebral palsy and then I have to tell them what it is. A lot of kids ask about his wheelchairs and why he can't walk. They ask if I ever get to ride in his wheelchair or if he has ever run me over. I hate it when people ask if I have l disability too! But otherwise, I like to answer their questions. —Emily P., 13, Indiana.

I often don't bring it up to my friends because I can never find the right time or words. I question how I should refer to him and it makes me mad at myself for not knowing how to say it or not just coming out and saying it. But if they ask me, I tell them. —Michelle M., 15, New Jersey

I tell my friends "on his planet he's a rock star, but he doesn't quite get how things work here. In other words..." Then I explain his behavior and his diagnosis so they don't get weirded out when they meet him, because you can't see his disability. —Miri L., 16, Illinois

After a new friend meets my brother, they ask what's wrong with him the next time we're alone. I tell them the truth and all I know. They usually say "oh" and don't ask about it again. —Nora G., 13, Virginia

I guess I tell them (my best friends surely know) or they figure it out by themselves. Sometimes people come over and laugh at the goofy things he does or roll their eyes. It's sort of frustrating. —Brooke W., 13, Virginia

I tell my really close friends everything because they are the ones that are really there for me. Sometimes kids at my school just ask out of curiosity. It doesn't bother me when they ask questions. It makes me realize that there are people in my high school that really do care about the situation. —Cassandra W., 15, Iowa

I tell my friends that my sister has cerebral palsy and how this affects her. I almost always tell them this outright at some stage, but I imagine they pick up more information along the way as they get to know me. I believe that any question that is polite and well-asked by a person I am connected to deserves to be answered. —Ariella, 16, N.S.W.

I tell my friends the cold hard truth, and they've never snickered or sneered. They're compassionate. They do ask questions sometimes, which are good—I want to educate them. —Lindsay K, 15, California.

I tell my friends exactly what my sister's disability is. They ask questions, and I encourage them to ask questions. I think if you are curious about anyone, you should ask; it's not insulting to me. I enjoy telling others about my sister. —Emily D., 18, Virginia

I don't get many questions, but when I do, I just say that he learns things a little slower than everyone else. And no, it's NOT contagious! —Katelyn C., 16, Virginia

I tell my friends that Stephen has Down syndrome, and then explain that he has an extra 21st chromosome in every cell of his body. Therefore, he learns slower and has a hard time doing exercise. Many of my friends have asked specific questions, and I always do my best to explain. I like the analogy of adding too much sugar to a cake. You still have a cake—it's just a "different" cake. —Kevin T., 14, Virginia

Mostly I just give them the facts. I do, however, have a couple friends who I can talk to about how I'm dealing with it all. Some friends do ask questions but mostly it all kinda goes over people's heads. —Alli J., 15, Ohio

I tell them that she can't talk or understand people—but I also tell them that she is still fun and cool. —Calen P., 14, Michigan

It is very hard to describe autism to my friends because it is such an abstract concept. I basically tell them that she lives in her own little world. The most frequently asked questions are "What is autism?" and "Do you know why it happened?" Since we don't know why Julie is the way she is I can't answer either question as fully as I would like to. —Emily N., 17, Oregon

My friends are always asking questions about him. They all find him very interesting. I tell them everything I know about him so that they can understand him more and treat him more like a regular person. —Megan D., 18, Texas

Well, I had this new friend come over, and she was kinda looking at my brother weird and I quietly told her he was autistic. She said, "What's that?" And I told her that I don't know how to explain it (because I didn't want to say it in front of Clint) and later on explained it to her. And ever since, she thinks Clint is the cutest thing in the world! (By the way, she is this REALLY popular girl in our school.) —Melisandre P., 14, Kansas

I tell them that my brother has Down syndrome, which affects him both physically and mentally. Sometimes they ask questions and I am always pleased to answer. Questions only mean they are interested and want to learn more. I take it as a positive sign. —Lindsay D., 17, North Carolina

Most kids don't recognize that my brother has a disability, but I make sure that I let all of my friends know. I tell them that my brother has Williams syndrome and some things—like fine motor skills—are harder for him, but overall he is just like a normal kid. —Emily I., 15, Washington State

The only question any of my friends has ever asked is, "Do you think she knows she has a disability?" and I didn't really know so it was hard to answer it. I don't really tell my friends straight-out "she has a disability." I figure when they meet her they will know and if they have any questions they will ask. —Kristin S., 19, Virginia

When I first meet people I just say, I have a sister, her name is Caroline. I let the rest unfold. That's what siblings of typically developing children do. When most kids meet someone new, they don't give away the story of their siblings' lives. It comes up in conversations; their stories unravel. Why should it be different for me? —Caitlin M., 14, Maryland

I tell them that Down syndrome is a mental disability that affects Erik's speaking, communicating, and overall intellectual level. They don't ask questions much—I think they might be nervous that they will offend me. —Emily J., 14, Colorado

Of course I tell my friends about Phillip's disability. If I don't tell them before they meet him, they'll ask questions afterward. I'm always happy to answer their questions. —Christiana R., 13, Wisconsin

Reader, write where you can!

What is your pet peeve?

I hate when teenagers have no clue what's going on in their family. I also hate when teenagers try to be mature by doing sexual things that they aren't ready for. —Caitlin M., 14, Maryland

Being ignored. I don't mind it if I am told "...not now" or "...later," but when I am flat-out ignored it kills me. —Catherine C., 13, California

I hate it when people add an "R" into a word that shouldn't be there, like "Warshington" or "idear." —Kat F., 16, Washington state

Does this sound weird to you? "My sister is spina bifida..." "Oh, him – he is Down syndrome." A person cannot BE a disability. They do not introduce themselves and say, "Hi, my name is spina bifida." This sort of talk, aside from being grammatically incorrect, puts the disability and the negativity that goes along with it, before the person. It effectively conveys their limitations as more important than their strengths. Another example of this is "handicapped person." Suddenly, they are a disorder, a negative thing, before they are an individual. My sister is not a disability; she is a young person who just happens to have a disability. —Jenna H., 17, N.S.W.

I am absolutely crazy about being on time to the exact minute. —Matt M., 15, Illinois

When someone calls me perfect or disses one of my friends. —Martha P., 13, Connecticut

Meanness. I get so annoyed by people being mean. It just annoys the crud out of me. —Emily D. 18, Virginia

Hypocrites. —Alicia F., 17, Illinois

Having someone come in my room without knocking. —Lydia Q., 13, Massachusetts

Cracking knuckles in a silent room. —Ashley S., 13, Minnesota

I just can't stand it when the kids put things in their mouths that aren't supposed to be there! It is soo gross and it just bothers me! —Michelle O., 14, Virginia

When people who don't know what you're going through say, "I know how you feel." It just drives me up the wall. I'd rather they say something like "I don't know what you're going through but I can imagine and..." You know? —Alli J., 15, Ohio

Well...I work in our church nursery

I hate it when people walk with their toes hanging over their sandals. —Nicole P., 15, Pennsylvania

My biggest pet peeve is probably when people use the words "retard," "cripple," and "spastic" as general insults to people who are none of those things. It annoys me because it is inappropriate and unnecessary. Another pet peeve of mine is when people leave taps dripping... —Ariella, 16, N.S.W.

People who ask questions even when they know the answers, just to get attention. Also, skinny people who say they are fat when they only weigh like 100 pounds annoy me. —Christiana R., 13, Wisconsin

People who lie. Carly H., 17, —Georgia

IBT (Imitation Baby Talk) like "potty," or "toofers" (my mom's IBT word for teeth), etc. It annoys me to no end. —Alethea R., 13, Minnesota

Losing things—and I am always losing things. —Erin G., 14, Alberta

I can't stand phony people. —Ty H., 17, Washington State

I hate people who dye their hair blonde when they have dark hair, and then they let the roots grow out. It looks horrible! —Sarah S., 18, Pennsylvania

I have many! People who make statements about right and wrong while refusing to acknowledge that what they are saying is simply their opinion; people who take on a cause and talk a lot about it but have clearly not done their research. Other kinds of people that irritate me are people who think they're better than others, people who act stupid to seem cute, and people who talk in a monotone. Yeah, that's about it. —Maggie W., 17, Wisconsin

People who throw around big vocabularies just to intimidate others. —Monica R., 15, Massachusetts

People who are manipulative and talk behind each other's backs. —Stephanie B., 16, Maryland

People who don't do anything to their hair; they just do the same thing every day or don't do anything with it at all. —Nancy R., 13, California

People who don't know someone—and haven't taken the opportunity to get to know them—but decide to judge them anyway. —Lindsay K., 15, California.

People who leave their car blinker on when they don't need to turn and their windshield wipers on when there is not enough water to wipe off. —Amy McK., 16, Tennessee

When my brother puts his dirty, sticky fingerprints on the CDs. —Brooke W., 13, Virginia

When someone says that they are going to do something and they don't follow through. —Michelle D., 16, New Jersey

When people truly bully other people, it really bothers me. —Kevin T., 14, Virginia

When someone doesn't finish their sentence. —Lauren O., 16, Georgia

It's got to be when people use the word "retarded" in a derogatory sense. —Elizabeth T., 19, Oklahoma

Squeaking teeth, my sister does it all the time!! —Kate F., 13, Wisconsin.

The word "retard" makes me crazier than anything else in the world. —Miri, 16, Illinois

I absolutely have no tolerance for people throwing "retard" around. My friends never do and if my friends or I hear someone using that word to describe something negative, we see it as trashy and uneducated. That word hurts me and people seem to just throw it around. —Ali N., 18, Massachusetts

When my sister, who sleeps in the same room as me, makes a mess in my room. She makes a mess of her clothes and I get blamed for it. —Leah K., 13, Iowa

When people pick or bite their nails. — Emily I., 15, Washington State

When I'm sitting on the couch or bed and someone else is like bouncing their feet or fidgeting. I get so frustrated. —Kathryn C., 14, Illinois

My biggest pet peeve is when people use words incorrectly. For example, "Oh, that's so gay" or "Oh, that's so retarded." It drives me up a wall that the people who say these sorts of things are ignorant to the point that they don't understand that they are offending people who are gay, retarded, and/or who know someone who is. Why can't people just say "stupid" or "boring" like they really mean!?! —Emily N., 17, Oregon

When people don't call back on the phone—it deflates me. And for some reason I can't listen to people giving directions—it aggravates me. —Allison S., 17, Connecticut

When people snort their noses instead of using a tissue and blowing their nose. It plain and simply ticks me off. —Daniel C., 17, Illinois

A watch—I hate not knowing what the time is!!! —Ariella, 16, N.S.W.

A book, to chase boredom away. —Alethea R., 13, Minnesota

What item must you have with you all the time?

A hair tie because I can't always tolerate my hair being down. —Kelsea R., 15, New Hampshire

Chap Stick! I hate it when my lips hurt. I have lip-gloss or Chap Stick in every bag, backpack and several in various pairs of pants because I have to have it all the time. —Kristin S., 19, Virginia

Chap Stick, at all times I must have, I probably have at least 15 varieties at this moment somewhere, but I constantly lose them, so I'm always buying more. —Amelia C., 18, Minnesota.

My keys and school ID card. —Amanda M., 19, Washington State

I always wear a friendship ring that I got for my birthday. All my closest friends have an exact copy. —Michelle D., 16, New Jersey

—Melisandre P., 14, Kansas

A book because I love to read. —Britny G., 16, Missouri

I always have to have a watch on. I'm always worried about being late/ being too early. —Katie J., 19, Illinois

A pen. And a notebook, if I can help it, but I can always write on my hands if I need to. I am constantly making notes concerning the characters I'm working with, or the plot, or something or other. I'll always have one—in my pocket, in my purse, in my hair. Always. —Maggie W., 17, Wisconsin

I always have my cell phone on me. Often I don't know what I'd do without it, but sometimes my parents call too much and I want to throw it! —Nicole P. 15, Pennsylvania

It would either have to be a cell phone or a book. —Melisandre P., 14, Kansas

A pen and piece of paper! At all times! No exceptions! —Lindsay K., 15, California

My "God connection" is what I must have at all times. I would be lost without it. —Elizabeth T., 19, Oklahoma

I must have a paper and pen with me at all times. I like to draw and I love to make lists, and without paper where would I be? —Monica R., 15, Massachusetts

Lip-gloss...definitely. —Martha P., 13, Connecticut

I always have a chain with my St. Benedict medal on it. I put it on, got it at a Life Night at my church one Sunday, and I haven't taken it off since. —Stephie N., 15, Arizona

A ponytail holder. Gosh, if that hadn't been invented, I think I'd go crazy! —Katelyn C., 16, Virginia

My purse! Inside are my make-up, wallet, body spray, and gum! —Alicia F., 17, Illinois.

My cell phone. I don't know what I'd do without it. —Lauren O., 16, Georgia

A little book of pictures I have of all of my family and friends! Whenever I am away from my family, I look at all of the pictures I have and it makes me feel like I am home again! —Michelle O., 14, Virginia

A radio. —Nancy R., 13, California

A shirt. —Erin G., 14, Alberta

My bracelets. —Laura P., 15, Virginia

Memories of "Daniel." —Mandi D., 13, Wisconsin

I must have clothing on!!!!!!!!!! Other than that, I don't know. —Leah K., 13, Iowa

Money, because if anything goes wrong, it can get you out of almost any problem. —Jemma J., 18, Berkshire

My wallet because without it I simply feel naked. —Daniel C., 17, Illinois

Cell phone. Lost without it. Car keys also; but if I didn't have those I couldn't get where I was without them, so. ;) —Allison S., 17, Connecticut

I have to bring my CD's and portable CD player with me. —Amy S., 15, Washington state

My cell phone. I like to be reachable at all times! —Emily I., 15, Washington State

My glasses! I'm practically blind without them. —Brooke W., 13, Virginia

I am absolutely obsessed w/Skechers. Wherever I go, I usually am wearing Skechers. —Margaret C., 14, Illinois

My ID. —Megan D., 18, Texas

My cell phone or Chap Stick, but that's when I'm not carrying my purse. —Kathryn C., 14, Illinois

My toe ring. I never take it off—not even in the shower. I swim with it on too. —Christiana R., 13, Wisconsin

My watch. It drives me nuts when I forget it!!! I am always looking at the time. —Teresa H., 13, Minnesota

My cell phone. When I don't have it, I feel like something is missing, I'm just that pathetic I guess. —Sarah S., 18, Pennsylvania

My wallet and money card. —Cassey C., 15, southland

My Burt's Bees chap stick. —Amy McK., 16, Tennessee

My head. —Kate F., 13, Wisconsin.

Underwear! —Carly H., 17, Georgia

A pen and paper for jotting down my observations of the amazing world around me. —Jenna H., 17, N.S.W

My cell phone. —Rebekah C., 17, California

My lucky ten pence. —Dave S., 14, Michigan

A book to read! —Stephanie B., 16, Maryland

My CD player. —Calen P., 14, Michigan

My electronic organizer. I can put in phone numbers, addresses, and write down ideas or lyrics that pop into my head. —Leslie C., 16, Washington State

My brain. —Ty H., 17, Washington State

My watch. If I don't have a way of telling time, I will be hopelessly lost and you might just find me wandering aimlessly halfway around the world with no idea where I am supposed to be. —Miri L., 16, Illinois

My soccer ball. —Kevin T., 14, Virginia

Probably my glasses, 'cause I can't see without them. —Emily P., 13, Indiana

Reader, what about you?

My sunglasses. I can't seem to go anywhere without them... especially when I'm driving! —Alli J., 15, Ohio

Can you imagine what it would be like if your sibling didn't have a disability?

It is not very difficult for me to imagine, because my sister had 8 years to develop her personality before her disability set in. I imagine her being very smart and playing an instrument, probably piano or cello (I don't know why—it just fits). She would do a lot of volunteering, especially environmental stuff. However, I don't know what I would be like if her "accident" never happened. A lot of what I do is because of what happened to her, so even though I've often imagined different personas, none of them seems to fit. —Catherine C., 13, California

I don't like to imagine it, because then I wouldn't be the same person I am now. I think there would definitely be sibling rivalry because of how close we are in age. But I think I would feel like a part of me was missing. —Christiana R., 13, Wisconsin

I suppose it would make my family just like any other family, although we might have a bit more money than we do now. I'd probably have many more fights with him but I wouldn't necessarily favor it. I'm perfectly happy with the way my life is now. —Maggie W., 17, Wisconsin

I can very easily imagine what it would be like if Arianna didn't have disabilities. Part of me yearns for that, but part of me thinks that this happened for a reason—to make me a stronger and better person and to teach me to be more grateful for everything I can do—however simple it may be. —Lindsay K., 15, California.

I could, but why would I? I am happy for who he is and the person he has become. —Carly H., 17, Georgia

I have tried this on long, boring days, and believe me—it's scary! I think it would be great for Caroline to be able to do things that she currently cannot, but things wouldn't be the same. I have come to accept my sister's disability and my unusual lifestyle. I love my life, and the only reason I can see to think of changing it would be for Caroline's sake. —Caitlin M., 14, Maryland

I have no idea what it would be like if Alex didn't have a disability. I actually think about this a lot, and I guess he'd be in college right now, since he's 22, and he's really smart. He's a big dreamer, too. My hopes are that he would be happy, and excited about the future, but, then again, that's what I hope for him anyway. —Stephanie B., 16, Maryland

I know that my life wouldn't be as interesting if Heather didn't have a disability. But I also wouldn't have as much stress in my life as I do now, having to deal with the teasing or odd looks towards my sister. —Ashley S., 13, Minnesota

It is easy to picture my brother without Down syndrome because I often forget that he has a disability at all. He is so much like any other kid his age that even when I am helping him with schoolwork I forget that he has a disability. —Michelle D., 16, New Jersey

I try not to, as it pains me so. But yes, I have thought of it occasionally—I could think of nothing I would rather have than Andrew to have been typical. —Allison S., 17, Connecticut

I would be spoiled for one, and I wouldn't be who I am today. —Kayla L., 13, Arizona

Life would be different. I always wanted one of those older sisters who was there—like a mom—and would always give advice and made you feel cool. I never really did get that, because Robin needs her space and "alone time." With my younger sister, I try to be the person for her that I always wanted and I'm hoping I'm not doing too bad at it. :-)
—Kelsea R., 15, New Hampshire

No, I can't because I have lived 15 years with him. Yeah, there are rough spots, but I have found that I get through them all. There are great things about my brother. He is always smiling and he passes it on to me. And there are hard things; like he can't read or write. But there are always going to be hard things about having any kind of sib. I love and admire my brother for who he is. —Emma F., 15, Michigan

I don't want to imagine it. I like him the way he is. My family has been blessed with my brother, and I would never ever want him to be normal. As mean as that may sound, I believe he's completely changed my views, and brings sunshine to the lives of everyone around him. He's perfect just the way he is, disability or not.
—Katelyn C., 16, Virginia

Of course. I would probably be on time to places more often. Our family room would be open way more of the time. We would probably argue with each other. Even my pantry would be different. My life would change.
—Matt M., 15, Illinois

Actually, I can't. My family—with everything from arguments to our current moving plans—is centered on my brother more than half of the time. It would be weird for him to have no disability—we'd have to talk about different things. —Laura P., 15, Virginia

Sometimes it's hard to sit back and watch my sister being the way she is. However, I love her so much that if she was "normal" our relationship wouldn't be the same. If my sister was normal, I think I would be kind of a jerk because I would not be used to people with disabilities.
—Margaret C., 14, Illinois

Yes. With Down syndrome, Jeremy likes movies, girls, friends, games, vacations, Big Macs, karate, and being the center of attention. Without Down syndrome, Jeremy would like movies, girls, friends, games, vacations, Big Macs, karate, and being the center of attention. Not having a disability could never change "Jeremy." It might change his body and mind, but his soul would remain intact. —Lindsay D., 17, North Carolina

Sometimes I think about this. I bet he would still like video games and be good at reading. Would Grant be cool, nerdy, unpopular, or mean? I don't know. Sometimes I wish he was normal, sometimes not. He embarrasses me sometimes. Then other times, he's quite cooperative.
—Brooke W., 13, Virginia

It would be really different and I'd probably be sharing a room with my sister and she wouldn't be treated like they treat her now. My parents are always worried about something happening to my sister, like rolling off the bed or choking, and they worry too much about me too. I think I'd have more freedom. —Amber C., 13, California

Nope. People ask me that all the time. I think my life is normal, I couldn't even think about how it could be any other way. —Sarah S., 18, Pennsylvania

I would not be where I am today. Without my experiences with my sister, I would not have the same interests in school and life. Also, family life would be very different—no schedules around the house, and the locks on the food closets would be gone. —Emily N., 17, Oregon

To be honest, I just can't. I admit there are downsides to being a sibling of someone with a disability, but I can't see my life without that. I believe that Sarah's disability has taught me so much and I don't want to find out what kind of a person I would be without it. —Stephie N., 15, Arizona

I have friends who are twins and sometimes I think that my twin sister and I would possibly be similar to them. I do know that my life would be very different though, because—for a start—I would still be living in Israel where I was born, and not in Australia. —Ariella M., 16, N.S.W.

No way! Everything would be so different! I can't even begin to imagine it. —Cassie W., 13, Colorado

I think I would be so bored that I would have to fill in for all of the craziness that goes on in our house. —Daniel C., 17, Illinois

Yeah, it would be quiet! No, that's not true—I'm loud enough for the both of us. But seriously, I don't think life would be as interesting without Lise. I mean there are like a million kids without Williams syndrome but there are only a couple with it and, of course, only one Lise. —Erin G., 14, Alberta

Reader, what about you?

She has had her disability for so long that I don't think I could, but all I know is that it would be sooooooo wonderful! She is so beautiful and I love her smile. It would be so nice to see that smile more often. =(—Leah K., 13, Iowa

I think about this often, but I do not know what my life would be like without Jackie. I do know that my life would not be as enriched as it is now.

Whenever I used to make a wish (when blowing out candles, for example) I wished for him to be "normal." I thought it was something I could alter. I confided this to a friend who helped me realize that I love him for who he is and I should just wish for his happiness—which is now what I wish for. —Jemma J., 18, Berkshire

—Emily D., 18, Virginia

Does your sib ever frustrate you? How?

Even though she is older than me, she gets away with things that I would get blamed for because "I know better." And it frustrates me when she doesn't understand the reason behind things that we have to do. She wants to do her own thing and gets upset when she can't. —Kristin S., 19, Virginia

All the time. He can be very stubborn and argumentative. He doesn't like to change his behavior and it can be really annoying to argue with him about the same things every day. —Amanda M., 19, Washington State

I think everyone gets frustrated with their sibling at one time or another, whether they admit it or not. But when Adrienne does get on my nerves, I can't stay frustrated for long! She has the ability to make anyone smile.— Lauren O., 16, Georgia

I get frustrated during the summer because my family and I cannot go to the beach. It is too hard to push Monica's wheelchair through the sand. —Martha P., 13, Connecticut

I get irritated when we argue and she refuses to see logic and rationale in my flawless and utterly reasonable points of view ;) and frustrated when she seemingly doesn't make an effort to include herself in social situations, when she is obstinate, sulky and when she pulls the "I'm a teenager and I'm here to annoy you" line. —Jenna H., 17, N.S.W

I do get frustrated—not at him, but at the situation—when I don't understand what he is trying to tell me. He gets frustrated too and I feel bad for him and then he throws a fit and I know he's hurting inside. —Rebekah C., 17, California

I know he is smart and he can talk really well when he wants to—but sometimes my mom babies him or he acts so lazy. And sometimes he gets mad at my parents and takes his anger out on me, just because he doesn't really know any better. —Jill B., 18, Florida

I often have to answer the same question over and over to get Stephen to understand. Overall, though, he is more of a blessing than an annoyance. —Kevin T., 14, Virginia

It bugs me when Dylan can't do something without help, like making himself something to eat. It seems like he always needs help with something, and it just bugs me sometimes. —Alisa, 18

All the time—but God knows how many times I must frustrate him. Especially with his yelling and his constant playing of video games (which he always turns up very loud, since he can't hear). Sometimes the frustration is nonstop. —Allison S., 17, Connecticut

Many times, Emily wants to express herself but can't; as a result, she will burst into tears and sometimes get violent. This is hard for her and for me, too. I long to know what Emily wants to tell me. What secrets does she hold? —Monica R., 15, Massachusetts

When he has his mind on something, he has to do it and won't give up. It's especially frustrating when he's doing something dangerous and you can't get him to stop. —Kayla L., 13, Arizona

Of course, but Jared, my brother without special needs, frustrates me too! Everyone gets frustrated or embarrassed, but I like to turn those moments into learning experiences. Yeah, sometimes Scott acts weird in public or is impatient, but I try to move on and love him for who he is.
—Carly H., 17, Georgia

My brother sometimes comes into my room and messes things up or takes something from my desk—even though we ask him over and over to not go into my room.
—Emily I., 15, Washington State

My sib screams a lot. Once, on the way to the movies, she started screaming. I tried to ignore her and my dad told me to pat her stomach. I did that for a little while and she kept on screaming. When we pulled into the parking lot, my dad lectured me on how inconsiderate I was being. My head was throbbing, my sib was still screaming, and I just wanted to scream at her to shut up.
—Catherine C., 13, California

Grant always seems to frustrate me one way or another. At dinner, he likes to copy me by drinking from his glass at the same time I do. Hey, after a while it gets on your nerves!
—Brooke W., 13, Virginia

Who doesn't? But I usually become frustrated with Jackie when I am frustrated about something else. It's a sibling thing.
—Emily D., 18, Virginia

Most normal siblings fight but she doesn't understand I should defend myself.

He sometimes expects me to do anything he wants, but when I can't because of homework, he gets mad. I feel bad, but I'm also frustrated because I want him to understand that I don't have the time.
—Emily J., 14, Colorado

Often! The most frustrating thing is when she hits me I can't fight back to defend myself. When my sister hits me, she doesn't understand the consequences. I have to control myself and not hit her back. I have the right to hit her back.
—Emily N., 17, Oregon

Oh yeah! She can't communicate as well as we'd like her to, and whines for things she wants until she has them. Sometimes, it's hard to figure out what she wants, even if it's only juice! —Lindsay K., 15, California.

My sibs frustrate me when they ask me to do things they can do on their own—such as getting a drink of water or washing their hands or telling me they have to go to the bathroom. It just gets really old! —Kate F., 13, Wisconsin.

My sib frustrates me when he won't walk. He loves being outside, but when it's time to come in he becomes a "limp noodle" and it seems impossible to get him in the house.
—Cassandra W., 15, Iowa

My brother acts out a lot, and he can become aggressive, which is really frustrating. I try to give him chances to socialize but all he wants to do is play computer and it makes me crazy. I constantly have to defend him from bullies, but he never tries to improve the situation himself.
—Miri L., 16, Illinois

Oh yes! She can't give herself a bath, so that is usually my job. Every night I can't just sit down and relax because I have to bathe her and it's kind of weird giving someone my own age a bath. I can't do what I want to do because I have to take care of her, like right now I have to go give her a bath and stop answering questions. —Anna H., 15, North Carolina

She gets away with lots of things that my parents feel she can't help doing—like making loud noises at the dinner table, pulling people's hair, and making messes. And if I do something by mistake (like spilling something), I get in trouble, told that I'm too clumsy, and need to pay more attention. It annoys me when I get yelled at for things my sister gets away with. —Amber C., 13, California

Yes, Matthew has plenty of times. Since he is deaf, it is hard to make him understand certain things sometimes. —Britny G., 16, Missouri

Oh, gosh, all the time! Sometimes he has an attitude. Developmentally, he's going through his adolescent stage and wants some independence. I worry, because I feel like an older sister (when really, I'm younger)... and he thinks I'm being bossy, and gets mad at me, which is always frustrating. —Stephanie B., 16, Maryland

Yes! My sister often carries on about a particular person or event. She becomes obsessed with her helpers and carers, and talks about them constantly, often repeating the same thing over and over and talking about them at times when the conversation is on a completely different topic. She doesn't seem to realise that no one else is as interested in it as she is. —Ariella M., 16, N.S.W.

It is often the little things such as when I try to have a conversation and he tells me to leave him alone. —Michelle M., 15, New Jersey

Sometimes I get frustrated when my sister won't concentrate on homework when my parents or I are trying to help her, and she'll just randomly spit out stupid answers that she knows are wrong. —Sarah S., 18, Pennsylvania

Sometimes he can't move fast enough or can't get himself ready fast enough. He needs help getting on his shoes and coat and seatbelt, and sometimes I don't feel like taking care of him when my parents aren't around. —Nora G., 13, Virginia

Sometimes Matthew wants to hang out with me and my friends, but I just want it to be us girls. Sometimes I need time away from him and he doesn't always accept that! —Nicole P., 15, Pennsylvania

Yes, my sib likes to push my buttons—he mimics my younger brother and me and enjoys irritating me in public because other people think it's cute, and I hate that! He also does it when my parents aren't around so that he doesn't get in trouble. —Emily P., 13, Indiana

My sister is very stubborn and, as my mom says, "has attitude to burn." So these things can get in the way and she can sometimes be hard to work with—but what sibling isn't at times? —Stephie N., 15, Arizona

They both frustrate me when I'm getting them ready for school or church. They don't move! And they put their clothes on backwards or won't put them on at all if I don't stand over them. Also, my brother's noises and my cousin's moods frustrate me. He just gets in moods where he behaves very badly—hitting and using stupid, repetitive language. —Elizabeth T., 19, Oklahoma

Yes, when she is disobedient and runs away from me when I need to change her diaper (she isn't potty-trained). —Leah K., 13, Iowa

Sometimes it frustrates me when my sister cries or grinds her teeth (her nervous habit) when I'm trying to get a big assignment done or I'm in a bad mood. I get upset and then feel bad because inside I know that that is her only way to communicate. —Caitlin M., 14, Maryland

Yes, because I feel like sometimes she gets more attention than me and that everyone cares more about her. But in the end, I understand. —Nancy R., 13, California

There are many times when I'll be home watching him, and I'll want to do one thing, while he wants to do another. Of course, I have to do what he wants to make sure he's safe. Or, he'll get in one of his pouty moods. It's very difficult to deal with sometimes. —Katelyn C., 16, Virginia

In more ways than I can count! However, it is not always his fault. It is frustrating because he cannot always express himself. —Alicia F., 17, Illinois.

When I was 13, she used to smooch with her Raggedy Andy doll. I couldn't take that. I would go get my mom and have her tell Janae to stop. Also, Janae moves so slowly. When we walk places together as a family, it takes forever. —Ty H., 17, Washington State

Reader, write where you can!

When Jeremy gets emotional, it bothers me. Sometimes when he's tired or highly stressed he begins to cry and it feels like such a small matter to me and I think "Jeremy, buck up and take it like an adult." I want him to act 19 but I understand that in some ways he is only at the age level of a 7-year-old. This knowledge makes me feel so cornered and trapped. I want him to be expressive, just not in the ways that a 7-year-old would. Although we all cry at times of tension. Maybe Jeremy is just trying to let me know that we're all human. —Lindsay D., 17, North Carolina

When I argue with my parents at the dinner table, David will really want to get in on the conversation, but usually doesn't have anything that would add to either argument. He'll just say something that he feels strongly about, which usually gets me to yell, "That has nothing to do with what we're talking about!" I always feel really bad afterwards, but it is still frustrating. —Katie J., 19, Illinois

Sometimes. She is very stubborn and often wants to have her way. She doesn't always get it, but when she doesn't she gets mad. She also talks a lot sometimes and takes forever to say something. —Megan D., 14, Michigan

Yes, because I feel like... but he will say at the end that he enjoyed it. —Jemma J., 18, Berkshire

...get there—but he will say at the end that he enjoyed it. —Jemma J., 18, Berkshire

When we try to persuade him to do something we know he likes doing but he refuses point blank and complains even when we get there

Getting out of class. —Lauren V., 14, Connecticut

What are some advantages—good parts—of having a sibling with a disability?

I get to meet so many great people, not only people with disabilities, but also people who work with them. My sib's teachers and aides are some of the nicest people I've ever met. They have given us ideas that have helped Keaton and our whole family. They are more than just teachers, though. I can honestly say that they are great friends. —Cassandra W., 15, Iowa

You get more clothes because she doesn't care about them. —Lydia Q., 13, Massachusetts

If my sister wasn't a part of my life, I would be so ignorant about people who have disabilities. —Margaret C., 14, Illinois

It gives you a different outlook on life. You don't take anything in life for granted. Jeremy helps me to slow down and just take a moment to relax and love life. —Lindsay D., 17, North Carolina

If you meet other kids who have sibs with special needs, you'll know what they are going through. —Amy S., 15, Washington State

It makes you more aware of other people's feelings and situations. It makes you more accepting of a wide variety of people and shows you that those with disabilities are just the same as everyone else. It also gives you a curiosity into what "normal" means in a larger sense than just disability. Being a sibling has shown me things that I would never have known otherwise, and I would hate not to know those things and therefore not be the person that I am. —Ariella M., 16, N.S.W.

I learn about patience, understanding, and acceptance. I am surrounded by sincere, generous, and loving people. I am part of a close-knit community. I am different. I get to participate in this book and help others, and the list goes on. I am so the luckiest sister alive. —Carly H., 17, Georgia

One thing is that we have a handicap sticker for parking. She also brings happiness to our family. —Matt M., 15, Illinois

—Lauren O., 16, Georgia

Reader, write where you can!

You take life more seriously and know that life is a gift from God. —Leah K., 13, Iowa

I always look like the good kid next to him. I have also learned so much about patience and compassion from him. —Miri L., 16, Illinois

He changed who I was and opened my eyes about life. —Alicia F., 17, Illinois.

Having a sister who is such a caring person. Adrienne will be the first to notice when I'm upset and I'll be the first one to comfort me.

I have a unique life. No one else can describe how it feels to have a sibling with a disability unless you are a sibling yourself. —Kathryn C., 14, Illinois

It's been such a learning experience and I've met a lot of great people that I can't imagine living my life without. —Kaleigh H., 16, New Hampshire

You don't fight nearly as often, your sib doesn't mind hanging out with you, and you don't have to be perfect around them because they will always love you, no matter what, and will always think you're cool! ☺ —Michelle O., 14, Virginia

You learn a lot about understanding and to value what you have. You also get to do fun activities (such as Camp Easter Seals) that you wouldn't be able to do otherwise. —Kevin T., 14, Virginia

It's opened my eyes to many talents I wouldn't have known I had. It's given me many insights into what a gift it is to be who you are. And it's given me the chance to express opinions on disabilities that I never would have had without my sibs. Plus, my parents put less pressure on me when they have Nathaniel and Sophia to worry about. —Alethea R., 13, Minnesota

I think growing up with a sibling who's disabled enables me to have a gratitude for life, and even when I have my ups and downs, to know that everything is going to be alright. —Lindsay K., 15, California.

sounds awful, but we cut everyone in line when at theme parks because of Andrew. —Allison S., 17, Connecticut

I've learned tolerance and respect, traits others may never learn and qualities that I value beyond everything else. —Erin G., 14, Alberta

It has really formed who I am and how I see things—and has exposed me to a world bigger than my own. —Rebekah C., 17, California

The advantages are easy! I'm different from other people because of it, and I'm involved in a world that most people just gawk at. It's definitely shaped my values. No matter how selfish it might sound, I'm so thankful that I've grown up with my brother the way he is! —Maggie W., 17, Wisconsin

You don't have the little brother that picks up and listens to your phone calls, then tattles on you. —Katelyn C., 16, Virginia

Like many other people with Williams syndrome, my brother is really friendly and outgoing, so I have met many people through him I may not have met any other way. Another advantage is that we have gotten to take some pretty fun trips to the Williams syndrome conferences. —Emily I., 15, Washington State

Your world is opened up to many different kinds of people. It really puts things into perspective. Not only have I learned about disabilities from my brother. I've also learned about the world—and even myself. —Michelle D., 16, New Jersey

My sib helps put things in perspective. —Catherine C., 13, California

I think David's made me a better person. Definitely a less judgmental one. —Katie J., 19, Illinois

You become sensitive to other people's needs and more understanding and accepting of people's differences. You also get to be part of special groups like Sibshops. —Christiana R., 13, Wisconsin

Everything is about that sibling. Everything revolves around his needs. —Alisa A., 18, Oregon

What are some disadvantages—not so good parts— of having a sibling with special needs?

As much as I love my sister, it is hard to do normal activities. If we go to the store, she makes noises or grabs a toy and everyone stares. It makes me feel like I'm invisible, yet everyone can see me when they stare. Also, we can't go on vacations because it is hard to be in the car with her for a long time, and unless we want to get kicked off the plane, we can't take her on one. —Margaret C., 14, Illinois

Having to modify your plans so that they can do things with you. Like you can't go on a walk around the lake because one can't walk. Or you can't do a haunted house because one can't see. —Kate F., 13, Wisconsin.

I don't get enough attention, and it is always very tense and crazy at my house. His behavior is frustrating, and when people bully him, I have to stick up for him. —Miri L., 16, Illinois

Frustration, thinking about what I could have had with a "normal" sibling; and worry, especially about what's going to happen after my parents are gone... but I try not to dwell on these things, because there's only so much time in the world, and I want to make the best of it! —Stephanie B., 16, Maryland

Because Stephen learns and moves slower, having a sib with a disability makes you go slower too. I like to get things done quickly, and sometimes I feel as if Stephen is holding me back. —Kevin T., 14, Virginia

It limits my family in many ways. Only 2 of us can be away at a time; someone always has to be home with him. Usually only one parent can come to see me at school events. —Jill B., 18, Florida

Because he also has special health needs, he sometimes has to spend time in the hospital. I don't like that. —Mandi D., 13, Wisconsin

All the rude stares and comments me and my brother and sister hear and see about her. —Ashley S., 13, Minnesota

I wasn't able to grow up with a normal older sister to learn from. An older sister would have shown me more on what to expect on what was to come in life and school. I had to figure it out by myself. —Ty H., 17, Washington State

My brother has many doctor and therapist appointments and it seems like we are rushing to one of his appointments all the time or sometimes my mom isn't able to pick me up because my brother has an appointment. —Emily I., 15, Washington State

Sometimes she's annoying and uncompromising. She's about the most stubborn person I have ever met. —Erin G., 14, Alberta

He chews on a basting brush for stimulation and that thing smells. And when he gets excited and flings that thing around, he gets his slobber all over you. —Tyler L., 15, Arizona

Not ever having a "normal" sister relationship. I find it hard to explain to people about how my relationship with my sister works. —Emily D., 18, Virginia

Reader, what about you?

Some disadvantages are not being able to go do the things that normal families get to go and do. Also, my parents are more stressed than most parents. A big disadvantage is getting hurt when my sister lashes out at me. —Emily N., 17, Oregon

My parents are not as available to take me places or do things with me because it takes a long time to load up Charlie in the van. Also, I feel very different from my peers and find myself getting frustrated with their superficiality or fakeness. I've seen a lot more than most people have, which puts me in a very different place. Sometimes I can feel pretty alone there. —Rebekah C., 17, California

The constant work. He always needs help with this or that and he always wants to be by me so I almost never get any private time. The worst is when he spills weird liquids he's found in my room, or when he screams when I play a videogame or watch TV. —Daniel C., 17, Illinois

Really there aren't that many. Sometimes when we go places, she might act up and that can be embarrassing, but that is about it. —Teresa H., 13, Minnesota

Often when people meet my sister before me, they assume that I also must have some form of mental retardation. —Monica R., 15, Massachusetts

I used to get teased in school more than my sister did, and it was hard to have friends. I was afraid they would make fun if they ever came over, but now it's totally different. If they want to laugh, then they aren't my friends anyways. —Kelsea R., 15, New Hampshire

Even though he's 18, he can't be left alone for long. He can take care of himself just fine but he isn't too good at decision making such as answering the phone or the door. So whenever I want to go out, I have to make sure that someone is watching my brother. —Lindsay D., 17, North Carolina

Having to watch the treatments. —Lauren V., 14, Connecticut

You always feel like you need to take care of them and have to think about them before yourself. Like if my friends want to do something with me, I always make sure I don't have to watch my sister. —Kristin S., 19, Virginia

I feel like they suck all of the energy out of you. And you have to watch them and they can get into your things and tear them apart. —Christiana R., 13, Wisconsin

You have to be ready for change at any time and sometimes it means not getting as much attention from your parents. It also means making sacrifices to help out your sibling or your family. —Alli J., 15, Ohio

She has life/death issues and she is in pain a lot. There are also lots of hospital trips and an exhausted mom! —Leah K., 13, Iowa

We can't go places that aren't wheelchair accessible and sometimes she doesn't understand, or ignores the fact that she has to be quiet during plays or performances. Sometimes we have to leave places early because we forgot her formula or she is shrieking or just being really annoying. —Amber C., 13, California

When I tell people that my little brother has a disability, some act like I have it. I also don't get to have a normal relationship with friends 'cause he needs to be watched constantly. —Kathryn C., 14, Illinois

Describe a perfect day.

When the Packers win, and the team you hate loses. —Jacob C., 13, Wisconsin

It would include food! Sunny, not too hot and I would spend the day with people I love like my friends or family just hanging out and eating great food! —Megan D., 14, Michigan

Going out in my boat with my family out to some exotic island. Go scuba diving on a beautiful reef all morning and horseback riding in the afternoon. Then we would camp and roast marshmallows and wake up early in the morning and watch the sunrise. —Jill B., 18, Florida

It doesn't have to be a sunny, warm day on the beach, or a nice walk in the park. To me, a perfect day would be when all of my friends and family are together having a great time talking, singing, dancing, and just having fun! —Michelle O., 14, Virginia

Start out sleeping late, and then go shopping with all my friends with an infinite shopping budget. After that, we would all get manicures and pedicures and later we would go out to dinner and then to a huge, happening dance. —Emily I., 15, Washington State

A perfect day would last forever, but would never be boring or repetitive. I would feel energetic, swim in clear aqua waters, and eat every dessert I wanted without ever gaining an ounce or feeling full. The entire day I would be surrounded by family, friends, and of course the love of my life (who, incidentally, I would meet that day). —Lindsay D., 17, North Carolina

A perfect day would be in the spring and with green grass, peach or cherry trees and close to a blue lake. There would be birds chirping and a slight wind. My sister would be there without her disability! —Leah K., 13, Iowa

I would wake up at 11, and then I would go see a Counting Crows concert. Then I would watch SNL and finally go to bed. —Margaret C., 14, Illinois

Get up really early to catch a flight to California—after picking up all my friends along the way. We would stay in the highest-class hotel and order room service. Nobody would fight and we would all laugh and talk about memories and how much we love one another. And then I would come home to find that my brother said his first word. Ali N., 18, Massachusetts

My perfect day would be in fall. There would be leaves scattered around and a light breeze in the air to blow them around. There would be a sun, but not too bright or too dull. —Ashley S., 13, Minnesota

Everyone would be in a great mood and our schedule would be relaxed. There would be no emergencies and both of my little brothers would be healthy and happy. We would all just hang out and everything would be totally calm. —Rebekah C., 17, California

Go to school, get all your major papers back, and have a 100% on every single one! And then, no homework. You could then go to your friend's house with a ton of people and have an awesome time. —Emily J., 14, Colorado

Nothing super extravagant or anything incredibly special—just be a day where I could hang out with my friends and have fun. —Stephie N., 15, Arizona

It's a bright sunny day on the Chesapeake Bay. It is low tide and the skim boarding is perfect. All of my friends and family are down at the bay as well. My friends and I skim board and build huge castles until nightfall. —Kevin T., 14, Virginia

Sleep in until noon. No school. A good breakfast. Hang out with my friends at the skate park or a motocross track. When it gets cooler build bike jumps behind my house with a tractor so it is easier and have no one complain about ripping up their fences and back yards to be able to get enough speed for the huge jump. Stay up late and hang out with my friends. Go to bed. —Tyler L., 15, Arizona

I'd wake up late in the morning, then have a breakfast of chocolate chip muffins and sausage. Then I learn there is no school that day! I go to a movie with my friends and my mom lets me get anything I want at the snack bar. After that, I get to go to Six Flags. All the rides are open and since it is a beautiful, warm day, the water park is open too. I win a prize at the game booths. When it is time for dinner, we go out to Red Hot & Blue restaurant for barbecue and my parents treat us to ice cream at Baskin Robbins. When we get home, my favorite show is on. When the show is over, I fall asleep very quickly and get a good night's sleep. —Brooke W., 13, Virginia

Watching the sunrise on the porch swing with a good book in hand, my dog Puddles at my feet, and a Sierra Mist within reach. Nathaniel and Sophia would behave themselves so my parents could relax for the first time in who knows when. Oh yes, and a flawless report card would arrive in the mail. —Alethea R., 13, Minnesota

I love all the seasons. In the winter, I love coming in after being out in the snow and sitting down with hot chocolate and watching TV. Or in the summer relaxing in my pool and getting a great tan. The possibilities are endless. —Kathryn C., 14, Illinois

Sleeping in until 11:00 a.m. and taking a nice long shower without my little sister using up all of the hot water. Then I would go with my friends to the mall, hang out for a while, and finally playing videogames at my house. Naturally, there would be no school to interfere with the day's activities. —Daniel C., 17, Illinois

Who has had a perfect day? I guess the closest to a perfect day would be to eat vanilla bean ice cream in the middle of a summer field with my girlfriend. —Ty H., 17, Washington State

My whole family would be together, with no negative feelings in the room. ALL of us laughing and joking around. It would be fun! —Megan D., 18, Texas

Reader's perfect day:

His aggressiveness. —Mandi D., 13, Wisconsin

If you could change just one thing about your sib (or your sib's disability), what would it be?

I believe that even though we are not perfect, we are who we are for a specific purpose and every part of every person's nature is designed to serve this purpose. So, I wouldn't change Nathaniel and Sophia at all, because I love them just the way they are. —Alethea R., 13, Minnesota

That he could enjoy what every other teenage boy likes to do, like playing football and hanging out with his mates. —Jemma J., 18, Berkshire

My sibs' awareness. Neither seems to have a conscience. I would like them to have a desire to learn and to better themselves. They both seem not to really care. —Elizabeth T., 19, Oklahoma

Emily and Liz's attitudes. They always make it seem like getting a glass of water is like climbing a 50-foot rock wall. Everything has to be a BIG deal! —Kate F., 13, Wisconsin.

I often wish he would act more mature. He can act very silly and childish and it can be embarrassing. —Amanda M., 19, Washington State

I'd make it easier to have a deep conversation with Alex. I feel like he can't relate to anyone—he simply can't put himself in anyone else's shoes. He says that he can relate to people, but he always links it back to some obscure thing that doesn't always make sense. Alex also sometimes has a hard time putting his thoughts together and organizing his words so that they make sense, which can be frustrating when you're having a conversation or trying to get some information. —Stephanie B., 16, Maryland

I wouldn't change a thing, because God made him different to teach us to look at the world in a different way. Just because life with a sibling who has disability isn't as glamorous or as common as having a sibling, without a disability doesn't mean it has to be less rewarding. —Christiana R., 13, Wisconsin

His stubbornness. Stephen is extremely stubborn and gets on my nerves when he is being stubborn. If you do one thing wrong to him he'll turn as stubborn as a mule, and u can't get him to do anything willingly for a while afterwards. —Kevin T., 14, Virginia

—Alicia F., 17, Illinois.

to not be in a lot of pain. When he does, etc. —

He would be perfectly typical. No disabilities at all. —Allison S., 17, Connecticut

I wish that he could trust people to be nice to him again. —Laura P., 15, Virginia

I would like for Monica to be able to speak. I think it must be awful not being able to say what you want. —Martha P., 13, Connecticut

I would change that he doesn't have GE Reflux and could eat chocolate and ketchup,

I wish he didn't have alopecia because sometimes he literally has absolutely no hair ANYWHERE. And he's really self-conscious about that. —Kat F., 16, Washington State

I would love if Caroline could talk. I can tell that she has so much to say, and sometimes I'll see her, trying so hard to talk, using every muscle in her body. But the words just won't come out. —Caitlin M., 14, Maryland

My sister's hygiene. She doesn't know how to shower herself or wipe decently after using the bathroom. Because of this my family is faced with a wide variety of transmitted....uhh... pests, such as head lice and pinworms. Yuck! If we didn't have to deal with these, life would be much easier. —Emily N., 17, Oregon

I would change her communication skills so I could know what she thinks about me and everyone else. I would like to have long conversations with her—know her perspective of life, and what she wants to do when she gets older. —Michelle O., 14, Virginia

I'd give her better problem-solving skills. Her current solutions include kicking, screaming, tantruming, yelling. —Erin G., 14, Alberta

I wouldn't change anything about Adrienne; she is an amazing person just how she is. —Lauren O., 16, Georgia

What would you change, reader?

I would take her whole disability away—and if I couldn't, I would take away the life/death issues. —Leah K., 13, Iowa

WOW! Really, I can't think of anything I really badly want to change about Jessica. She is SO wonderful. UM, maybe have her be a little better listener. —Teresa H., 13, Minnesota

I would make it so my brother was happy and felt good about himself. —Miri L., 16, Illinois

I would definitely change my brother's listening skills! I often wish that he would just listen so that I don't have to ask him or tell him something 50 million times. —Michelle D., 16, New Jersey

I'd change how rigid she is in her schedule, so she'd be more willing to do different things that she now won't try. —Kristin S., 19, Virginia

I would make it so Riley did not have to take all the medications. —Cassey C., 15, Southland, N.Z.

If I could change one thing, it would be that things came easier to him. He often has to spend more time on schoolwork than I do and he has to try so much harder. —Nicole P., 15, Pennsylvania

That he didn't have the disability. His and my life would be so normal. Everything would be boring and there would be no commotion in our house. —Kathryn C., 14, Illinois

Why would I want to change my sibling? He is not perfect, but no one is. I would rather accept him for who he is. —Carly H., 17, Georgia

If taking away his disability wasn't a possibility, then I would want him to not screech when he doesn't like something. I'd also like to increase his attention span. —Brooke W., 13, Virginia

Arianna's limited eyesight—she's legally blind. —Lindsay K., 15, California.

What do you see for your sibling's future? And what part do you think you'll play in that future?

I see him in a group home here in Iowa, leading a happy life. I see me visiting him and bringing him home at least once a week and me working at the group home on weekends. I know that a group home may sound like a horrible thing. But if he gets accepted and if the people are great, he'll have a stable environment and he'll be able to do more of the things that he likes to do. He also won't have to go through the confusion of our household. If he goes, it will be very painful, but I think it could be a great thing for all of us to be happy and to get along. —Cassandra W., 15, Iowa

I worry sometimes wondering how old Charlie will live to be. If he makes it to manhood I wonder if he'll be independent enough to live on his own. I really hope so. I hope he finds a good woman and maybe adopts some kids (his disability may be genetic).
My role on paper is when my parents are no longer capable I (and my older sister) will be in charge of Charlie's trust fund, living arrangements, and life management. A big role. I'll always be here for him and he'll always be a big part of my life.
—Rebekah C., 17, California.

I hope my brother will go to college, get a decent job, and become a little bit more responsible and less depressed as he gets older. My sister, I hope, will end up in a group home somewhere with a job that's repetitive, like a fast food restaurant or coffee shop, where she can work to support herself and have spare time for her writing.
—Alli J., 15, Ohio

I can see my brother graduating from high school and working in a place like Blockbuster. He knows almost every movie and he would love working there. I'll be an involved brother, like I am now. I will visit him often, and do my best to make sure he is OK. —Kevin T., 14, Virginia

I can see many possibilities. He might live near my parents, or go far away to college. More than anything though, I hope he'll find someone who smiles when they see him. —Laura P., 15, Virginia

I don't often think about her future. I don't really want to know what it will be like because she's not getting much better. I guess I see her living in an apartment with a full-time nurse.
I think I will play a part in her adult life but I don't know how.
—Catherine C., 13, California

I see great things in both of their futures. They will marry, have great jobs, and make great contributions to society. —Elizabeth T., 19, Oklahoma

I see him either working in Blockbuster or at like a Radio Shack, because those are the things he is interested in. But I don't know anything else yet. I am really worried about it. I hope I can help him out along the way. —Melisandre P., 14, Kansas

Hopefully he will get a job, or do something for the community that will help everyone. I want to be there whenever I can; I don't want him to forget me at all or think I don't love him. —Kathryn C., 14, Illinois

I hope David will continue to work at Walgreen's and the grocery store and keep having fun with his friends and Special Olympics. I would like to live near him, in case he needs anything. I would also like to have him over a couple times a week for dinner. —Katie J., 19, Illinois

My mom is working on getting a program set up for him. When my parents can't take care of him anymore, I'd like my brother to live with me and my family. —Jill B., 18, Florida

I think he might work in a grocery store. Hopefully he'll learn to read well enough to be able to shop, but if not that's OK. Eventually he'll live with me and my family. I'll always be there for him. —Leslie C., 16, Washington State

The future is so unpredictable, but most likely, my parents will care for Nathaniel and Sophia as long as they are capable. I'll probably go off to college, start a career and a family, and visit whenever it's possible. When my parents can't care for them anymore, I'll probably help choose a place for Nathaniel and Sophia to live, because I don't think I'd be able to provide the care they need, as much as I'd like to. It's painful to think about, but I will still make them a priority in my life. —Alethea R., 13, Minnesota

Hopefully, Scott will live with 2 roommates in a small, safe community surrounded by nice people. He will be able to use public transportation to travel to and from his job at the local grocery store. I will live nearby and visit him occasionally, but will also lead my own life. I am aware that I may have to take on more responsibility for him than most sisters, but he is definitely worth my time and love. —Carly H., 17, Georgia

My bro will hopefully get married, have kids, and have a job. That's one possibility. He could also end up being highly dependent because his people skills—or lack thereof—will keep him from finding and maintaining a job or a relationship. Either way, I suppose I'll just have to support him and advocate for him when he needs it. —Miri L., 16, Illinois

It's hard for me to picture Sarah's far-off future right now because she is only 4. I'm more focused on her finishing preschool and going into kindergarten. —Stephie N., 15, Arizona

My sister will always be in my life. She will be included in the decisions I make and the paths I choose. I see her in every aspect of my future. —Emily D., 18, Virginia

A nurse constantly in her house helping while I make money to help pay for her stuff. —Dave S., 14, Michigan

I think my sister will grow to be an accomplished woman. She'll be living in her own apartment. She'll be working a steady job at some store. When my parents are gone, I'll probably be taking care of her. She'll have staff helping her at her apartment. She will call me if she needs me. I'll be able to live my life with my family, because she will have her own life too. —Ty H., 17, Washington State

Reader, write where you can!

I think he may live with my family (my husband and kids) as we grow older or maybe in a group home. I see the home as a very active place that is constantly planning activities in the community, and a place where he will make some of his best friends. Above all else, I see it as safe and loving. Possibly he will have a part time job. Whatever the future holds I know that my sib will stay in my life as long as we're alive. —Lindsay D., 17, North Carolina

I HOPE he will get a job at the library (where he loves to hang out) or something like that. Maybe he'll get his own apartment. I bet I'll check up on him every week. But I hope by then he is a lot more independent than he's now. —Brooke W., 13, Virginia

I beat the crap out of this kid in 6th grade because he was making fun of my little brother. —Tyler L., 15, Arizona

What annoys you the most about how people treat your sib?

How they make fun of her for the way that she looks and for things that she can't help. —Matt M., 15, Illinois

I dislike it when we are out together and people address questions regarding my sister, to me. For example, at a restaurant, "What would she like to eat?" Just because they see the wheelchair and assume its occupant is incapable of communicating, when in fact she can quite competently assert herself. —Jenna H., 17, N.S.W.

How they treat him like dirt. Like he is nobody. He has feelings just like any other person does. —Alisa A., 18, Oregon

I like how people always tell me how cool he is. But, then, when they see him, he gets nothing but a quick "Hi" from them. If they really think he's so cool, I'd think they would be nicer and more sincere to him. —Nicole P., 15, Pennsylvania

I am annoyed to no end by people who hear my sister has special needs and automatically assume she is stupid. —Monica R., 15, Massachusetts

I hate when people talk to him and treat him as if he is 14 months instead of 14 years old. He can do so much, but he won't if people allow him to be a baby. He is lazy and likes being a baby. I try my best not to allow him to slip into that mentality. An example is when I won't allow him to speak in one-word phrases. —Elizabeth T., 19, Oklahoma

I hate it when people baby my brother! I know that he has a disability, but he is still 13! Some of his teachers tickle him and let him play with their hair. They'd get in trouble if they did that to any other kid! I just wish that people would treat him like a 13-year-old. —Emily P., 13, Indiana.

I hate it when we're walking in the mall and people stare at her. I don't mind so much when little kids do it, because they don't know better, but when adults or people my age do it, it ticks me off. She's not a freak show, she's a human being, so take a picture, it'll last longer. —Caitlin M., 14, Maryland

I hate it when people get on their high horses about disabled kids. It's right to have an opinion, but to lecture others is too much for me. One of my friends gets livid when someone says "retarded." Although I think people who say this often make themselves sound more uneducated or uncaring than they are. I don't find it wrong. It doesn't make me uncomfortable—that IS what disabled people used to be referred to medically. Freedom of speech and all that. Just because one says "retarded" it doesn't necessarily mean they do not respect retarded people. —Allison S., 17, Connecticut

People endlessly bully and exclude my sib because of his weird social skills and behavior. It makes me so mad when other people hurt him because while he can't always help his behavior, they can, and being cruel is a far worse behavior than any of my brother's. —Miri L., 16, Illinois

They treat him like he is the sweetest thing in the world when he—just like everyone else—can be mean and nasty. —Amanda M., 19, Washington State

It really annoys me when random strangers come up and speak to my sister like she is a baby—assuming that they know everything about our lives and that they have the right to talk to us in a way that makes my family feel uncomfortable. These people do not know us from a bar of soap—they have no right to ruin our day by talking to my sister in a way that is really inappropriate. —Ariella M., 16, N.S.W.

My sister has fetal alcohol syndrome because her birth mom used to drink when she was pregnant with Catherine. That annoys me so much. How could someone do that to an unborn person? Every sip of alcohol she took hurt Catherine. I mean, I am so glad that Catherine is a part of my family and I know she has a better life with us than with her birth mom, but if you're going to ruin someone's life, then take responsibility for it. —Margaret C., 14, Illinois

—Stephie N., 15, Arizona when people judge my sister based solely on the way she looks. They don't even take the time to get to know her personally. This isn't true for all people, but it really annoys me

When people call kids "retards" a knife goes through my chest. I hate it because people are so arrogant when they say that. Most of the time I tell them that it is unacceptable to use that word, but sometimes I don't say anything because I am too tired of saying it. —Emma F., 15, Michigan

When they call him a retard. It seems so small but it hurts so much—even if they don't call him it to his face. Something about the word severely bothers me. —Lindsay D., 17, North Carolina

Reader, what about you?

People see Charlie and look away—like he's not even there. I guess they are trying not to stare, but I wish they would just treat him like any other 4-year-old. Smile at him, say "hi," and ask how old he is. When kids point and ask a question about Charlie, their parents grab them and whisper "don't stare!" then take them away. —Rebekah C., 17, California

When doctors don't take you seriously until they see evidence right before their eyes. —Leah K., 13, Iowa

He likes to say silly things, so people are always trying to get him to be loud or say things he shouldn't. They aren't being mean, just annoying. —Leslie C., 16, Washington State

When someone says or does something that's so mean it makes him cry at night—and nobody can get him to stop. —Laura P., 15, Virginia

Sometimes people make faces and stare. I don't think that's right because it's not like they are horrific dogs or anything! They are just people that need a little extra help here and there. —Kate F., 13, Wisconsin.

They won't hold his hand because he's got slobber on it. Kayla L., 13, Arizona

It annoys me that people try to make my sister perfect. People do not accept that she will never be able to do things perfectly, so they try to get her to do stuff that she can't do. This just makes her very frustrated. —Emily N., 17, Oregon

Yes they do, and I'm grateful for it. —Cassie W., 13, Colorado

Do your parents include you in discussions about your sib? How do you feel about that?

My parents sometimes include me in conversations, but most of the time I have to listen in on discussions with doctors or discussions between my parents. For example, I found out about one of Sarah's surgeries when the doctor called to remind my parents of the surgery and I answered the phone. I do wish that my parents would include me more because I'm going to find out what's going on eventually. —Stephie N., 15, Arizona

In our house, it's a normal dinner discussion topic. I am happy that they do include me because it shows me that my opinions matter and I am important too. —Emma F., 15, Michigan

I have always been involved in discussions about Jackie. Now that I am a little older, we talk about what Jackie is doing, how she's acting, and how the medication is working, etc. I think every parent should include every member of the family when it comes to their sib. —Emily D., 18, Virginia

My parents feel like I worry too much about things that are out of my control, and so they generally don't involve me in discussions about Alex. They definitely keep me updated, though, and let me know how they're feeling about certain situations. —Stephanie B., 16, Maryland

I basically include myself in discussions about my sister. When we have consultants over for meetings, I add my input and ask questions if I feel the need. I enjoy being a part of the decisions involving my sister. I feel like I can give her a voice. We are about the same age and I am going through the same type of changes as she is, so I can share (a guess) of how she is feeling about certain things. —Emily N., 17, Oregon

Reader, write where you can!

If I am very curious at the time about what they are discussing then yes, I will be included. It is a good feeling that somehow, I can help in a different way, and I have a different point of view than they do. —Kathryn C., 14, Illinois

I'm glad my parents include me in discussion about my brother because one day I'm going to have to watch out for him. David is pretty independent, but there are some things I need to help him with. My parents let me know what I should keep an eye out for. —Katie J., 19, Illinois

My mom includes me a lot—sometimes I think I'm the only one who she talks about Eric with. Sometimes I wish I could butt into her conversations with my dad about Eric. I am glad that I have a voice, because I want to make him happy—and that is getting to be a hard thing to do. —Laura P., 15, Virginia

In most situations, they include me, but then I think there are also those discussions where just the parents need to be involved. Being included helps me understand things. —Kelsea R., 15, New Hampshire

I am extremely pleased with my parents including me in discussions about Adrienne. I am just as much a part of Adrienne's life as they are and always want what is best for her. —Lauren O., 16, Georgia

Yes; most of the time I am the one asking all the questions. I am happy with being in these discussions because I learn more about my sib. —Emily P., 13, Indiana.

I am always included in discussions about Caroline. It's very important to me to be able to be a part of my sister's life. Whenever I can, I try to attend her IEP meetings. —Caitlin M., 14, Maryland

They talk openly about what Janae might be dealing with in her life. There has also been some pretty serious stuff that has happened that my parents have not told me about, but I know about it because I could tell they were upset so I listened from a distance. —Ty H., 17, Washington State

My parents include me when there is something I can offer. If there isn't any way for me to help, they don't tell me very much. But I know everything anyway, because I want to know, and where there's a will there's a way. —Miri L., 16, Illinois

It's nice to know that my parents care enough about Emily and me to ask my opinions, even if they don't agree with them. —Monica R., 15, Massachusetts

They do, which is sometimes good because they can hear my point of view, but sometimes it's bad because my parents like to point out how different they are from me and how I need to make adjustments to fit their needs. —Alli J., 15, Ohio

My parents were respectful and kind enough to include me in discussions about my brother from the very start. While it is sometimes painful, including me helps me understand and accept my brother and his situation. —Allison S., 17, Connecticut

If I want to know anything I can just ask. My parents are really open with me. —Amber C., 13, California

Sometimes, but most of the time they don't. It's kind of frustrating not always knowing what they are saying about him. I am a member of the family, too and I deserve to know what's going on with him just as much as they do. I mean: what if they aren't always there to take care of him? How am I supposed to take care of him if I really don't know anything about him or the problems he has had in the past? Or what meds he is allergic to? That kind of stuff. I need to know too and I don't think that they realize that. —Alisa A., 18, Oregon

Yes. We talk about what may happen with my brother if God forbid something happens to my parents, or when he's done with school. I like being a part of it, because I feel that I have helped raise my brother in some ways. —Jill B., 18, Florida

My parents don't really talk about my sister more than they talk about my brother and me—at least I don't think so. I pretty much know what is going on. I like knowing what is going on. —Megan D., 14, Michigan

Not usually, unless they have a concern and wonder if I've noticed anything. I like it that way: Lise's business is her own. I wouldn't want my parents talking about me to her so why should they talk to me about Lise? —Erin G., 14, Alberta

Yes, they do and I am happy to know what is going on but am sad to hear about it because the news isn't always good. —Leah K., 13, Iowa

Sometimes; I don't get the gory details, but enough to feel good that they value me as a part of his life. —Daniel C., 17, Illinois

Yes, now that I'm older I'm involved in a lot of the conversations. Since I attended the high school Debbie now goes to, I know which teachers will be able to conform their teaching styles to assist my sister and which won't. —Sarah S., 18, Pennsylvania

It's nice to know that my parents care enough about Emily and me to ask my opinions, even if they don't agree with them. —Monica R., 15, Massachusetts

Yes, they don't burden me with the parental responsibilities, but they include me in discussions about him because I am a part of the family, too. —Carly H., 17, Georgia

Has your sib ever embarrassed you?

Last year, my brother and I were in the same gym class. We were playing dodge ball, and I accidentally hit him with a ball. He then got mad at me and started to come after me in his wheelchair, screaming at me in front of everyone. I was embarrassed because all of my friends were there. I realize now how funny we must of looked running around the gym. —Emily P., 13, Indiana

My brother is really outgoing and sometimes likes to tell made-up stories. One time he got really mad at me and decided to tell all the neighbors that I was pregnant, which was a complete lie! He told people that one night I came home real late and then the police came, took me in, and found out I was pregnant. The neighbors believed this story. The worst part was I babysat for all their kids and they trusted me so they were all quite disturbed by this story. My mom cleared everything up with them and now we all just laugh about it. —Emily I., 15, Washington State

My favorite was when my sister was at a hotel with my mom. At the hotel's buffet breakfast, my sister went to get milk and announced—in a very loud voice—that the milk dispenser "kind of looks like a tampon!" —Alli J., 15, Ohio

I don't know where to begin. My brother told my friend about a surprise party we were throwing her. He has said VERY inappropriate things to my friends—more times than I can count. He has fully combusted and acted out in front of my friends a million times. He is like a big ball of embarrassment on legs. —Miri L., 16, Illinois

Julie used to flip her shirt up and play with her hair upside down in the store, and people would give us funny looks. This was probably the most embarrassing thing that she did when she was younger. Now, she hits me (and others) in public; it is not so much embarrassing but more uncomfortable. People stare at her for something she can't control, and I know they are thinking that she is a bad child. —Emily N., 17, Oregon

Just recently at my Aunt Lorraine's funeral, my brother was doing all he could to comfort us. He would take tissues, wipe away our tears, and rub our backs. He even held a tissue to my mom's nose and told her to "blow hard," just as my mom does for him when he needs it! —Michelle D., 16, New Jersey

No, but she has barfed on me a couple times when dancing with her. —Dave S., 14, Michigan

I have tons of good "Grant" stories. At my piano lesson, Grant—who says what he thinks--pointed at a rather large man and said, "He ate too much." My mom and I were mortified and Grant got no Nintendo for the day as a punishment. Another time, on a trip to the library, Grant didn't make it to the bathroom in time and made a mess in his pants. He took off his underwear but left them on the library's bathroom floor. When Dad went to the bathroom, he saw his underwear there (luckily) and picked them up. —Brooke W., 13, Virginia

My friends and I were watching movies one night and all of a sudden, he came bolting downstairs to us, and he had nothing on! I was so embarrassed. My friends are like, "Does he do that often?" —Kathryn C., 14, Illinois

The time I remember most is when we were at this huge store looking for light fixtures or something boring. I took my sister to look at something a little more interesting and she started shrieking! This lady from the next aisle must have thought that someone was being kidnapped or murdered because she yelled over asking if everything was okay. I yelled back that everything was okay and tried to shut my sister up. As I walked back to my parents, she shrieked the whole time, and people looked at us like we were crazy. —Amber C., 13, California

When I was 10 and 11, I hated going to the mall because she'd scream and try to sit down and just make everyone stare at us. She's completely different now, and I hate how I used to be so embarrassed by her doing that. It doesn't even bother me now if she gets a little upset when out shopping. If people are that bored with themselves that they have to stare, then let them. —Sarah S., 18, Pennsylvania

Of course—they both have. Once, we went to Disney World for my birthday. My brother loves Mickey Mouse, so we went to see him. However, my brother went crazy! He made noises and ran around the building, with Mickey chasing him. With my cousin, once I took him to play tennis with a few friends from church and school. He was loud and obnoxious and kept yelling "hit it harder—and put some hot sauce on it!" —Elizabeth T., 19, Oklahoma

Sometimes she has, like when we were in middle school and we would both go to the dances. Sometimes it would embarrass me that she would just dance and wouldn't care if other people would make fun of her. I think she thought they were having fun WITH her—except they were making fun OF her. —Kristin S., 19, Virginia

The only time that my brother has embarrassed me is during conversations at funerals. When we're talking he'll bring up other people who have died and just say, "Well, so and so is dead too." —Katie J., 19, Illinois

The only time I can really remember that Alex embarrassed me was at my grandfather's funeral. My uncle (a monk) was giving the service, and he asked if anyone had anything to say... and lo and behold, my brother stood up and walked to the podium. My mom and I held each other's hands so tightly that they turned white. Everything turned out OK—Alex talked about how my Pop Pop took care of him when he was little and sick, and how they would do things together. It was a nice speech, and I guess I was more terrified than embarrassed, but I'm proud that Alex did a good job. —Stephanie B., 16, Maryland

oh, gosh yes, all the members of my family have embarrassed me at one time or another! Erik will sometimes tackle me and lay on top of me which is kind of gross and embarrassing, but you have to see how he doesn't understand that that isn't entirely appropriate. —Emily J., 14, Colorado

No. He is who he is, and that's nothing to be embarrassed about. —Kayla L., 13, Arizona

Sometimes she will start telling a story that starts out true, but then she might change it so that they will laugh or to make it more dramatic. Then people think something that isn't true at all, and that can get pretty messed up. —Teresa H., 13, Minnesota

Um, once at school, Harry visited me when I was with these hot guys and Harry asked one of them to be his wife! I was so embarrassed! —Alicia F., 17, Illinois.

My sisters will randomly scream out. Not screaming mad but just screaming. One time at church, when I was maybe 7 or so, my sister screamed and everyone turned around. So my older brother, Matt, told me to stare back in a mean face at the lady in front of us. So when she turned around again I gave her a really mean look and she was so embarrassed and quickly turned around.
—Margaret C., 14, Illinois

Oh yes indeed they have. When we first moved to our street there were just 3 houses and the neighborhood boys used to play street hockey. I would go out to watch—just to get to know them. Well, Liz decided to really get to know them and walked out to the center of the court with her pants down to her ankles and shirt up around her neck. Let's just say that it didn't take us long to meet the neighbors.
—Kate F., 13, Wisconsin.

Sometimes she says things out loud that might be funny but also embarrassing. One time in church, her shirt slipped up so her stomach was hanging out and she loudly said, "Look, I Brittany Spears!" Believe me, she doesn't look anything like Brittany Spears! Another time I was playing basketball and my sister yelled "Nice buns!" at me. Fortunately, not many people understand what she is saying but my family and I do!
—Megan D., 14, Michigan

My sib embarrasses me almost every time that I go out with her. Personally, I don't like laughing at what she does.
—Matt M., 15, Illinois

She has embarrassed me plenty of times. One that really stands out is when we were at a Christmas service at church and we sat near the choir. My sister got mad and slapped the cymbal on the drums in the middle of church.
—Matt M., 14, North Carolina.

When my sister and I were 7, my family went out for dinner one night. We had just started eating when my sister started choking on her food. She was choking so badly that my parents took her outside the restaurant. I was left alone at our table. Meanwhile, came up and asked if he could clear my parents' barely-touched plates away. Although this doesn't sound at all embarrassing to me now, I was extremely self-conscious at the time, and the whole situation seemed absolutely terrible to me then. —Ariella, 16, N.S.W.

When my brother and I were younger, our family vacationed in Florida at my great aunt's condo. We were surrounded by senior citizens and were trying to have fun in the pool. Well, my sib wasn't 100% potty trained yet and he pooed in the pool! I yelled at the top of my lungs to my mom "MOM, Matt pooed in the pool!" and she was going to just die—not before she killed me though! I've never seen so many old people move as fast as they did out of the pool. —Nicole P., 15, Pennsylvania

Well sort of... He used to embarrass me when we were in a quiet place like a doctor's office and he'd shout, "Megan, I need to use the bathroom!"
—Megan D., 18, Texas

If Janae is around when I am performing on my cello or guitar, she cheers really loud. That is embarrassing.
—Ty H., 17, Washington State

Yep! My brother just jumps around a lot, waves his arms, and hums. Everybody stares. It is really funny watching how people just can't get their eyes off him. —Cassie W., 13, Colorado

We were at Heartspring (speech services), there was this girl who is African American, and Clint had just noticed that her skin color was different than his, so he literally ran to her and started to rub her skin! It was so embarrassing at the time, but now I look back and I can't help but smile! —Melisandre P., 14, Kansas

Well, you have to understand, I am not easily embarrassed. However, this one time Lise plugged my piano teacher's toilet so bad she had to call a repairman and we had to pay a lot of money to fix it. I laugh every time I think about it. —Erin G., 14, Alberta

Reader, what about you?

Yes quite a lot. Once when were out in public, Riley pointed at me and in a big loud voice (as Riley has) said, "He's got skiddy undies!" It is funny now but not then. He also talks about body parts with great delight. —Cassey C., 15, Southland, N.Z.

No, she has never embarrassed me before. —Leah K., 13, Iowa

When she was younger, my sister was intensely afraid of big stuffed animals and oversized shop dummies, like the larger toys in FAO Schwarz. Shopping trips were a nightmare as we had to weave our convoluted way through department stores, avoiding giant Lego people and blow-up T-Rex figures to save her having an embarrassing panic attack! —Jenna H., 17, N.S.W.

The best one I can think of was when my little brother began running through the house naked when my friends visited. It seems funny now, but I still prefer to go over to my friends' house. —Daniel C., 17, Illinois

My sib is VERY social. He loves to be the center of attention. He likes to say "hey" to everyone we meet. It is really embarrassing at the time but as I look back at all the times he has done it, I laugh. —Amy Mck., 16, Tennessee

Not really. All my friends say that he is really cute. —Tyler L., 15, Arizona

Well, my sister has these episodes when she gags on her food and makes a really loud choking sound. Sometimes, when my family and I eat out, Monica does this and everyone in the restaurant stares at our table. —Martha P., 13, Connecticut

Do you know lots of other sibs and if so, how do you know them?

I have met most of the sibs I know online, through SibKids. However, I met some Australian sibs through The Northcott Society—an organisation which provides disability services—at a 'Sibcamp' that I helped instigate. —Jenna H., 17, N.S.W.

The only other person I know with a sibling with disabilities is a friend I've known since first grade—before the births of either sibling. —Allison S., 17, Connecticut

I know a few. I've been to a lot of sibshops in Vancouver and here in Calgary. I also attended a sibshop in Seattle a few years ago. —Erin G., 14, Alberta

I know about 10 other sibs, from my SIBS group here in New Hampshire. We all hang out and talk and it's a nice way to see what other teens my age are thinking about their brothers or sisters with special needs. —Kelsea R., 15, New Hampshire

I know a few other sibs. I have met them mainly at school and church and later found out they had a sibling with disabilities. However, I have met some sibs by just going to activities specifically for kids with special needs that my brother attends. —Emily I., 15, Washington State

I don't really know a lot of other sibs. I have met some, but I could never really relate to any of them. I think that just because two people share one experience doesn't mean they have anything in common. —Caitlin M., 14, Maryland

I know 2 boys with special needs through Riley. I went on a camp last year for kids that have special needs brothers or sisters with SibsSupport New Zealand. —Cassey C., 15, Southland, N.Z.

I go to the International Fragile X Conference and I met a few, but never established much of a connection. Here in Tulsa, I have a friend I went to high school with who is a sib. We can only relate to each other on a miniscule level because our lives are so different. —Elizabeth T., 19, Oklahoma

I know a bunch of other sibs from SibKids! I love SibKids so much... it has opened so many doors for me, and made me think. SibKids has shown me that I'm not alone. —Stephanie B., 16, Maryland

Actually I don't. My family provides much of the support I need. Other than that, I mostly keep to myself. —Alethea R., 13, Minnesota

I have met lots of other sibs through Sibshops, which I've gone to for 4 years and now help run. There is also a student in my grade who has 2 brothers with autism but he doesn't seem to want to talk about it. I sometimes have lunch or talk with older sibs who I look up to as role models. —Emma F., 15, Michigan

Because of SibKids, I've met—or rather heard from—tons of siblings around the world who I would have never had otherwise met. I also know a few sibs of my friends. It's really great to know I'm not alone. —Laura P., 15, Virginia

I know about 7 others through my Sibling Support Group that I attend 2 times a month, 12 months a year. —Kaleigh H., 16, New Hampshire

I am a part of SibKids, so I know lots of sibs from all over the world, but only through the computer. It's nice having people who understand where you're coming from. Most of my friends don't want to hear it or don't know how to respond when I have concerns or worries about my siblings, health, or home life.
—Rebekah C., 17, California

Yes, I know a bunch of sibs from lots of ways—my sister's school and through her sports program. I meet them when I help them out. —Matt M., 14, North Carolina

No, I don't. I have seen some, but I don't know them that well, unfortunately. I would like to though, and need to get to know them. —Melisandre P., 14, Kansas

I know some through my school, but I'm not really the best of friends with them. I know a few from picnics and such, but I don't really keep in touch with them that much.
—Katelyn C., 16, Virginia

some of what I go through on a daily basis. —Monica R., 15, Massachusetts

My best friend since 2nd grade has a little brother with Down syndrome. We met because her mom asked my mom about good schools in the area. We don't talk about our brothers very much, but when one of them makes a big accomplishment, we tell each other because we know that the other will understand how important it is. —Katie J., 19, Illinois

I don't know too many other sibs near where I live. The ones I know, I know because I spend a lot of time with their brothers and sisters who have special needs. I know a ton of people from SibKids, but we've never met except online. —Miri L., 16, Illinois

some of what I go through on a daily basis. It's nice to know someone else can understand some of what I go through on a daily basis.

I know many other sibs through Sibshops. My mom is the executive director of Fox Valley Sibling Support Network here in northeast Wisconsin. We have regular Sibshops for kids ages 6 – 16 and extra SuperSibShops for kids age 11 – 16 just so we can get away from the little kids. SuperSibs sometimes go bowling or play laser tag. We even spent the night at a hotel once. I also go to a weekend camp every year called SibCamp.
—Christiana R., 13, Wisconsin

I feel like we both share a special bond.

I have 2 cousins who also have brothers with fragile X and know other sibs through meeting Scott's friend's sibs, writing a book, and holding sibling workshops. I enjoy meeting other sibs— it's comforting to share similar experiences. When I meet with other sibs, I find I both contribute and learn. —Carly H., 17, Georgia

Yes, I do. There is a sibling workshop that I attend every year. We do crafts, discussions, games, and eat pizza. We do the best part is that we can feel like ourselves. We talk openly about what bugs us most about our sib and what we love most about them. —Ashley S., 13, Minnesota

A girl in my Biology class has a sister with Down syndrome and I feel like we both share a special bond.

No. —Emily D., 18, Virginia

I met a lot of kids who have siblings with Down syndrome when I went to the National Down Syndrome Conference last year. —Nicole P., 15, Pennsylvania

How is your sib treated by kids in your community?

Kids have never been mean to Caroline, at least not after they've met her. Sometimes we get those awkward stares in the mall, but usually it's the adults who don't accept her. Kids just jump on in and play with her, and if she can't do something, they help her. Watching that makes me so happy.
—Caitlin M., 14, Maryland

Alex's "community" right now would probably involve Special Olympics and where he works. People treat him well—he has friends, and people are good to him. There are always the token jerks, but Alex is big enough to understand that they don't matter and ignores them.
—Stephanie B., 16, Maryland

I think she is accepted. I think because she is very positive and my friends are always saying how sweet she is. Everywhere we go in our town people know who she is.
—Kristin S., 19, Virginia

Terribly. They bully him mercilessly.
—Miri L., 16, Illinois

Kids are very friendly towards her, but not many invite her for play dates anymore. —Lydia Q., 13, Massachusetts

Most people understand that he has difficulties doing some tasks and are very helpful. They'll ask things like "How's Phil?" or "Is Phillip going swimming today?" It's a really cool feeling.
—Christiana R., 13, Wisconsin

The kids in my community generally treat my sister okay. I cannot remember a time when anyone said anything nasty to her face—but on the other hand, they don't really say much to her at all. My sister is very quiet when she is around people she doesn't know. Because of this, I think people who don't know her don't realise how smart she is and they underestimate her.
—Ariella M., 16, N.S.W.

Whenever neighbor kids come over to play they are really good about trying to include him in what they are doing, and they never complain if we ask them to play something else so that he can join in. —Cassandra W., 15, Iowa

At first, kids may be skeptical of Scott, because he is different. But once they see him interact with people he knows, they are immediately attracted to him. Again, positive attitudes are contagious. —Carly H., 17, Georgia

Really, I think like any other kid. I mean there are always going to be those kids that tease you, but everyone has those. —Teresa H., 13, Minnesota

Good, I think. I think the only thing that ever happened was when someone told me I got my retardedness from my sister. —Megan D., 14, Michigan

Since 5th grade, my brother has been included in regular classes. He also is a Boy Scout and has participated in our church youth group for several years. He gets along better with adults, so he doesn't have a lot of friends his age, but a lot of people from school or various activities make a point of saying hi whenever they see him.
—Amanda M., 19, Washington State

Arianna is treated curiously by children in the community. Some are curious about her because she's different and others don't know any better.
—Lindsay K., 15, California.

There are mixed reactions. The neighborhood kids only see him if they come to play with my other brother or sister and most ignore him after a few moments. But some like to watch him because he is so different—and he is a sort of amusement to them. Although I am hurt sometimes, I don't blame them. I wonder how I would see Andrew if he wasn't my brother. Some kids do enjoy him, though, because he is brilliant with playing video games, despite all his handicaps. It's almost savant. —Allison S., 17, Connecticut

Reader, what about you?

David is treated like a movie star by kids at home. Everyone knows him and says hi to him. But kids from school rarely, if ever, ask him to hang out with them. —Katie J., 19, Illinois

The kids I know in the high school seem to be really nice to her. A lot of people who know me like her and will stick up for her if anyone ever says anything. —Sarah S., 18, Pennsylvania

The kids in the neighborhood do not ask my brother or my cousin to play. They just laugh at them because they cannot ride a bike without training wheels. My cousin, because he has better communication skills, seems to make friends at the neighborhood pool. —Elizabeth T., 19, Oklahoma

Now that she is older, people treat her just fine. When we were younger, a few kids teased her and called her a retard. Once I got kicked out of Boy Scouts because this punk kid called her a retard. I punched him in the face. No one calls my sister a retard. They know I will kick their ass. —Ty H., 17, Washington State

The kids in my community and all my friends are nice to my brother. But sometimes the kids on my bus talk behind his back or make fun of him when he is not around. —Emily P., 13, Indiana

Ugh! People who don't really know my siblings can be so mean! My brother sometimes cries easily and kids call him a sissy and try to make him cry, which just makes him sadder. And my sister…well they just think she's really strange and then ask me or my mom why she's like that. But when they know them, they are usually pretty nice to them. —Alli J., 15, Ohio

Adam used to like playing with the other children in our street, until one of them starting bullying him. The rest of the children followed suit so now he very rarely goes out apart from to go to and from school. —Jemma J., 18, Berkshire

Most kids don't really understand, but they are pretty accepting. Sometimes kids will ask if Steven has his own language. But if someone teases him, I'll be the first one to explain it to them and set them straight. —Jill B., 18, Florida

When kids know them, they generally treat them like any other kid. Kids who have never met them may be scared or uncomfortable around them, and may treat them poorly. That's why I introduce and explain about Charlie and my foster brother to kids whenever I get the chance. —Rebekah C., 17, California

A doctor--more precisely, a surgeon or pediatrician. —Catherine C., 13, California

What career choices sound good right now?

I would really like to work in a museum. Those jobs are hard to get so I'm planning on getting my PhD in psychology and teaching at a university. —Katie J., 19, Illinois

A physical therapist, because I like interaction with other people and I love the idea of helping others. It also helps to keep me involved in athletics. —Lindsay D., 17, North Carolina

A microbiologist or possibly a researcher for a drug company. —Daniel C., 17, Illinois

I want to be an opera singer, but I honestly don't know if I'll make it, because of the attitudes that people in the music business can have. I just can't see stabbing someone else in the back so I can move up the ladder. I want to do something with music, though, like conducting, or maybe something with English or science, like teaching. —Stephanie B., 16, Maryland

High-powered attorney, college professor, housewife and/or mother, and the American ambassador to France sound really nice right now. —Elizabeth T., 19, Oklahoma

Forensic pathologist—more commonly known as a medical examiner or coroner. It is a long haul, 13-15 years, but it really interests me. —Amanda M., 19, Washington State

A professional musician. I would like to be discovered and share my music with others. I sing a bit like James Taylor. —Ty H., 17, Washington State

A nurse helping children, a translator, a florist, or a cosmetologist —Nancy R., 13, California

A journalist or a writer. I would like to write columns for magazines, newspapers, etc. and I would also like to write fiction. —Melisandre P., 14, Kansas

Engineer or zoologist —Kevin T., 14, Virginia

I think it would be cool to be a youth minister at a church. I think it would be fun to be able to have a job where you can spread the word of God to younger people. —Michelle M., 15, New Jersey

A production, set, or costume designer for movies and theatre or a special ed. teacher. —Miri L., 16, Illinois

A book editor or possibly something in the disability field. However, I am starting to think that the second option is unlikely. —Ariella M., 16, N.S.W.

Fashion Designer is number one right now although I would LOVE to be a professional singer/actor, but that is really hard to do. —Teresa H., 13, Minnesota

Maybe a special education teacher, a physical or occupational therapist (all the fun sensory toys) or maybe something totally different like being an archaeologist, historian, or an author. —Alethea R., 13, Minnesota

Orthodontia—at the moment I am going to school to be a dental hygienist to see if I like the dental field enough to go to school for 10 years. —Alisa A., 18, Oregon

It would be awesome to be on Broadway, although it's not very realistic. I also want to be a speech pathologist and work with kids who have special needs. —Margaret C., 14, Illinois

Journalism and the Life of a foreign Correspondent appeals to my adventurous side. —Jenna H., 17, N.S.W

Right now, I would LOVE to work for the F.B.I. because you can make a difference in someone's life by solving a crime, and helping someone out in bad times. ☺ —Michelle O., 14, Virginia

I wanna be everything! Politician, author, political speechwriter, inclusion specialist, and teacher are my top five. I would also really like to open a school. —Caitlin M., 14, Maryland

I'm torn between two loves: medicine and English, so right now, I'm considering anything involving pediatrics or being an English professor. —Lindsay K., 15, California.

An astronomer. —Matt M., 15, Illinois

Registered nursing. One area that is really appealing to me is pediatric rehab, especially at an in-patient center like a children's hospital. —Rebekah C., 17, California

I would like to be a doctor, to help other children beat cancer. —Lauren V., 14, Connecticut

An on-air radio personality—a DJ! —Megan D., 18, Texas

I'm majoring in hospitality and tourism management so I guess that's the career path I'm on right now. —Kristin S., 19, Virginia

Adolescent psychiatrist sounds pretty good—or a nutritionist for teenage girls. —Alli J., 15, Ohio

I want to be an English teacher at my school when I get older! —Leah K., 13, Iowa

A professional dancer, teacher, or physical therapist. —Kathryn C., 14, Illinois

Social worker, youth minister, or something along those lines, where I can directly help people and work with kids. —Maggie W., 17, Wisconsin

History professor or rock band manager. —Calen P., 14, Michigan

Right now, I really want to be a social worker or an interior designer. I had wanted to be a teacher or a photographer, and in a way, I still do. All of my choices are different, but they're all working with people and that's really what I want to do: work with people and make them happy. —Cassandra W., 15, Iowa

Something in the computer industry, because there's so much money there. —Jemma J., 18, Berkshire

I will own my own vending machine business when I turn 16! —Tyler L., 15, Arizona

Will this question ever go away? (I'm a freshman in college…) Business marketing right now. However, I know I want to work with people and use some of the social skills I've learned as Scott's sister. —Carly H., 17, Georgia

Going into cosmetology and finally opening a salon one day. —Kelsea R., 15, New Hampshire

Reader, what about you?

Something with animals! I seem to work great with them. —Cassie W., 13, Colorado

Right now, I kind of want to be a geneticist or a lawyer, and I would write and do art in my spare time. I am interested in research to find a cure for C.P. and other disabilities, or at least something to help them. —Emily P., 13, Indiana

Well, I'm majoring in pharmacy, so that seems pretty good! —Sarah S., 18, Pennsylvania

Working with young children may be a fun career, but politics would be fun too. —Emily I., 15, Washington State

Water ski. —Lydia Q., 13, Massachusetts

Something you said you'd never do but did anyway:

Join the symphonic band at my high school. —Matt M., 15, Illinois

Get in huge arguments with my parents. I used to see TV shows where the teenage daughter would get in arguments with her parents and I said I'd never be like that. Guess I didn't understand being a teenager. —Catherine C., 13, California

I always said I'd never kiss a boy until I found a really special one, but high school hit, and of course, that never stayed true... —Katelyn C., 16, Virginia

I said I would never be a cheerleader. I thought that they were air-brains who were popular because of their looks and that they were all too loud, too peppy, too cheerful, and too annoying. —Cassandra W., 15, Iowa

Give in to peer pressure. —Rebekah C., 17, California

I said I would never pierce my ears, but 2 years ago, I did,...now I have 5 holes in my ears. —Katie J., 19, Illinois

Care what other people think about me... but it's kind of inevitable, especially because I'm sensitive, and I can't help it! —Stephanie B., 16, Maryland

I said that I'd never go on the Extreme Scream ride at the Puyallup Fair but I ended up going on it with Susan. —Amy S., 15, Washington State

Wear shin guards! Now I play soccer competitively. —Cassie W., 13, Colorado

Cut my hair. —Erin G., 14, Alberta

Be on a sibling panel sponsored by Arc. It was more fun than I thought, as I did find it neat to meet other sibs. Still, I'm not so sure I'm glad my mom talked me into it. —Alethea R., 13, Minnesota

I told my best friend everything, but then I told my self, but then... —Emily N., 17, Oregon

How about you, reader?

I told myself that I would never tell anyone a few secrets about myself,

Go white water rafting after the first horrible experience. But I did it again last summer and loved it. —Emily D., 18, Virginia

When I was little, I vowed to my parents that I would not become a rebellious teenager. —Martha P., 13, Connecticut

98 ★ Something you said you'd never do but did anyway:

Bleach my hair blond. Eventually,
I did and now it looks really good.
—Daniel C., 17, Illinois

I said that I wouldn't go on a roller-coaster ride, but did anyway. I was really scared afterwards. —Leah K., 13, Iowa

I said that I wouldn't do the "freshman fifteen" when I went to college...but I did. It's so sad. —Elizabeth T., 19, Oklahoma

Hmm...I remember saying that I would never like boys...that has certainly changed! ☺ —Michelle O., 14, Virginia

Get carsick. When I went to California I was asked if I got carsick and I said "Nope, never" and—of course—on that very trip I got sick. —Alli J., 15, Ohio

Eat liver. It's not bad as long as you don't know what you're eating. —Lindsay D., 17, North Carolina

Get sick on a boat —Dave S., 14, Michigan

Be embarrassed to go places with my parents. —Laura P., 15, Virginia

To go rock climbing and that was awesome. —Kathryn C., 14, Illinois

I said I'd never ever scold my brother, but I seem to do it a lot. —Christiana R., 13, Wisconsin

Get my belly button pierced. I ended up doing it on my own and my mom made me take it out the same day. —Kelsea R., 15, New Hampshire

I said that I would never, ever, ever go on a skycoaster (something where people get you in these suits and they pull you up 11 stories and you fall 70 mph to the ground almost hitting the ground then it jerks you upward). —Melisandre P., 14, Kansas

Fail my driver's test. I swore I wouldn't. —Allison S., 17, Connecticut

To watch her struggle at stuff. —Dave S., 14, Michigan

What is the hardest thing to do as a sibling?

Feeling trapped by my brother—as though my life will amount to nothing more than worrying about him; his limitations were inflicted physically and bleed down to me mentally. —Allison S., 17, Connecticut

Seeing your friends' siblings and their families. You get a reminder that the reality is that your sibling and family aren't like them and that most people do not have the challenges that you do. —Elizabeth T., 19, Oklahoma

It's seeing other siblings interact. I watch them talk to each other, exchange advice, confide in each other, and even fight, and realize: I won't ever have that kind of sibling relationship. —Alethea R., 13, Minnesota

Answering questions. My brother's disability is not one of my favorite subjects, but I'd rather tell the truth than mumble something to someone and have them think the wrong things. But sometimes people don't want to be near my brother after they know. —Nora G., 13, Virginia

Always having to be understanding and not saying anything that might in some way offend my sister. —Kelsea R., 15, New Hampshire

It is hard to discipline my sister because it is weird to punish your sister. It is not like other sibling relationships; sometimes sibs play a bigger role in our brothers' and sisters' lives. —Emily D., 18, Virginia

Going to school acting as if everything is all right—even though a lot is going on in my mind. —Mandi D., 13, Wisconsin

Explaining his disability to kids around his age. —Katelyn C., 16, Virginia

The hardest thing to do as a sib is to put up with Stephen 24/7. He is mainly nice and happy, but when he isn't, everyone in my house is in for trouble. —Kevin T., 14, Virginia

Letting Alex make his own mistakes. I feel like an older sibling, and sometimes even a parent, because I don't want him ever to be sad... and sometimes I just have to let him live his own life and stop trying to protect him! —Stephanie B., 16, Maryland

Make a decision for them that you know is the right thing, but you know they're never gonna like it. —Jemma J., 18, Berkshire

Changing diapers! —Megan D., 14, Michigan

Having to hear people making fun of your sibling. It is really hard; I don't think my brother knows they say those things, because they don't say it to his face. I hope he doesn't know. It is just hard for me to take it, so it would be extra hard on him. —Melisandre P., 14, Kansas

To sit back, relax, and realize that while your sibling needs your help and care, they are not your responsibility. —Caitlin M., 14, Maryland

It is hard to take care of my sister everyday. Just one day can be extremely stressful. —Matt M., 15, Illinois

Possibly the hardest thing to do as a sibling is watch other people with their "typical" siblings—seeing what they do together and how they talk to each other—and knowing that that will never be you or your family. Dealing with other people's negative and ignorant reactions is also pretty hard as well. —Ariella M., 16, N.S.W.

It is hard to be patient with them, but I think that having a disabled sibling has made me more patient than most of my friends. —Alisa A., 18, Oregon

Not wishing my sister was "normal." At least once a week I find myself saying, "I wish Emily was normal." Nevertheless, I know that if Emily were "normal" my life would not be the adventure that it is today. —Monica R., 15, Massachusetts

It is hard to be supportive of your sib even though you feel like killing them, and reclaiming your life, attention, parents and sanity. —Miri L., 16, Illinois

Keeping a positive attitude for your disabled sib and your other siblings when it feels like your world is falling to pieces. —Rebekah C., 17, California

Finding the balance of challenging Scott to help him grow and learn, without pushing his limits. —Carly H., 17, Georgia

Understanding sometimes what's going on or why something can't be done. It's hard when you can do something like go to the mall by yourself with friends or get your driver's license and because your sib has a disability, he/she can't. —Kaleigh H., 16, New Hampshire

To stand back and watch your sibling be different. Don't get me wrong, I never said that Sarah being different was a bad thing. But, it's hard to see all the other kids talking, walking, and riding bikes before her. It's a feeling that is hard to explain, but all you sibs know what I mean. —Stephie N., 15, Arizona

Watching your sibling go through treatments and trials and not being able to do anything. —Lauren V., 14, Connecticut

Trying to be a good role model and trying to put up with them all the time. —Teresa H., 13, Minnesota

To see him struggle. When I see that he is having a hard time or is extremely frustrated it only makes me frustrated for him. I want so badly to help him and it bothers me when I can't. —Lindsay D., 17, North Carolina

To be mad at your siblings, because no matter what they do you still love them. —Megan D., 18, Texas

My brother who has a disability is older than me so, in a way, I have to act older than I am. —Amy S., 15, Washington State

Watching her suffer when she has a migraine or gets poked and I can't do anything about it! —Leah K., 13, Iowa

Changing Riley's colostomy bag when Mum isn't there to do it. —Cassey C., 15, Southland, N.Z.

To try and love your sibling when they are destroying your stuff. —Daniel C., 17, Illinois

Leaving for a long period of time. When I leave, my sib always goes around the house saying: "Sissy? Sissy?" and it just melts my heart every time!! Or going somewhere with my family when I know my sib wouldn't be able to go with us because of his disability. —Cassandra W., 15, Iowa

Not being allowed to pummel the people who are mean to my sib. —Laura P., 15, Virginia

When I have to clean up after my siblings "because they don't know how to" or for some other dumb reason. It doesn't seem fair for siblings to have to do extra work because their sibs have special needs. —Alli J., 15, Ohio

To be unable to tell them things and know they understand. —Alethea R., 13, Minnesota

To see him struggle so much, it's like you want to do it for him but you can't. —Alicia F., 17, Illinois.

Watching him when my parents are gone and I want to do something else. —Kayla L., 13, Arizona

I feel bad because he gets frustrated. —Emily J., 14, Colorado

Understanding my sib. He has a very difficult time speaking and I can't understand him sometimes.

Sweetest thing someone has done for (or said to) you:

Six of my closest friends and I went to a corn maze—basically just a cornfield haunted by a bunch of boy scouts. Well, we got VERY lost and finally a boy scout came and found us. Luckily, our new friend stuck by us for 3 hours. Plus, he spent 10 dollars on us and surprised us with candy bars. If I ever see him again, I really need to give him a thank-you card! —Martha P., 13, Connecticut

I told my science teacher that my family was in crisis over my brother. I was really upset and she sat with a highly emotional me for 2 hours and got me excused from the class I missed so we could talk. It was so sweet of her, and helped a lot. —Miri L., 16, Illinois

About a year ago, I had my first onstage appearance in a school play. My friends came to watch, and after the show, one of them gave me a single red rose. It made my day! —Emily N., 17, Oregon

My freshman year there was this guy I liked and he liked me. We were talking about our childhood and I said I remember playing at this park that I used to love to go to. Then he asked me what my favorite flower was and I said roses because my middle name is Rose. Two weeks later, he asked me to meet him there and in woodchips, he spelled out "will you go to homecoming with me?" And he had a dozen roses! —Alicia F., 17, Illinois

Someone told me I was very pretty and had a heart of gold and beauty of an angel. —Nancy R., 13, California

My Space Camp counselor gave a very flattering speech to the entire camp when I won the Outstanding Camper award. She described me as a shy but very bright boy who she would look to see later on in life doing great things. —Daniel C., 17, Illinois

My best friend has never stopped being there for me. Even when it could hurt him to hear what I'm saying, or even when it's not convenient for him to listen, he's always been there right beside me. —Stephie N., 15, Arizona

When I was in 5th grade, I sang in the school talent show. Afterwards, a little kindergartner came up to me and gave me the biggest hug I have ever had! ☺ —Michelle O., 14, Virginia

A couple years ago someone sent me a dozen roses anonymously with a note that read "Thanks for being a great friend." Even though I don't know who sent them it makes me happy to know that someone appreciates me. —Amy McK., 16, Tennessee

They said that I had a voice like Dolly Parton. —Mandi D., 13, Wisconsin

My boyfriend called me in the middle of the night just to say he loved me and was thinking about me. I thought that was really sweet. ☺ —Alisa A., 18, Oregon

Once, when I was being left out at a camp, one of the girls with the group that was leaving me out decided to leave the group and came to get me. —Kate F., 13, Wisconsin

When my (now ex-) boyfriend wrote me a poem. It was one of the most beautiful things I've ever heard. —Nicole P., 15, Pennsylvania

When readers of my book (My eXtra Special Brother) tell me that I have inspired them to develop closer relationships in their families. —Carly H., 17, Georgia

Told me they still love me even after they know everything (good and bad) about me. —Rebekah C., 17, California

At school Last year, my friend made me some Cookies and had a teacher give them to me so I didn't know who they came from. I found out Later on, but it was so Cool! —Leah K., 13, Iowa

Well, it's not the sweetest but it's the best thing that someone's ever done for me: when I didn't have anywhere else to live, my grandma took me in. —Amy S., 15, Washington State

Being rather sensitive of stomach, I was panic-stricken when, at the age of about 8, I stepped on a large, fresh dog poo in the school playground. My very practical, self-sacrificing and considerate friend Katherine obligingly got rid of the problem in the privacy of the girls' toilets with the aid of a stick. She saved me from embarrassment, not to mention spewing, which I fear would have been a likely outcome otherwise. A very sweet thing my sister did at age 9 was writing a heartfelt letter to me explaining how devastated she was that I was changing schools, and that she would not have me around any more. —Jenna H., 17, N.S.W.

Someone told me that I'm her model. What better thing can be said than, "I want to be like you?" —Lindsay D., 17, North Carolina

For our one-year anniversary my boyfriend, who goes to West Point, surprised me by coming home, and showed up at my babysitting job with a dozen roses...in uniform. —Katie J., 19, Illinois

Probably making me pancakes when I'm sick (my mom), editing my novelette when she has no idea how to edit (my friend), or Letting me crash in her office after a bad day (my orchestra teacher). Props to you guys. —Maggie W., 17, Wisconsin

Two of my friends sent me flowers for my birthday last year, my freshman year of college. It really made my day. —Amanda M., 19, Washington State

When Riley says he loves me, then tries to kiss me and won't stop until he has. —Cassey C., 15, Southland, N.Z.

A kid was making fun of my little feet, when another boy came up and gave me a hug and said, "It's okay, you may have little feet, but you've got a big heart." —Katelyn C., 16, Virginia

Reader, what about you?

When my best friend Erin came over to my grandma's house where I was staying while my sib was in the hospital. She came over at 10 o'clock at night just to give me a hug because she knew I was really upset about my brother. —Cassandra W., 15, Iowa

Her laugh, because she's always so damn happy!
—Lindsay K., 15, California.

Is there something about your sib that just makes you smile?

She has an infectious laugh, so deep and sincere that if something's particularly funny, tears will shoot out of her eyes and she'll sit there, shaking helplessly with silent laughter until—needing to breathe—she makes a loud exclamatory sigh. It's such a pure expression of delight and emotion that it makes me grin too. —Jenna H., 17, N.S.W.

He has these two cowlicks in the back of his head that spin different ways. No matter how many times we brush it, his hair sticks up. —Christiana R., 13, Wisconsin

Whenever he knows I am mad or sad he comes up to me and gives me a hug. I think that is so cute. —Kathryn C., 14, Illinois

His singing and his one-man versions of his favorite movies that he puts on in his room. —Amanda M., 19, Washington State

EVERYTHING about Adrienne makes me smile! She's the actress of the family. Her facial expressions and body language are particularly hysterical! —Lauren O., 16, Georgia

He is so funny sometimes without meaning to be. He always acts self-confident even if he isn't at the time. Nora G., 13, Virginia

I love it when David sings when he's doing something. Sometimes it's just running up the stairs after renting a new movie, other times it's in the shower. When he sings it means he's really happy. —Katie J., 19, Illinois

His smile—it's so big and broad that when I see him come through the door, it's as if he's reminding me to smile. —Emily J., 14, Colorado

His face, his sweet face. His flat feet, his stubby fingers. Harry always makes me smile. —Alicia F., 17, Illinois.

Her constant high spirits, and her knowledge on birds and flowers. It amazes me and that's one of the many great things about her. —Kelsea R., 15, New Hampshire

He is so honest. Sometimes too honest. I can't help but laugh when someone asks him if he likes their new haircut and he says "no." Or when he says something totally sweet right out of the blue. —Miri L., 16, Illinois

When Riley pulls faces. —Cassey C., 15, Southland, N.Z.

It always brings a smile to my face when she races in the Swimming Special Olympics competitions because no matter if she wins, or comes in 3rd place, she always comes out of the water with the biggest smile because she got to do what she loves to do! ☺ —Michelle O., 14, Virginia

Yes. Stephen's ability to prove how intelligent he is to other people. Sometimes when my other brother spells a word, Stephen will say "You spelled that wrong" or "No, Austin, it is spelled _ _ _ _." It makes me very happy to see him have such unexpected intelligence. —Kevin T., 14, Virginia

My sisters' obliviousness because it's like having comedians around. They often just don't get things and it's funny how they'll ask questions or attempt to do something. Or use words they don't understand and then not use them right. —Kate F., 13, Wisconsin.

He always tries to give me advice when I'm upset, and it just makes me feel better. —Stephanie B., 16, Maryland

His purity. —Allison S., 17, Connecticut

When he's crying or mad at me, I copy him perfectly and it makes him laugh and smile. I can copy so well now and it makes my friends mad! —Kat F., 16, Washington State

When he says something that makes us all laugh until we cry—which happens often. My sib's laugh is just the cutest and funniest thing in the world. No matter how sad or mad I am it always makes me laugh. And then we just sit there laughing at each other.!! —Cassandra W., 15, Iowa

I love watching him play sports and seeing how incredibly able he is. He also has this laugh that can change my day. When he gets hysterical and starts laughing, it never fails to make me happy. —Michelle D., 16, New Jersey

It always makes me smile when my sister uses big words. She doesn't have very good communication skills, but every once in a while she will use a word that isn't even a regular word in my vocabulary. Emily N., 17, Oregon

Her sense of humor. I don't even know if she tries to be funny, but some of the stuff she says is so funny! —Kristin S., 19, Virginia

—Laura P., 15, Virginia

Yes, my sister Heather is so beautiful. She will never need makeup. She is just so cute. Another thing is that if you don't feel good she'll rub your back. Also, when somebody cries, Heather cries too, to show her sympathy for them. —Ashley S., 13, Minnesota

The way she makes me apologize when I get mad at her and the funny ways she says words—like ridiculous, she says "dediculous." —Anna H., 15, North Carolina

My sister makes me smile sometimes with the sly, cheeky comments that she makes when you least expect it. She has a great sense of humour.... And people don't often realise that about her, which just makes her comments all the funnier!!! —Ariella M., 16, N.S.W.

How caring he is when he wakes me up in the morning, he's so cute about it. —Katelyn C., 16, Virginia

The thing about my sis is the funny stuff she says sometimes and the big words she uses. With my bro it's that he always wants to cuddle and make up after fights. —Alli J., 15, Ohio

I just love when I come home from college on weekends and my sister runs up to me to give me a big hug and pats my head. It's awesome. —Sarah S., 18, Pennsylvania

My sister's ability to do the socially unexpected and unacceptable never ceases to make me smile. —Monica R., 15, Massachusetts

Yes! His laugh, his smile, when he talks, when he sings, when he dances, when he hugs me, when I see him happy, or when I see him trying to do something new. —Jill B., 18, Florida

When he smiles or tells me he loves me (although it's very rare and I usually have to prompt him to get him to say it). —Jemma J., 18, Berkshire

Reader, what about your sib?

Whenever he smiles! I love those times, especially when it's me who makes him smile . . . . I feel useful. —Maggie W., 17, Wisconsin

When he tries to use big words he doesn't know and says something really funny. —Emily I., 15, Washington State

Anything about your sib that just pisses you off?

He always has to be the center of attention. If the subject of a conversation has nothing to do with him, he'll change it to something that does. It really annoys me, especially when the rest of the family is having an interesting conversation and he butts in. —Amanda M., 19, Washington State

Whenever my personal items are destroyed. Also, whenever I am studying, he is loud but when I don't have to work, he is so quiet. —Kathryn C., 14, Illinois

Definitely. He can be very possessive, since his possessions are something he can directly control. So if I want to borrow a CD, a pair of boxers, you name it, he will do everything in his power not to lend them to me. Hmm, maybe that's exaggerating; he just lent me his Red Hot Chili Peppers CD. Anyway, generally I have to go to my mom and ask her to veto his possessiveness. —Maggie W., 17, Wisconsin

When she comes and lays on the just-made bed, or when she lays on top of me and she won't get up. —Ashley S., 13, Minnesota

I can't stand when he doesn't listen to me! Even something as simple as "please come downstairs," or "put on your shoes before you go outside" can turn into a huge battle. —Michelle D., 16, New Jersey

His constant whining—if he wants anything he'll just yell "MUM" until she replies. —Jemma J., 18, Berkshire

I hate when my sister misbehaves intentionally and other people (my parents!) say she can't help if and it's something she can't control. And I get really pissed off when they later start going on about how great she is and look at all she can do and she's improving and blah blah blah. —Amber C., 13, California

How rigid she is in her schedule. She never wants to change. She has to wear this shirt on this day, even if it has a hole and a huge stain on it! I just don't understand why she can't change ever! —Kristin S., 19, Virginia

His not minding his own business always pisses me off. After my parents are finished being angry with me, Stephen decides to reiterate what my parents said and add some of his own comments, such as "No friends over, Kevin." It just gets plain annoying. —Kevin T., 14, Virginia

Reader, what really ticks you off?

When she yells at my Mom for TRYING TO HELP HER!!!! —Erin G., 14, Alberta

Sometimes when I'm trying to have fun with my friends, she needs quiet time and we have to make sure we aren't loud and joking around too loudly, because then she sometimes gets upset and I get in trouble. —Kelsea R., 15, New Hampshire

Sometimes he makes faces at me when I'm trying to talk to him because he doesn't want to listen. That really pisses me off. But I mean hey! he is my brother so I suppose it's only normal. —Lindsay D., 17, North Carolina

I hate when my sister has a tantrum in stores and everyone stares. I hate how she doesn't understand that she can't have something when she wants it! I hate when she grabs my hair and other people's hair. As mean as this might sound and as much as I love her....I hate how we can't go on vacation because of her. —Margaret C., 14, Illinois

My sister is quite obstinate and argumentative at times, and when her protests against something are irrational and unjustified, I get annoyed. Preferring peace, I tend to do my best to brighten her mood, swaying her attention away from whatever is upsetting her, sugarcoating my conversation. However, as she gets older I am expecting more of her, including an ability to cool her own temper and make compromises. I am no longer content to pander to her emotions and am sick of having to make false merriment and tailor my comments in order to keep her happy. I can only hope that this is a teen thing, and harmony will be restored in a couple of years. —Jenna H., 17, N.S.W.

When my sib hits me—he doesn't know that he's doing anything wrong. When he does it, he thinks he's playing, but it really hurts. —Cassandra W., 15, Iowa

The noises! Oh the noises! My brother and cousin make the weirdest, most "retarded" sounding, annoying noises. Plus, they are made at the worst times like church, bedtime, or in the early morning. —Elizabeth T., 19, Oklahoma

Yes, when I'm trying to get him to do something that he is supposed to do, and he just sits there and stares at me like I'm not even there. —Megan D., 18, Texas

It pisses me off when my sister carries on and on about people that she is looking forward to seeing or events that she is waiting for. She talks about them continually, even though no one else is interested (after the 107th time of her saying the same thing) and we all tell her to be quiet. —Ariella M., 16, N.S.W.

I feel terrible saying this, but it really ticks me off when she cries or grinds her teeth (her nervous habit) when I'm trying to get something done. Sometimes I get angry at her and then I feel REALLY bad because I know it's her only way to communicate. So either way I feel bad. —Caitlin M., 14, Maryland

So much. The yelling, the noise from the video games, the smelly diapers. I often feel trapped by him, as though my life will have to revolve around him. I don't want to be stuck caring for him after my parents are gone, and yet I feel guilty for saying it. I don't like having to take so much care of him, I don't like having to wonder what he would have been otherwise. I don't like that he may keep me from other opportunities. And I don't like that I can't accept it. —Allison S., 17, Connecticut

My sib likes to mimic me and bug me until I get mad. He keeps going even after I ask him to stop. He knows how to push my buttons. —Emily P., 13, Indiana

That would have to be the constant screaming. My parents don't even try to silence my brother and it really gets annoying when he decides he wants to do his scream next to you. —Daniel C., 17, Illinois

The way she asks questions over and over again. It's like she can't remember the answer so she asks it a million times. And the way she can't give herself a bath and I have to do it. —Anna H., 15, North Carolina

I hate it when he gets mad at me for something I can't do anything about. —Emily J., 14, Colorado

Sometimes it seems like Matthew gets his way a lot. —Britny G., 16, Missouri

When my sib goes through my stuff, or wants to butt in where he's not welcome, that makes me frustrated. And, when I have to drag him along if I'm going out with my friends. —Nicole P., 15, Pennsylvania

I get mad when I get into trouble for things that Vickie gets away with. I try not to get mad because I know that she just doesn't know any better about some things, but sometimes I just lose it! —Michelle O., 14, Virginia

What confuses you the most about the opposite sex?

That if you give a guy any form of ball or Frisbee they can be entertained for hours at a time. —Catherine C., 13, California

How they can seem so sweet at first but then turn out to be total jerks. —Lindsay D., 17, North Carolina

The need for males, particularly the adolescent variety, to constantly prove themselves to each other. This frequently seems to involve eating copious amounts of food or bizarre displays of jumping on and pummeling each other. Others in the clan hoot and emit strange grunting noises, egging on the contestants. Also, the somewhat limited ability of young men to hold a conversation can be disappointing. Young women, of course, are devoid of such strange rituals and characteristics. By the way, does my bum look big in this? —Jenna H., 17, N.S.W.

Why they think boys are rude slobs. —Dave S., 14, Michigan

How they hate to go shopping, but love to go hunting. —Megan D., 18, Texas

Everything! I don't have enough room to explain. Maybe I will write a thesis on it some day. —Emily D., 18, Virginia

Why are boys my age always trying to get attention or act macho?! —Leah K., 13, Iowa

Boys have this way of making you think they are so stupid. But then, they do something incredibly sweet and completely throw you off. —Miri L., 16, Illinois

How women think. —Kevin T., 14, Virginia

God, boys think girls are complicated! They need some serious psychoanalysis. Boys want love but they don't—they all need therapy, all of them. No offense, boys; I may be ragging on you but it doesn't mean I don't adore you. —Allison S., 17, Connecticut

Most of them are obsessed with one physical feature in a girl (you guess) and I still wonder what's up with that. —Kat F., 16, Washington State

EVERYTHING!! But the one thing that confuses me the most is how a boy can act like such a tough guy, but when he's not around his friends, he is the sweetest most caring person ever, and that even he's shy sometimes too. —Cassandra W., 15, Iowa

Everyone I know seems to think that all guys are one way and all girls are another. I think everyone is different, and different things confuse me about different people. —Caitlin M., 14, Maryland

All of the emotions and basic illogic involved in women's reasoning. It is a proven fact that guys are more logical, step-by-step thinkers than women and this confuses many women. —Daniel C., 17, Illinois

Why they don't pick up subtle hints. —Alli J., 15, Ohio

Why they think fake burping is just the coolest thing. —Méisandre P., 14, Kansas

Why is it so hard to communicate? —Alicia F., 17, Illinois.

How guys always answer with one-word answers. If you ask them what they did during the day, they usually answer with "nothing" or "I dunno." —Emily N., 17, Oregon

Males have this funny habit of sending "mixed signals." A guy will do something that makes a girl think that he is interested in her. Then, he will do something else that sends the opposite message. Are guys just not conscious of this? If you are interested in a girl, act interested! If you aren't, then don't act as if you are! It just complicates the situation and keeps us guessing. —Elizabeth T., 19, Oklahoma

I don't see why when a guy likes a girl he has to be so annoying! Why can't guys just come out and say, "Hey, I really like you!" —Martha P., 13, Connecticut

The way they can hide emotions, or just avoid having them (and yes, I'm incredibly jealous). —Erin G., 14, Alberta

Why they won't accept that without women, they'd go extinct because nobody would fix them a sandwich or wash their clothes. Basically, we women do all the real work. —Laura P., 15, Virginia

I guess the one thing I don't get is the fascination with cars and sports. —Rebekah C., 17, California

Sigh. So many things. It seems like one minute they might like you and the next, they don't. —Lindsay K., 15, California.

Why they are so embarrassed by their period. I mean it is natural. They don't have to make up some lame excuse why they were being "moody." —Tyler L., 15, Arizona

What doesn't? —Calen P., 14, Michigan

It's like boys never listen, or they take something the wrong way. They must think we are mind readers and, umm, last I checked I wasn't —Kathryn C., 14, Illinois

Why are guys so into sports on TV? I like watching sports when friends of mine are playing, but why watch every game on TV?! I'd rather be sleeping. —Nicole P., 15, Pennsylvania

Guys hardly ever call when they say they will. —Christiana R., 13, Wisconsin

I wonder why women are more vulnerable to consumerism. —Ty H., 17, Washington State

Their odd obsession with having to pay for everything whenever you go anywhere with them. I understand that they are trying to be polite, respectful, and all that; but it would be cool if I had to pay for myself once in a while. —Stephie N., 15, Arizona

Reader, what confuses you?

How do the people at your school/church/ after-school group treat your sibling?

My sister and I go to different schools. I have been at the same tiny school since kindergarten, so everyone has kinda known about Caroline since day one. But it's hard when I have to go to a new place, like camp, and have to explain it to everyone. It gets tiring. I wish I could just gather the whole camp together and make a big speech about it. But I hate it when people's reaction is, awwww that's so sad. —Caitlin M., 14, Maryland

I am proud of Janae—she didn't want to hide away in a back room at high school. She wanted to hang out just like everyone else and that took a lot of courage. Even though there were ignorant staff and peers, she just held her head up and went about her day. It takes a great personal strength to ignore those who don't want to see you succeed. For example, Janae wanted to eat lunch with a wide group of friends, but her special education teacher told her that she had to eat at the table just for disabled students. Janae would not obey her teacher. She persisted at sitting with the school class leaders, cute boys, and a group of talkative girls. —Ty H., 17, Washington State

At church when she makes noises (she does not know better) some people look back at her with a kind of nasty look. But then, most of the other people there know she is not trying to be rude and understand that she has a disability. —Calen P., 14, Michigan

They have never met him. I don't think they would treat him well at all. In fact, most might be silently disgusted, or at least poke fun. I wouldn't blame them, mind you—they don't know any better. —Allison S., 17, Connecticut

People who don't know my brother has autism don't have very much tolerance for him. Kids at school treat him terribly. But the adults who know him best—like some teachers, Hebrew tutors, and relatives—just love him to death. There's a huge range in people's responses to him. —Miri L., 16, Illinois

At my school, everyone knows that there's something's "wrong" with Nathaniel and Sophia but they don't really talk about it or call them "retards" or anything and that's good enough for me. At church, people stare at us because Nathaniel and Sophia look like normal kids who should be able to behave and don't. Some people understand, some don't, and some try to. —Alethea R., 13, Minnesota

In middle school and even in high school, some people made fun of her. They didn't do it right in front of her or call her names, but when she'd say something, they would laugh about it or pretend to act like her. —Kristin S., 19, Virginia

I have only come across a few people who don't treat my sister very nicely. All my friends, teachers, and youth ministers absolutely love her. One of my best friends even considers her a second sister and wants to kidnap her. —Stephie N., 15, Arizona

Other people play with him, love him, and respect him —— just how my family treats him. We set the example: positive attitudes are contagious. —Carly H., 17, Georgia

People used to call him names in elementary school and I would yell at them and defend him. But, when he was in 4th grade, two popular boys became friends with him. They defended him too, and everybody's attitude towards him changed. That made Clinton happier, more confident, and more outgoing. So, when we changed schools, everything was still good because Clinton had changed and everyone liked him. —Leslie C., 16, Washington State

Most of the kids at Eric's school don't treat him well at all. I guess they're just too young to understand. In fact, we're contemplating moving so that Eric can be at a school that will better suit his needs. At church, everyone is very helpful and they really care for him. —Laura P., 15, Virginia

Everyone is always extremely nice to Jeremy because Jeremy is always nice to them. They often exchange kind greetings and a hug (maybe even a kiss). Even though people are nice to Jeremy, he rarely gets invited to birthday parties or houses to spend the night. They don't call Jeremy and ask to hang out. —Lindsay D., 17, North Carolina

Most of my friends treat him pretty well, but at church, we do tend to get a lot of stares. Matt doesn't like staying in one place for a long time, and gets a little rowdy... and he's never really been good for one whole church service since he was a toddler. —Katelyn C., 16, Virginia

Well, there are always going to be mean people in this world, so everywhere Jackie goes there are going to be jerks. High school is an awkward time for everyone, so some people deal with it by putting others down, and do not treat special needs kids with the respect they deserve. But at our church, everyone adores Jackie and shows her Christian love. —Emily D., 18, Virginia

They treat my little brother with respect and kindness. If they don't then they will have to deal with me. —Daniel C., 17, Illinois

My friends are very good to my brother. They often help my mom by watching and playing with him when she needs help or just because they want to. Some call just to talk to him! —Michelle D., 16, New Jersey

Reader, write where you can!

My sister has a great group of friends through her church youth group who are very supportive of her, and another group at school. Her social situation has improved as her peers have matured and been able to overcome the barrier of the wheelchair to form friendships with her. —Jenna H., 17, N.S.W.

The people in our church and school group treat Vickie really well. Most of them understand Vickie and know her limits. Vickie really enjoys helping out, so at school, they have Vickie put out things on the sign outside because she is so good at spelling. At church, she helps out with the desserts at Community Meal. With all of the things she does, I think she feels very important in our community. —Michelle O., 14, Virginia

Everyone in our community loves Adrienne. Her hugs, laughter, and big smile leave everlasting impressions on everyone she meets. People want to be happy and Adrienne's happiness is contagious; when you are around her, you just can't help but smile! —Lauren O., 16, Georgia

At my middle school, the kids were very critical. They made fun and teased him. But not to worry, I spoke up and told them off. At my high school, my friends and teachers were much more understanding and supportive. They were very proud of me for my strength and they were so encouraging. —Jill B., 18, Florida

My brother is quite the social butterfly and is known by quite a few people at our church. He loves to talk and always has to say hi to everyone he knows. It can be hard to drag him out of church sometimes. People are very nice to him and always make a point of saying hi to him. —Amanda M., 19, Washington State

They treat them like any other person. They don't baby them or act like they have cooties or anything, I think that our town is very generous. —Kate F., 13, Wisconsin

Most people I know treat my brother well because he is a friendly person and once you meet him, you can't forget him. He's just that kind of person. But sometimes I think that some people treat Dylan nicely just because he is my brother, and I think that's sad. —Alisa A., 18, Oregon

My brother went to my high school, and most of the people there treated him very well. He made some awesome friends that he still keeps in touch with. Some people were cruel, but that's high school—it's inevitable to have people who are immature and just plain mean. —Stephanie B., 16, Maryland

When we are out shopping, people aren't always kind... at all...and it makes me want to look at them the same way or walk over there and say something to them, but I can't. That just makes matters worse. My sister has learned to deal with it, so I have to try and learn to--as much because it hurts and upsets me. —Kelsea R., 15, New Hampshire

They think he is so funny. Of course, they don't know what he is like at home. —Cassie W., 13, Colorado

Everyone we know treats my brother with a lot of respect. We know a lot of people who understand and are always very concerned when something goes wrong. I don't think that we could ask for better people to be around us! —Cassandra W., 15, Iowa

I try very hard not to tell the people I meet about my sib so that they won't treat him or me differently. —Lauren V., 14, Connecticut

Most of them haven't met my sister but their general reaction is the "smile-and-nod." I explain to them what she's saying and then they warm up to her. My one friend just loves her. —Erin G., 14, Alberta

"Hey" or "Whatever." —Brooke W., 13, Virginia

What are some words or phrases you use the most? "Man." —Michelle M., 15, New Jersey

My sister and I also say "of life" after a lot of phrases. We aren't really sure why, sometimes we'll just say, "I just got back from college of life," or "How was school of life?" It's pretty funny. Lately we've been saying "of death" after a few things too just to be crazy like that. —Sarah S., 18, Pennsylvania

"Eh?" "I'm just saying." "Sucka foooou." "Jeeze of Pete." "For the love of Mike." "Hola." "Babe." "Honey." —Emily D., 18, Virginia

I always say "It's all good" around little kids or my sister because if they make a mistake, a lot of the time they get really mad and think that they have disappointed you in some way. Whenever I say that, it seems to calm them down. —Michelle O., 14, Virginia

I live by the motto "Everything happens for a reason," so I tell people that phrase when they think something horrible happened. I also say "Poodle" often because it is an inside joke between my best friend and me. —Emily N., 17, Oregon

I like to use a variety of words and phrases I hear off of the TV. and internet like "burnination." I throw in some quotes from famous writers but many people my age just don't get it —Daniel C., 17, Illinois

When my mom asks, "Are you ever going to clean your room?" or "Are you going to start your homework soon?" I'll say "Yeah, eventually." It drives her crazy. —Amy S., 15, Washington State

I use the phrases "I know, right?" and "Do you want a medal or a chest to pin it on?" a lot. —Monica R., 15, Massachusetts

"Get over it." "Cool." And "peace." —Ali N., 18, Massachusetts

"What?!", "Ya Think?", "Cute," "Umm, no," and "Hey Baby." —Ashley S., 13, Minnesota

"Barnacles," "fudgesicle," and "crap!" Also, "Ding-dong, the witch is dead!" —Alicia F., 17, Illinois.

"Grr" (the actual word), —Kayla L., 13, Arizona "neato," and "awesome."

"Just kidding." —Calen P., 14, Michigan

"Daniel, are you listening?" —Mandi D., 13, Wisconsin

"Basically what it comes down to..." "Not gonna lie..." "That's cool and by cool I mean totally sweet." —Katie J., 19, Illinois

"Well, you know what? Life isn't fair! Get over it!" I use this whenever my friends start being drama queens about everything. —Kathryn C., 14, Illinois

Rather than saying yes or of course I always say "Definitely" or "yup." —Christiana R., 13, Wisconsin

I use: "Dude," "monkey," "sweet" (as in cool), and "jenk" (stuff). —Kevin T., 14, Virginia

My best friend just recently got me into saying the word "fabulous." —Stephie N., 15, Arizona

I quote Dorie from Finding Nemo all the time. I like to speeeeeeaaaaak whaaaaale like Dorie. I also pull out random quotes and lyrics from songs all the time. I have a juvenile sense of humor, what can I say? —Miri L., 16, Illinois

"Potentially."
"My Dobermans."
"Me too."
"That's good."
"I see." "Here, let me explain it like this ..." —Maggie W., 17, Wisconsin

"Arg!" "All extra..." "Ding dang it Bill Bailey!" "Reciprocity." —Elizabeth T., 19, Oklahoma

"Geeze," "heck?," or "What the heck?" —Alisa A., 18, Oregon

"Good lord!" "Oh my gosh!" "Schnikes" and "Hiya" —Alli J., 15, Ohio

"Aighty tighty," "freaky," "evil," "no pressure." —Teresa H., 13, Minnesota

Sometimes at the end of a sentence I say, "And yah." —Leah K., 13, Iowa

"Shoot a Monkey!" —Britny G., 16, Missouri

I say "same difference" when I mean "same thing" and I use the word "nudnik" which means "being a pest for the sake of being a pest" in Hebrew. —Ariella, 16, N.S.W.

"Obviously" and "You don't even know." —Emily I., 15, Washington State

"Swanky," "fabutan," and "Don't mock me!" —Erin G., 14, Alberta

I say "ouch," a bunch when someone says something harsh. —Lindsay D., 17, North Carolina

I say "outta control" way too much and "aw geez" a lot too. —Michelle D., 16, New Jersey

I say "humorous" instead of "funny." —Caitlin M., 14, Maryland

I like to use the word "humorous" instead of "funny." I just think it's a better word. —Caitlin M., 14, Maryland

I say "sweet," or "that's so random" a lot. —Anna H., 15, North Carolina

"Prossibly" (a word I made up—a mix between possibly and probably). —Stephanie B., 16, Maryland

"Come on baby girl." —Dave S., 14, Michigan

I use "d'oh," "loser," and sometimes "tisith" now. —Matt M., 15, Illinois

Reader, what phrases do you use?

"You might regret that you do it but you will regret it so much more if you don't!" —Melisandre P., 14, Kansas

I love to use the words "dude," "sweet," "sick," and anything French. —Lindsay K., 15, California.

"Cool," "Hecka'," "Hella'," "OK," "Whoops," "Whatever." —Rebekah C., 17, California

"Spiffy." That's my word. —Kat F., 16, Washington State

"Whatever," "I'm bored," "Awesome." —Amber C., 13, California

I don't do it to be a total valley girl, but I always say "like." —Margaret C., 14, Illinois

Has something ever happened to your sib that scared you?

When my brother was younger, he had to have eye surgery so that he wasn't cross-eyed. The doctors said that everything went OK, but when Matthew woke up, he was crying frantically because he couldn't see. He asked if the doctors had taken his eyes out. I felt so bad and for a second or two I wasn't sure if he was blinded. My mom reassured him he'd have his eyesight back in a few hours, which made me feel so relieved. —Nicole P., 15, Pennsylvania

Yah, there were lots of times when Charlie got sick and we weren't sure if he'd make it. I hate it when he's that sick or when he can't breathe and turns blue on the way to the hospital. It makes me cherish every moment I have with him. —Rebekah C., 17, California

My sibling went through a rough period where he would get these outbursts of anger. He would get violent, throw things, and hit people. Often just my mom and me were at home, because my dad was at work. My brother often destroyed a room and my mom and I would be left in tears cleaning it up. It was a very frightening time for me because I was scared of my brother and what he would do next. I just wanted it all to stop. And eventually it did, thankfully. —Michelle M., 15, New Jersey

Adrienne is currently battling scoliosis. The thought of her possibly needing back surgery is scary. She would have to be in the hospital for a couple of weeks and require many therapy sessions to learn how to walk again. —Lauren O., 16, Georgia

Yes, when I was 9 my brother had a stroke in the very same week that my grandpa passed away. It was really scary because my parents had to be out of state with my sib and we were being kind of "passed around" the family so we would have a place to stay and always have someone to talk to. —Cassandra W., 15, Iowa

Once she had a stroke-like thing and was in the hospital. She had lots of seizures and we weren't sure if she was going to be able to do the few things she could do ever again. She couldn't even talk for a while. My parents were very upset. Eventually after lots of therapy, she started talking and returned to her normal self. —Megan D., 14, Michigan

Actually it was quite recent, when he got bitten by a copperhead snake and had to be taken to the emergency room. Also, when he started a fire in the house and I was just two rooms away from him. —Kathryn C., 14, Illinois

Another autistic kid who has a problem with my brother walked up to Adam in the playground and, without saying a word, kicked him in the face. This really opened my eyes to the differences in severity of autism. —Jemma J., 18, Berkshire

At 12 months, my brother disappeared into himself. They called it autism. —Ali N., 18, Massachusetts

Yes. Too many times to count. —Kayla L., 13, Arizona

The morning of my 14th birthday party, he had a seizure while working with a table saw and cut his finger off. My friend and I were woken up because the ambulance had its sirens going off at 7:30am. —Kaleigh H., 16, New Hampshire

Reader, write where you can!

When Stephen went through open-heart surgery, I was very scared. I was rather young then, but I can remember saying "How can Stephen live without a heart?" At that time, I didn't know that they were just "patching" his heart, but even now, I would be afraid of him going through such a major surgical operation. —Kevin T., 14, Virginia

In 1999, my sister was supposed to have a day-only appointment at the hospital, but ended up staying for 5 weeks. For a long time, the doctors weren't really sure what the problem was and the situation was so unexpected that no one really knew what was going on and everything was hectic and unplanned—all of these things making that time quite scary. —Ariella M., 16, N.S.W.

When Harry was born I thought I was going to lose him. He was born with a hole in his heart and needed open heart surgery. We didn't have insurance at the time, but Harry did have his surgery. —Alicia F., 17, Illinois.

My brother was laid off last Friday, and it was terrifying... because I realized just how unstable the work force is. I'm so scared that he won't be able to support or provide for himself, and I'm constantly worrying about what's going to happen to him after my parents pass away. —Stephanie B., 16, Maryland

Once when I was little, Monica had a seizure in the middle of the night. My parents had to rush her to the hospital because she was not breathing and left me at home with a babysitter. My mother and sister stayed in the hospital for a week while I sat at home, wondering what had happened. —Martha P., 13, Connecticut

Jeremy often wanders off and I can't find him. It happens at super-populated places: malls, Disney World, hotels, grocery stores, and football games. I begin to worry about him and start to catalog in my mind all the different horror stories I've heard about lost kids. I frantically try to collect myself and try to calmly think of the most plausible place he might be. Even more disturbing is when I come across the wreckage of my parents in a similar state of mind. —Lindsay D., 17, North Carolina

My brother became really depressed and my mom and I found him trying to hurt himself several times. We had to watch him constantly to make sure he didn't hurt himself. Those were the scariest few weeks of my life. —Miri L., 16, Illinois

Yes, once a guy with disabilities visited my sister at her apartment and tried to have sex with her. —Ty H., 17, Washington State

A couple years ago, my brother got really dangerous. He had to leave our home, and was placed in a hospital in Portland. It scared me because he couldn't control himself or what he was doing. It was scary not knowing if he would ever get to come out of the hospital, and that I might not have been able to see him whenever I wanted to. —Alisa A., 18, Oregon

Ever feel invisible?

I'm too out there to be invisible! —Ty H., 17, Washington State

A lot of the time. Sometimes I feel as though my parents don't care about what I do or don't do. They are so preoccupied with my brother and all of his friends that I don't really seem to matter. Almost all of my time is spent in my room watching my TV, listening to music, doing homework, or talking on the phone. You would think somebody would notice that I spend all of my time in my room, away from everyone else and all the problems that surround their lives. —Alisa A., 18, Oregon

Never. I get as much attention as my sister. Calen P. 14, Michigan

A few years ago, I would have answered this question with a huge YES!!!, but now I realize that there are many times when Caroline feels invisible, and that life doesn't need to be a big competition—the 3 of us can all pay attention to each other. —Caitlin M., 14, Maryland

Absolutely. My parents are very good about not intentionally ignoring me—but having a kid with special needs takes up a lot of their time. Even if I know they do, it seems like they don't care what I say or think. I can't stand being ignored. I don't mind it if they say "not now Catherine" but when they don't respond I really get annoyed. —Catherine C., 13, California

I seldom feel invisible because I provide so much for my brother and I'm a big part of his life. With only 2 kids in our family, my parents never make me feel invisible. —Christiana R., 13, Wisconsin

Definitely. Since I'm the oldest in my family, there are times when either Nick (who is the middle) or Arianna need the most attention. It's also hard having my mother on the phone talking to Arianna's doctors and therapists all the time. I don't spend as much time with her as I'd like to. —Lindsay K., 15, California.

There have been very few times that I have felt invisible, because my parents have always made an effort to ensure that I do not feel like that. However, one time a newspaper wrote an article about my sister's and my bat mitzvah—and only mentioned my name once, while writing heaps about my sister's speech and my mother's speech. When I saw this article, I was extremely angry with the woman who wrote it and it was the one occasion that I did feel invisible. —Ariella M., 16, N.S.W.

Nope, but that would be cool one day, ha ha ha. ☺ —Carly H., 17, Georgia

Lots of times because it seems Matthew gets a lot more attention than Cory and me— even though we have special needs, too. —Britny G., 16, Missouri

I'm a freshman in high school, so this happens all the time. I know my family loves me but sometimes I feel like no one cares if I'm there or not and sometimes everyone acts like I'm not there. I wish people saw me... —Margaret C., 14, Illinois

Sometimes, yes. Sometimes I even feel like I get in the way and make my parents' life harder. I hate that feeling. —Rebekah C., 17, California

I used to all the time. I hated my parents driving Lise places or spending time doing stuff with her. Now I think I understand better why they need to spend time with her, and I'm really glad that they do. —Erin G., 14, Alberta

Are you kidding? Of course! Whenever my sister gets really sick or is screaming my parents get all worried about her and it's like I don't exist. It's Naomi this and Naomi that and if I need something it is always after they have taken care of everything for my sister. —Amber C., 13, California

Yup. Especially one morning when I was late for school and whining that I needed a ride. My mom looked at me and said "I have to take care of my special needs children first!" That just cut me deep and I felt like I didn't mean anything to her. —Alli J., 15, Ohio

Sometimes I feel invisible when I come up with an idea to help my sister, but my parents won't listen to my thoughts. Other times I feel invisible at school when my friends are talking about being retarded—as in being stupid—while I am standing right there. —Emily N., 17, Oregon

Yes, but it is usually because I want to be invisible. There are times that I just want to not be seen so I can do my own thing. We all need some invisible time in our lives. —Emily D., 18, Virginia

No, not really, I'm usually pretty loud and I am good at making myself seen. —Megan D., 18, Texas

Only to myself. —Allison S., 17, Connecticut

Not completely invisible—more like...transparent. It's like they can't really see me sometimes. Since the majority of my family's life revolves around Sarah and younger kids (because there are so many of them and so few of me), there are times that I feel "not all there" and kind of left out. But I get over it. —Stephie N., 15, Arizona

Sometimes, but usually it's intentional—it's good to be by yourself for a while. —Stephanie B., 16, Maryland

My brother doesn't get really good grades very often and his occasional A's seem to mean so much more to my parents than mine. I can't help but feel bad. —Nora G., 13, Virginia

I don't think I can say that I feel invisible because I know and understand that Vickie needs more help than I do. My parents spread their loving care to the both of us and they do a pretty good job. —Michelle O., 14, Virginia

Ever feel invisible, reader?

Once in awhile. I live in a family of 7 with 5 kids, so it can get pretty hectic sometimes. Also, since I am one of the oldest kids, I don't need so much taking care of. I sometimes have to keep reminding my parents if I need something or they might forget. —Teresa H., 13, Minnesota

Sometimes my parents focus mainly on Adrienne. I understand that, at times, Adrienne needs more attention than I do. My parents are striving to make Adrienne an independent person, something that they know I have already become. —Lauren O., 16, Georgia

If you could meet one person, dead or alive, who would it be?

Celine Dion. I love her music and the messages her songs send. —Kelsea R., 15, New Hampshire

Elie Weisel; he is such an inspiring man. He works to encourage understanding between people. Even if it is not directly about special needs, his message is important for all people to hear and embrace. —Monica R., 15, Massachusetts

My grandma. She died when I was just born and I would have loved to get to know her. —Kathryn C., 14, Illinois

Either Simple Plan or Good Charlotte.

Princess Diana, she's one of my role models. —Kate F., 13, Wisconsin

Eleanor Roosevelt. —Nora G., 13, Virginia

—Ashley S., 13, Minnesota

Helen Keller. She's my favorite person to quote, and I think it would just be so amazing to meet someone with her strength and intelligence. —Laura P., 15, Virginia

Dan Marino—he was an awesome quarterback for the Miami Dolphins. He had a great attitude, win or lose. Marino also has a child with a disability, so he could probably give me insight on how to cope with Stephen. —Kevin T., 14, Virginia

Marilyn Monroe, so she could give me some tips for auditions and hopefully make me a better actress. —Christiana R., 13, Wisconsin

My mom's mom. My mom speaks so highly of her; I wish I had met her before she died. —Emily D., 18, Virginia

I want to meet the president and spend a day with him to see what it's really like. —Emily J., 14, Colorado

Colin Firth, the actor in Bridget Jones's Diary—he is so dreamy! —Katie J., 19, Illinois

Helen Keller. She had such a rough life and she had so many obstacles but she overcame them all. —Michelle O., 14, Virginia

Either Abraham Lincoln or Emily Dickinson. They both had complex personalities and contributed to society in different ways. —Lindsay K., 15, California.

Dr. Phil. Ever since he was on Oprah, I have fallen in love with Dr. Phil. He is smart, witty, and I love his strange Southern sayings. —Michelle D., 16, New Jersey

Albert Einstein. —Dave S., 14, Michigan

Hitler, to tell him exactly what I thought of him. —Margaret C., 14, Illinois

Jesus. I want to meet the man who died for all of our sins, and went through so much pain and torture just so we could live. It's amazing and I will meet him someday. —Cassandra W., 15, Iowa

John F. Kennedy. Though his presidency was over 40 years ago, I'm amazed by his stamina and charisma. I'd just love to talk to him about his whole life. —Sarah S., 18, Pennsylvania

Mother Teresa. She died when I was 7 and I have read a lot of books about her. Also, I would like to meet Hilary Duff and Chad Michael Murray. —Teresa H., 13, Minnesota

Matt Damon. I have always told my friends that it is my goal to have brunch with him one day. —Lauren O., 16, Georgia

My dad's mother, Isabelle; I've always heard what an amazing person she was and that I look like her but she died before I was born. —Rebekah C., 17, California

My grandfathers, I have never met either of them and it kinda sucks because they sound really cool. —Erin G., 14, Alberta

J.R.R. Tolkien. He died in 1973. —Alethea R., 13, Minnesota.

Marianne Curley—she is my all time favorite author! —Melisandre P., 14, Kansas

My grandfather. He died of cancer before I could talk. —Lauren V., 14, Connecticut

Jimi Hendrix. I would like to jam on the guitar with him and ask him how he played certain parts of his music. —Ty H., 17, Washington State

My grandmother on my mother's side of the family. I hear wonderful things about her such as her fabulous piano playing. —Martha P., 13, Connecticut

All the people that I talk to on SibKids, the listserv for sibs that I am a member of. I have got to know these people so well through emails and it would be amazing to one day meet them in person!! —Ariella M., 16, N.S.W.

My Grandpa. My mom always tells me how much we are alike, and how proud he would be of me if he were alive. —Stephanie B., 16, Maryland

Mel Brooks. His movies always make me laugh and he's an overall excellent entertainer. —Daniel C., 17, Illinois

Martin Luther King, Jr. —Alicia F., 17, Illinois.

My grandfather, because I have heard so much about him.
—Caitlin M., 14, Maryland

Napoleon Bonaparte or Joan of Arc. I think he seems interesting, and she's the best gung-ho woman and can-do-anything idol. I guess I'm a little bit of a history buff.
—Kat F., 16, Washington State

All of the Beatles. I have grown up listening to their music because my dad loves them. I'd have to bring my dad!
—Alisa A., 18, Oregon

Slash from Guns 'n' Roses or Alice Cooper. —Calen P., 14, Michigan

Probably some famous dirt biker, BMX biker, Travis Barker, Carmen Electra, or someone like that.
—Tyler L., 15, Arizona

The members of Blink 182. They are so funny!
—Kristin S., 19, Virginia

My grandfather, since I never got to meet him.
—Nancy R., 13, California

Reader, what about you?

My grandpa. He was my dad's father and I never got to meet him because he died years before I was born. —Emily P., 13, Indiana.

Malcolm X. After studying him and reading his autobiography, I've always wondered what would have happened to him if someone could have destroyed his misconceptions about the Christian faith.
—Elizabeth T., 19, Oklahoma.

Stephen Hawkings. I would love to talk to him about what his life is like. —Catherine C., 13, California

Leonardo da Vinci, James Dean, Sara Teasdale, Arthur Miller, Marilyn Monroe, and Jesus—group meeting. And I'd love to just observe Vincent van Gogh. —Allison S., 17, Connecticut

Jennifer Garner—or at least her character, Sydney Bristow... I am such a big Alias fan. .
—Lindsay D., 17, North Carolina

If you had a choice, would you get rid of all the disabilities in the world—or just the negative reactions to them?

I'd be very hesitant to do that. God doesn't make mistakes and so there is probably a reason for people to have disabilities. Just because we don't understand or know them doesn't justify changing a major aspect of life. —Elizabeth T., 19, Oklahoma

The disabilities, because even without negative reactions, the disabled people would still be living with the grief associated with their disability. —Emily N., 17, Oregon

The negative reactions to them. We need those differences—people and their lives are the ultimate teachers. —Allison S., 17, Connecticut

My brother doesn't complain about having a disability. It is part of who he is and he has learned to deal with it, just as our family has. I don't like how people call people "retards." I would like to get rid of the negative reactions and the name calling, people being disrespectful. —Emma F., 15, Michigan

I see so much magic in my brother; he's unlike anyone else I know. He looks at the world so differently and loves so much. I know other people with disabilities who have made life-altering effects on peoples' lives. They can make you see things so differently. I cannot imagine the world without disabilities; they give the world a balance. (This, by the way, does not mean that I'm glad people are disabled; I just think the world is a better place because of them.) —Lindsay D., 17, North Carolina

No way, the imperfections in life are what make it so beautiful. —Carly H., 17, Georgia

Reader, write wherever you can!

Just the negative reactions. We have to learn to tolerate one another, not just eradicate all the differences. —Erin G., 14, Alberta

I would get rid of all the disabilities in the world because then there would be no negative reactions towards disabled people. —Daniel C., 17, Illinois

I would rid the world of all disabilities because—even if all the negative reactions were gone—there'd still be things people with disabilities couldn't do. Like, David wants to go to college, and play on a school sports team, but he won't ever do either one of those. —Katie J., 19, Illinois

Although there are some disabilities that probably would be better if no one suffered with them, there are more disabilities that I would not get rid of at all. I am so thankful for disabilities and people with them. I would, however, take away the negative reactions any day. —Michelle D., 16, New Jersey

Most definitely the negative reactions. Everyone is different with or without disabilities. I feel the world would be filled with less color. —Alicia F., 17, Illinois

Disabilities make life rich and experiences different; they are not all bad. It's the reactions to them that cause problems. —Rebekah C., 17, California

I would never get rid of disabilities. People with special needs have too much to offer. I would definitely get rid of the world's negative reactions to them. I try as hard as I can to do that every day. —Miri L., 16, Illinois

I'd be opposed to getting rid of all disabilities, as it would invite a genetic "cleansing" of society. Indeed, we would have to consider just what constitutes a disability. Every human being has imperfections, little "disabilities," and it would be impossible to draw the line before we created a species where anything less than perfection was considered a physical or mental handicap. With that would come the loss of so many of the attributes that are the quintessence of being human. —Jenna H., 17, N.S.W.

It depends on whether the people with disabilities were happy or not. If they weren't happy, I would get rid of their disabilities, but otherwise I would just get rid of the negative reactions—because those are what can make having a disability miserable a lot of the time. —Ariella M., 16, N.S.W.

If people accepted people with special needs, open-armed, I think it would do so much more good than getting rid of all the disabilities. —Nora G., 13, Virginia

I'd get rid of all of the negative reactions to disabilities. Taking away disabilities goes against God's path. —Matt M., 15, Illinois

Just the negative reactions. I really appreciate the diversity in our world and disabilities are part of that diversity. The world would be a boring place if everyone was the same; people just need to accept individual differences. —Amanda M., 19, Washington State

I think the world needs to realize that everyone isn't perfect. If no one ever had a disability, no one would learn patience, hope, and persistence. If people just learned to help and understand, it would make the world a better place than if all disabilities just disappeared. —Amber C., 13, California

Personally, I think disabilities can bring out the best in people who have them and everyone around them. It can also bring out the worst! So I would probably say just the negative reactions. However, I don't have the perspective of a person with a disability. —Alethea R., 13, Minnesota

The disabilities. It would make life for the people who have disabilities so much easier. Plus, it would help their families. I know my family is worried about what will happen when they are not around. —Kristin S., 19, Virginia

Our world needs people who are different in it to make it interesting; if everyone were the same we'd all die of boredom. —Monica R., 15, Massachusetts

I would get rid of their disability because then they wouldn't have negative reactions toward them. A win-win situation. —Kate F., 13, Wisconsin.

Most embarrassing moment:

If it were embarrassing, why exactly would I tell it? ;-)
—Allison S., 17, Connecticut

You want me to pick just one? Once at an airport I spilled Sprite on my crotch and everyone thought I peed. I always say really bad things when there is a silence in the room; I do so many embarrassing things every day.
—Caitlin M., 14, Maryland

The THIRD time I broke my arm was when I was in a dress rehearsal for "Fiddler on the Roof." I had to run down the steps of a dark theater, wearing a mask and a long gown that was too big, and then run up some steps onto the stage... all the while screaming! Well, on the way down, I tripped on my dress and fell up the stairs to the stage, chipping my front tooth and dislocating the bone in my left arm on the way. It was so embarrassing (and painful!).
—Stephanie B., 16, Maryland

I went bowling, but I ran too far down the lane. So I slipped and fell down hard, while everyone watched.
—Lauren V., 14, Connecticut

I went to sit down and my friend kicked the chair away. I fell flat on my butt. It hurt so bad and all of the juniors and seniors were laughing. .
—Margaret C., 14, Illinois

Probably when I was leaving the swimming pool. I had my underwear and bra in my towel and didn't know that they fell out. These two older, hot guys came up to me and said, "Excuse me, you dropped these two items." I almost had a heart attack!
—Alicia F., 17, Illinois.

When my sib decided to drop trou in the middle of the neighborhood.
—Kate F., 13, Wisconsin.

When Scott and I were younger, he would throw temper tantrums in the middle of the cereal aisle at the grocery store. I hated it when people stared at Scott, even though they didn't mean anything by it. I was 10, but knew how to act in public. Scott, on the other hand, was 15, but he acted like he was 5. It was a tough problem for a little kid like me to figure out. —Carly H., 17, Georgia

I don't get embarrassed. Well, OK—Last summer my friend pantsed me in front of like 4 guys. It was more funny than anything else though. —Erin G., 14, Alberta

I wrote a letter to the guy I had a crush on and his friend took it and read it out loud to a lot of people at my school and after I had my next class with my crush.
—Nancy R., 13, California

In the winter of my freshman year, I was auditioning for a special choir. We had to sing solo and I was so nervous because I am not good at talking in front of people, let alone singing. I started out a little off and then everything went downhill from there. I got so upset that I had messed up beyond fixing. I started to cry, and then I literally ran out of the room. It was so embarrassing, although I have tried out for it again, and have also tried out for a number of musicals. —Cassandra W., 15, Iowa

One morning I was changing real quickly in the family room thinking I was the only one up. And in comes my brother with his friend (both about 23 years old). I jumped and ran out of the room so fast. I was 16. Then my brother and his friend gave me a ride to school and all the way there we didn't really speak and my face was bright red. —Rebekah C., 17, California

In high school, I had a cast 'cause I had fractured my ankle playing football. Then, in chemistry class, I fell off the stool 'cause I lost my balance thanks to the cast. Of course, my high school crush was sitting right next to me. —Jill B., 18, Florida

When I was 7, I went to camp for 3 weeks. I woke up early and had to go to the bathroom. I didn't want to wake anybody up so I stayed in my bed and, um, stayed a bit too long…. —Brooke W., 13, Virginia

When I was at a music recital and my boyfriend was there and my dad comes up and he starts talking to him! Oh my gosh, I thought I was going to die! My dad was being all mannerly and stuff like hi how are you doing (shaking his hand also)! I could not believe it! —Melisandre P., 14, Kansas

Reader, what's your embarrassing moment?

I felt so stupid and embarrassed when I asked a new friend of mine, Harper, where he lived, and he said near Detroit. And I followed by asking, "Is that in Colorado?" Yeah… not cool. —Nicole P., 15, Pennsylvania

When my little brother urinated on the sign of the Ford assembly plant—and I had to cover my little brother. —Daniel C., 17, Illinois

I was walking to my seat in band class, had my saxophone in one hand and my music in the other, when I tripped over a stand, fell, and knocked over a chair and a stand—in front of my whole entire class, about 80 kids. —Emily P., 13, Indiana

Playing kickball with a basketball and falling over it and breaking my ankle, and then having to crawl into the house because my mom didn't believe I was really hurt. —Kelsea R., 15, New Hampshire

What's the best advice you've given or been given?

Don't worry about the future. Or worry—but know that worrying is as effective as trying to solve an algebra equation by chewing bubble gum. The real troubles in your life are apt to be things that never crossed your worried mind, the kind that blindside you at 4 p.m. on some idle Tuesday. —Monica R., 15, Massachusetts

If God brings you to it, He will bring you through it. —Kathryn C., 14, Illinois

If you want to be happy, you have to find a way to make yourself happy. If you think negative, you'll live a negative life. —Miri L., 16, Illinois

Always be friends with a person before you date them or when the relationship ends you'll lose the friendship too. —Alli J., 15, Ohio

Don't be taken advantage of and it's OK to say no. —Cassey C., 15, Southland, N.Z.

"The bumblebee flies anyway" is my senior yearbook quote. And it's perfect. You see, aerodynamically, with body to wingspan, the bumblebee shouldn't be able to fly. But it does—the bumblebee soars. What the bee does not know to be impossible becomes more than possible—a reality. Such a lesson. —Allison S., 17, Connecticut

You are capable of anything you put your mind to. The only limits in life are the limits you put on yourself. Don't sell yourself short. And do what you know is best for you, not for anyone else. You have to take care of yourself first. —Rebekah C., 17, California

Follow your gut. What you originally think about a situation is usually the right choice. —Kristin S., 19, Virginia

Good advice from the reader . . .

Lauren V., 14, Connecticut

. . . the way of caring for yourself.

Choose your friends wisely. Don't wish to grow up to soon. —Emily D., 18, Virginia

It's OK to care about other people as long as that caring for others does not get in

To keep trying. Don't just give up after you fail once. Get back on the horse and try again. —Lindsay D., 17, North Carolina

Make the most of life—even if you think you can't. —Erin G., 14, Alberta

Don't care what other people think of you. Just be yourself and then you will know that people truly like you for you. And everybody's not gonna like you and everybody's not gonna hate you! —Kelsea R., 15, New Hampshire

Don't be afraid to speak your mind. As Dr. Seuss says: "Be who you are and say what you feel, because those who mind don't matter and those who matter don't mind." —Lauren O., 16, Georgia

Treat people with kindness. —Kate F., 13, Wisconsin.

Try to create a balance in your life. —Carly H., 17, Georgia

What will come, will come, and we'll have to meet it when it does. —Cassandra W., 15, Iowa

Have fun. —Dave S., 14, Michigan

Live each day as if it were your last—because someday it will be. —Stephie N., 15, Arizona

Be your own fashion critic. —Martha P., 13, Connecticut

Attitude is everything. —Kevin T., 14, Virginia

Try not to stress over the little things that don't need to be stressed over and do everything you are able to live life to the fullest. —Emily I., 15, Washington State

"What you don't have you don't need it now, what you don't know you can feel somehow..." (U2). —Catherine C., 13, California

Not to worry about things I can't control. —Stephanie B., 16, Maryland

Don't listen to what other people think. It's what's in your heart that counts. —Alisa A., 18, Oregon

Believe in yourself because if you don't, no one will. —Michelle D., 16, New Jersey

Never give up; anything is possible if you put your mind to it. —Megan D., 18, Texas

Where you see yourself in 10 years:

Hmm... I'll be 27 years old. I will probably be working as a nurse in a hospital or other healthcare facility. Maria will be 18 and Charlie will be 14. My parents would be 63 and 69. I'd imagine having Maria over to visit and helping my parents with Charlie when I can. I see my life going pretty well by then, as a mother, wife, and sister. Thinking about that is what keeps me going in life. —Rebekah C., 17, California

Living with my sister, working for the FBI and having the time of my life! ☺ —Michelle O., 14, Virginia

I will be married to my current boyfriend, Brian. We will be living in or near Chicago. I hope that I will have my PhD in Psychology by then, doing research at a nearby university. Brian will be in the FBI. Also, I hope we will have at least one child by then. —Katie J., 19, Illinois

I hope to have a nice house, nice car with a stable career and income, and someone to spend the rest of my life with. I'll live near my family, and I hope still to be in contact with many of my high school friends. —Cassandra W., 15, Iowa

Probably in University or on tour with a ballet company (cross your fingers!) —Erin G., 14, Alberta

In 10 years, I'll have just finished my masters in college. I'll be looking for a job at NASA. They're high, but not impossible, hopes. —Nicole P., 15, Pennsylvania

Hopefully I'll have my Doctor of Pharmacy degree and be raising a family of my own. —Sarah S., 18, Pennsylvania

Married and starting a family. —Lauren O., 16, Georgia

Up in a tree, reading a book, with my cat, sunbathing. —Kat F., 16, Washington State

I see myself in grad school, going into a field where I can work with kids and be useful at the same time. But I plan to still be learning 10 years from now. —Maggie W., 17, Wisconsin

At my high school reunion, having graduated from FSU with my degree in speech pathology, helping disabled kids to speak better. —Jill B., 18, Florida

That is way too far in the future! I'm not even sure where I'm going to high school. —Amber C., 13, California

Out of college, with a Bachelors degree, married, possibly with children. And a career in radio broadcasting. —Megan D., 18, Texas

I'll probably have traveled around North America. I might be in college, or have a job, or both. There are a lot of possibilities, so I'm not sure. I'll probably be living with my family, because I think I'd like that better than being somewhere else. —Leslie C., 16, Washington State

Working for a pharmaceutical company researching new diseases and trying to find cures for the super germs of the future. —Daniel C., 17, Illinois

Medical school. —Alli J., 15, Ohio

College probably--getting my doctorate or teaching college!

—Calen P., 14, Michigan

Having served in the Peace Corps, worked as a social worker, and married, with kids. —Emily D., 18, Virginia

In 10 years, I will be 27. I see myself finishing graduate school with a Ph.D. in physical therapy. I will be coming up in the world and supporting myself financially. I also see my brother who lives either nearby or in the same apartment. If we didn't live together, I would try to visit him once a day. I hope that 10 years from now I will be just as happy as I am now if not happier. —Lindsay D., 17, North Carolina

Married to a wonderful husband, have a job, and lots of friends. —Amy McK., 16, Tennessee

College—studying something I love. —Brooke W., 13, Virginia

In college, doing really well, and hanging out with a few really good friends. —Catherine C., 13, California

On the cover of a CD that has sold a million copies. —Ty H., 17, Washington State

I see myself engaged with a music degree from Julliard and my own Mercedes Benz. —Martha P., 13, Connecticut

I can see myself with my M.F.A. in English, heading on to graduate school, and possibly married. —Lindsay K., 15, California.

In 10 years, I see myself being eccentric and not having a real job. Boy, would that be nice! —Monica R., 15, Massachusetts

I see myself with a great job that I enjoy doing and engaged to an awesome person. I see myself keeping in touch with family and old and new friends. I see myself enjoying life and all the great things that it has brought me. —Michelle M., 15, New Jersey

I see myself living in a major city, out of college, and performing with an opera company or even conducting! Hopefully, I'd be more in tune with myself, and I'd be able to spend time with me. —Stephanie B., 16, Maryland

—Ashley S., 13, Minnesota

Living in a city, working as a lawyer or in law school. —Lydia Q., 13, Massachusetts

Reader, what about you?

Out of college, working on costume design for small theatres. I will be working with the Special Olympics as well and I will be running an awareness program about disabilities, primarily autism. —Miri L., 16, Illinois

Having a husband and having 1 or 2 kids. I would still be in law school. And we would be financially stable.

I've just graduated from college. I'm teaching during the school year and traveling around the world in the summer. —Christiana R., 13, Wisconsin

Helping my little sis get through tough times. —Dave S., 14, Michigan

What life lesson have you learned from being a sib?

Never take the little things in life for granted. You are so lucky to be able to feed yourself, clean and care for yourself, go to school, have a job, have a future, be able to breathe and speak and do everything you can do. You are capable of ANYTHING you put your mind to. And never give up. If Charlie can do all that he does, then I know I can do anything that I would ever want to do. —Rebekah C., 17, California

Just because a person may have a disability or be different doesn't mean they are any less amazing than everyone else. —Emily I., 15, Washington State

I have learned that people are all very different: some are accepting, some shallow, some a little smarter than us, and some take a little longer. Regardless, just about everyone has a bit of good in them that is worth trying to see. And, if you take a little time to find out, you'll also find out a little something about yourself. Michelle D., 16, New Jersey I learned that life is short; humans are mortals; to live each day to the fullest, and never think that you know exactly what will happen tomorrow. —Lauren V., 14, Connecticut

I have learned from Matthew always to try again and never let someone tell you that you can't do something. —Britny G., 16, Missouri

"Don't judge a book by its cover." Just because a person may look a little different or act a little different, doesn't mean that they should be ignored or treated badly. When some people look at my sister all they see is a person sitting in a wheelchair—but others see a fantastic person who has an amazing sense of humour and who has opinions about all sorts of things, if only someone took the time to listen... —Ariella M., 16, N.S.W.

To Love unConditionally. —Lindsay K., 15, California

Normal is just a cycle on the washing machine. No one is the same; we all have differences and excel in different areas. —Lauren O., 16, Georgia

Everybody is different, and everybody is doing the best you can. You have to be kind and compassionate even if someone is annoying, smelly, slow, fat, ugly, or nerdy. I try to live by the golden rule: Treat everyone the way I'd like them to treat Aaron. —Miri, 16, Illinois

Reach for the moon — even if you miss, you will land among the stars! (It's corny, but I love it) — Stephanie B. 16, Maryland

That everyone has special needs. —Megan D., 14, Michigan

Recently, I did a holiday club with children with disabilities and one kid stays in my mind. He had little understanding of the world around him, but he always seemed happy, and the innocence displayed in his big brown eyes was amazing. It made me wonder why we get so worried about things like money and work, and we forget the importance of what is around us. —Jemma J., 18, Berkshire

No matter how bad things are for you, there is always somebody with bigger difficulties. —Megan D., 18, Texas

To be understanding of other people's difficulties, and have empathy for those who—through no fault of their own—are faced with enormous challenges, and to value each person's unique attributes. —Jenna H., 17, N.S.W.

That the odds may be against you, but if you strive for success, it will come to you. I have watched Stephen beat the odds many times, and I remember that when the odds are against me. —Kevin T., 14, Virginia

Don't give up—because your sibs never do. —Lindsay D., 17, North Carolina

That everyone is beautiful and it doesn't matter who you are, what you look like, or how smart you are. All you need is a smile and a big heart. —Michelle

That life is not perfect and that you must appreciate what you do have. —Lydia Q., 13, Massachusetts

People like to shy away from their problems. Everyone does it in a different way, but they don't like to face them head-on. They will go to almost extreme lengths to avoid what to them is alien. —Maggie W., 17, Wisconsin

To trust people and to give them a chance. You never know what someone can do until you let them try. And, although the news may focus on the bad people in the world, there are so many more good, honest, and caring people out there. —Cassandra W., 15, Iowa

Things will be OK in the end. If it's not OK, then it's not the end. So keep pushing. —Kristin S., 19, Virginia

To live life one day at a time and focus on the little things that make you happy. There's no use in stressing over things you can't change! —Katie J., 19, Illinois

You aren't always going to get what you expect. Be flexible and open-minded. Think outside the box. Plan ahead. Stay focused and your hard work will pay off. —Christiana R., 13, Wisconsin

Reader, what about you?

I have learned compassion from my sister—and that being compassionate is the only way to get through life. —Emily D., 18, Virginia

I guess I have learned to be more responsible and mature--but I sure don't feel any of that. I feel just plain spent. —Daniel C., 17, Illinois

That no matter what I do he will always be there for me. He's my special light in the darkness; there when all other lights go out. —Kathryn C., 14, Illinois

—Emily N., 17, Oregon

To cherish people's differences, to act kindly towards all people and to teach people with patience.

That the impossible takes a little longer. (That's the Williams syndrome slogan, and I think it fits!) —Erin G., 14, Alberta

Do not take anything for granted—and smile! —Emily J., 14, Colorado

Go with the flow. —Monica R., 15, Massachusetts

That life is precious and delicate. It needs to be cherished and lived to the fullest because we don't know when it will end. —Stephie N., 15, Arizona

To accept that I am different than most of the people I know and I shouldn't try to be them. —Catherine C., 13, California

Everyone has a disability—whether it is on the inside or the outside—because no one but God is flawless. —Alicia F., 17, Illinois.

That God is in control. We don't know the hour we will die; consequently, I've learned to love and cherish each moment I have with my sibs. —Leah K., 13, Iowa

Happiest moment:

My happiest moment would probably have to be my Bat Mitzvah. The feeling of standing in front of all my friends and family, having just accomplished something that I had worked towards for several years, is one of the most special feelings I have ever had. Also the fact that it was something that my sister and I did together and that was challenging for both of us, made it special because there have been very few things that we do together. —Ariella M., 16, N.S.W.

Michelle Branch came to Portland, Oregon and played at Tower Records. And she signed my guitar, even though one of the people she was with said no. She did it anyway. —Alisa, 18

When I crossed the finish line at the cross-country conference meet, the last one of the season. I PR'ed (broke my own record) by 2 minutes and had made my season goal of finishing a race in under 20 minutes. —Maggie W., 17, Wisconsin

Finding out the person I liked liked me too! —Anna H., 15, North Carolina

Being voted MVP for my varsity softball team my sophomore year. I had worked extremely hard to become a better player since I was about 13 years old and this was the first time that I was recognized for my achievements. —Michelle D., 16, New Jersey

One day when my brother came up to me, wrapped his arms around me, and hugged me so tight. He said to me, "Jill, you're a good sister. You're my best friend. I love you." It brought tears to my eyes. —Jill B., 18, Florida

I felt so good when I helped at the Mile High teen/adult Halloween party. Everyone had such a great time, which made me feel so good. —Emily J., 14, Colorado

The time I first knew what it was like to be loved by someone not in my family. It felt so safe yet so dangerous at the same time.. —Monica R., 15, Massachusetts

So far, it's been a cruise we took celebrating my grandparent's 50th anniversary. They took the whole family! I had just finished a stressful school year and the vacation was perfect. Meeting new people, relaxing daily, and exploring the beaches was amazing. —Lauren O., 16, Georgia

When I went to my very first concert I went with my best friends to see Tori Amos live. Our seats were in the 6th row, and it was almost as if Tori was singing just for us. —Emily N., 17, Oregon

When I earned the rank of Eagle Scout. It had been a dream since I was in the first grade and just heard of the Boy Scouts. Finally achieving that rank gave me a joy that nothing since has been able to compete with. Daniel C., 17, Illinois

When Matthew took his first steps the summer after he turned 7. The doctors had said that he would never walk if he didn't walk before then.
—Britny G., 16, Missouri

At my school's talent show. I got up in front of the whole school in 7th and 8th grade and I sang. It was just great to see everyone looking at me and after I sang, I loved the applause.
—Margaret C., 14, Illinois

When my mom called me at 3:45 in the morning to tell me that I had a new baby sister. I really love both of my little brothers, but I had always wanted a little sister. I guess the saying "good things come to those who wait" is really true!
—Cassandra W., 15, Iowa

When I know that I make my sisters' day by spending time with them and making them laugh and just being there.
—Kelsea R., 15, New Hampshire

When we got Jessica from the airport, when Elizabeth was born, and when my parents brought Daniel home.
—Teresa H., 13, Minnesota

When I went to camp for the first time and met my best friend. —Lydia Q., 13, Massachusetts

Reader, what's your happiest moment?

It's really hard to pick just one. It seems that for all of life's bad moments, there are three times as many happy ones. —Caitlin M., 14, Maryland

Some of my happier moments have come as a result of seeing my sister master new skills, overcome obstacles, or learn to do things she could not previously. For example, mustering up the energy and will to transfer herself from her wheelchair to the sofa — a difficult task if you cannot use your legs, have poor balance, and a dislocated hip.
—Jenna H., 17, N.S.W

When my favorite author, Marianne Curley, sent me her autograph. She lives in Australia, I had emailed her, asking her about how much it would cost, and she just sent it to me! —Melisandre P., 14, Kansas

When I got 2 dogs for my 12th birthday. —Elizabeth T., 19, Oklahoma

When Riley is at school.
—Cassey C., 15, Southland, N.Z.

When I was performing onstage with the Junior High Connecticut Eastern Regional Chorus. I was singing my heart out with people that I had grown close to. —Martha P., 13, Connecticut

When my brother graduated from high school. There were 1,000 kids in his class and when David got his diploma, all of them yelled and cheered for him. They didn't do that for anyone else. —Katie J., 19, Illinois

When I got my Pointe shoes. When my teacher told me I could get them, I was so excited. I was about ready to cry 'cause I was dying to get them. —Kathryn C., 14, Illinois

When I became a Christian! —Leah K., 13, Iowa

When my soccer team won the championship in a tournament and we just really played great. —Matt M., 14, North Carolina.

When I became a big sister!!! —Mandi D., 13, Wisconsin

When my brother made it through his bar mitzvah, when I finished middle school, and when I stayed up all night lying on the grass under the stars talking to my best friend. —Miri L., 16, Illinois

My first-ever tryout for cheerleading freshman year. When I opened my letter and it said I made it, I was just full of joy. —Katelyn C., 16, Virginia

When my sister took her first step. —Dave S., 14, Michigan

When my brother and I walked across the stage on graduation day together to receive our diplomas. —Megan D., 18, Texas

Whenever I learn something new. Or when I am with the people I love. —Carly H., 17, Georgia

When my sister got her hip surgeries; since then, she hasn't had any more problems with her hips. —Nancy R., 13, California

When I won my President's academic award in the 5th grade. All of the teachers chose one student in their class and my teacher chose me! —Michelle O., 14, Virginia

If you had just one day when your sibling didn't have a disability, what would you choose to do on that day?

I would really like to have a long conversation with him. I would probably spend time together in a restaurant (so we can talk), then go to a movie (because he can't do that with a disability, and if he does then it is really frustrating). Go to an amusement park too. And just show him the world—or the state at least!
—Melisandre P., 14, Kansas

I would do real sister stuff: shopping, dressing up and doing a photo shoot, or have a spa day! And with my brother, there already are some days that it seems like he doesn't have a disability and we do stuff like go to the movies, play games, or other things like that. —Alli J., 15, Ohio

Talk a lot. I'd like to know his normal side. See if he is an annoying little brother or one you could live with. —Brooke W., 13, Virginia

Frolic around on the beach, swim in the surf, trek through a tropical Queensland rainforest, climb Uluru and marvel at the expanse of red ochre desert that is central Australia, then head to my grandparents' place for a traditional Sri Lankan feast with the family. —Jenna H., 17, N.S.W.

I would take Emily to lunch and then to the mall. Together Emily and I would discuss all the things we have wanted to talk about over the years but never got the chance to, like my boyfriends or her favorite music. —Monica R., 15, Massachusetts

I would try to bond with him in a way most sibs don't. We'd do something semi-rebellious that we would keep a secret from our parents. That would be something special we'd have in common. —Nicole P., 15, Pennsylvania

I wouldn't do anything special, I would just do as many ordinary, everyday things as I could. For half the day I would do something with my family, and for the other half I would do something with my friends and my sister – seeing what it is like to be a "real" twin in that situation. —Ariella M., 16, N.S.W.

I think we would just have a normal day. We lead every day now like there is no disability in the mix, so why should that day be any different? —Sarah S., 18, Pennsylvania

I would ask him how he feels. Scott has never been able to communicate his thoughts and emotions clearly. I've always been a little curious what goes on in his brain. —Carly H., 17, Georgia

I almost wouldn't know what to do because it would be like having a total stranger as a brother. I would probably play sports with him, actually strenuously, and walk with him to all kinds of cool places he wouldn't have gone before. —Kevin T., 14, Virginia

The first thing I would do is have him drive me around. (He can't drive). Then I would have him help me with my homework. Then we would go out for Mexican food and a funny movie. He would be able to pay for both the dinner and movie because he would be more comfortable with counting money. Then he'd drop me off at home and drive off to spend time with his friends, who invited him to come with them. —Emma F., 15, Michigan

—Christiana R., 13, Wisconsin I would just hang out with him or do whatever he's been trying to tell us over the years. wanted to do and talk to him about what he's

I'd tell them how much I love them so I could look back on that day and remember that for one day, they knew they were loved, and that for one day, I could hug them, and have them fully understand what that hug really meant —Alethea R., 13, Minnesota

Anything that he wanted to do! We would probably do things that we couldn't do as a family because of his disability. Because he loves to play basketball, I would even spend the whole day playing basketball with him. At night, I would take him out dancing, which he loves to do. —Emily P., 13, Indiana.

Basically, we would do the same stuff: watch movies and TV, wrestle, and play games. What would change would be the specifics like the games and the TV programs we'd watch. I guess I've always tried to treat my brother like a normal kid. That's my justification for beating him up all the time. —Elizabeth T., 19, Oklahoma

We could jam together and sing the blues. —Ty H., 17, Washington state

Take him scuba diving, 'cause he loves the ocean and fish. I'd love for him to see the beauty of the ocean reefs. —Jill B., 18, Florida

Well, my brother can't fly on planes 'cause he doesn't do well around a lot of people or in tight places. So on my day, I take him to Disneyland. I think he would really like that and everyone has to go to Disneyland sometime in their life. ☺ —Alisa A., 18, Oregon

140 ★ If you had just one day when your sibling didn't have a disability, what would you choose to do on that day?

I would just want to hang out with him and get to know him better. You know, just talk as two regular people do. So he could understand a bit more about me and I could understand more on him. —Daniel C., 17, Illinois

Take her somewhere that isn't wheelchair accessible, do something she normally couldn't do. We would also go somewhere so she could taste a bunch of foods she has never been able to have. —Amber C., 13, California

Take him dirt biking, driving, BMX biking, and all sorts of cool stuff like that. —Tyler L., 15, Arizona

Talk. I would want to tell her about everything "normal" sisters talk about. I would want to fill her in on everything I have done in my life that I never told her. I would confide in her. I would want to fight over the bathroom or the curling iron. —Emily D., 18, Virginia

I would take Alex out for coffee and to the music and bookstore, so that we could have really long and deep conversations about anything and everything (especially music!). —Stephanie B., 16, Maryland

I would take my sister to the mall. We would party and shop all day long. I would show her what things I like to do. —Emily N., 17, Oregon

I would take her on some roller coasters she can't get on. —Nancy R., 13, California

The most social thing that I could think of--- maybe like a frat party. haha. —Laura P., 15, Virginia

What would the reader do?

I wouldn't choose what had one day to do. I wanted to do. If she would let her decide what she wanted to do. —Catherine C., 13, California

Babysitting when I want to do something else. —Kayla L., 13, Arizona

What's the toughest thing about being a sib?

I don't know if this is part of being a sib or just a part of life. But it is the uncertainty, not knowing what's coming next, and the feeling of vulnerability if something does happen and that you're open to being really hurt. Also, not knowing if my little brother will wake up the next morning or when a kiss I give him will be the last. —Rebekah C., 17, California

Not being able to predict what his life is going to be like in the future. I have no idea what he's going to be doing, where he'll live, who he'll be living with, and what kind of role I'm going to play in his life. I worry about it a lot... maybe the extra worrying is the toughest thing about being a sibling. —Stephanie B., 16, Maryland

Having to worry about the future of your sib. —Melisandre P., 14, Kansas

Admitting that you don't always like your sib and that sometimes you yell at them and treat them unfairly. It's weird, but you can't fight with them like you could with a typically developing kid and so you are forced to share your anger with someone else, and then you feel like an idiot. —Caitlin M., 14, Maryland

The responsibility definitely stinks. I get few privileges for all the work I do for my family and my little brother. —Daniel C., 17, Illinois

Having to put up with him all the time. After a while, I became the second mom-- always helping my dad and mom. —Brooke W., 13, Virginia

Telling people I've just met that I have an older brother and them asking me where he goes to school. Then I have to explain that he has Down syndrome. I feel like they pity us. —Katie J., 19, Illinois

Seeing her suffer when there's nothing I can do except comfort her. —Leah K., 13, Iowa

Sometimes my family can't do things as a family because of the wheelchair. Like when we go to a basketball game, we can't all sit together because one parent and Sarah has to sit in handicapped seating. —Megan D., 14, Michigan

Standing back and watching all the other "typical" kids grow up while your sibling is left in the dust. It's hard to watch all the other kids learn to walk, to talk, and to ride bikes before your sibling does. It's a feeling that is very hard to put into words. —Stephie N., 15, Arizona

I think it's watching her fail. The look in her eyes would send a full-grown man into tears. Or her being denied opportunities that other kids have. —Erin G., 14, Alberta

Not getting the attention I was used to. —Dave S., 14, Michigan

Knowing that I will be able to do certain things someday that my sib probably won't get to experience, like going to college, driving, or even living on my own. —Emily P., 13, Indiana

Watching my sib go through treatments and not be able to do anything. —Lauren V., 14, Connecticut

The sacrifices you have to make. It means being flexible 24-7 and always being aware that there are often changes that need to be made. —Alli J., 15, Ohio

Dealing with everyday frustrations, like knowing that my brother isn't the smartest, most able person. Or the frustration I feel when my brother can't do something. Or how other people act towards him. And that I can't always help my brother—and many others, big and small. —Michelle M., 15, New Jersey

Always coming second to your sib. Often feelings and wants are put on the back burner so that things work out for your sib. —Amanda M., 19, Washington State

The questions from people, the stares. You've just gotta shut out the ignorant people, and focus on the beauty of your sib. —Katelyn C., 16, Virginia

Having to understand that she needs more attention and that she needs more help with things than I do at times. ☺ —Michelle O., 14, Virginia

Trying to understand why this is happening. —Britny G., 16, Missouri

Remaining patient with Jackie. Sometimes I forget who I am dealing with and lose my patience. When I do that, it only makes things worse. —Emily D., 18, Virginia

Seeing other twins together and the way they live their lives—seeing how close they are, and knowing that my sister and I will never be like that —Ariella M., 16, N.S.W.

Constantly having to understand. I'll adjust to a reality that I have to understand, and as soon as I have adapted, I have to adapt again. —Lindsay K., 15, California.

Supporting your sib—even when you'd really like to tear them apart because they're making you absolutely mad. —Miri L., 16, Illinois

Not being able to know what your sib would be like if they didn't have the disability. —Laura P. 15, Virginia

That I can't do anything to help him or make him better. Feeling helpless is tough. —Alisa A., 18, Oregon

Accepting the fact that you are different than most of the people you know and you shouldn't try to be them. —Catherine C., 13, California

Reader, this space for you!

Having to grow up and be a caretaker of your brother or sister. You become like a second parent and, as a parent, you want to see your child grow, prosper, and be able to enjoy everything there is about childhood. However, with the sib being disabled, you don't get to see that and there's not much you can do about it. —Elizabeth T., 19, Oklahoma

When he throws temper tantrums and people look at you like "Aren't you going to do something?" And the truth is, there isn't anything we can do about it; we just have to let it pass. —Cassandra W., 15, Iowa

Having to stand up and stick up for Stephen even when he has totally embarrassed me. —Kevin T., 14, Virginia

Probably seeing how other people see Erik. They see him as stupid. I see him as smart, but challenged. We all have our challenges. —Emily J., 14, Colorado

"Does he speak French?" —Katelyn C., 16, Virginia

What's the weirdest question you've ever been asked about your sib?

"How does she eat chicken through that?" This was after I explained that she can't eat through her mouth, so she eats through a thin tube that goes straight to her stomach and mainly lives on liquid formula. —Amber C., 13, California

The weirdest question is also the most common and hardest to answer: "Is he (or she) OK?" Once we even had a personal care attendant applicant for Nathaniel and Sophia at our house who took one look at me and asked if I was OK—meaning normal! —Alethea R., 13, Minnesota

"What's wrong with her?" "NOTHING!!" is what I want to shout at them. Then, my patience kicks in and I calmly explain that just because Adrienne may not be the same as them does not mean something is "wrong" with her. —Lauren O., 16, Georgia

"Is what he has contagious?" A younger kid, probably 5 years old asked me that once, so, of course, I sat down and explained everything to him. —Kevin T., 14, Virginia

"Can he at least count cards?" I guess this was in reference to the movie Rain Man. —Daniel C., 17, Illinois

Once at the airport, my brother was acting a little weird I guess--making a few noises and clapping. The attendant for the metal detectors asked us if he could walk through the detector. Why wouldn't he be able to do that? —Elizabeth T., 19, Oklahoma

"You shower with her?" It is a weird question to be asked because usually children only shower together when they are young, but my sister still can't shower on her own. Sometimes I have to help shower her and it is just easier to get in and shower with her. —Emily N., 17, Oregon

The weirdest thing is when people have no clue that we're related. Since I'm from Korea and Jeremy has blonde hair and blue eyes I guess it's a little hard to tell. One time this lady asked me, "Are you Jeremy's assistant?" I was like, "Oh, no. I'm his sister." —Lindsay D., 17, North Carolina

"What's the name of her disease?" (It's not a disease, let me explain again...) —Erin G., 14, Alberta

My sister was sitting in her wheelchair when someone came up to me and asked "Can she walk?" —Megan D., 14, Michigan

It was more of a comment. "Oh, I just figured that he'd gotten addicted to something and it messed him up." —Maggie W., 17, Wisconsin

☺ —Michelle O., 14, Virginia

"What's pretty bizarre!! I just think that's she can't learn.

When people ask if my sister goes to school. Just because she has a disability, doesn't mean

People don't really ask questions. They just stare. It's way worse. —Caitlin M., 14, Maryland

"Do sometimes you wish he wasn't your brother?" I think it's completely crazy someone would actually ask me that! —Rebekah C., 17, California

"Does she go to bed?" I think the person meant to ask how she went to bed – but it came out the wrong way and it was quite funny at the time! —Ariella M., 16, N.S.W.

"Does he speak English?" I was ready to smack him 'cause it was someone who knows that we only speak English in our house. —Kathryn C., 14, Illinois

I had a picture of her on my binder at school. And this girl was like, "Is that your brother?" —Margaret C., 14, Illinois

How about meanest? It would have to be "Is she retarded?" —Kate F., 13, Wisconsin.

Someone asked me if she was speaking Spanish when really she was speaking English. They just couldn't understand her. —Teresa H., 13, Minnesota

"your brother has a girlfriend!?" It's like people don't expect them to have feelings for other people too. —Alisa A., 18, Oregon

I haven't really been asked any weird questions. Most people don't really ask me anything at all—but I wish people would ask instead of wonder. —Kristin S., 19, Virginia

Well, because I have two sibs people often think that my parents did something wrong. I understand that, but one time an adult asked me if my parents were related...that was really ignorant —Ali N., 18, Massachusetts

Reader, write where you can!

"Why is she stupid?" One of the reasons that it is so stupid is the kid that asked never saw her. —Dave S., 14, Michigan

"Does he eat carrots?" —Christiana R., 13, Wisconsin

one guy asked if my parents were retarded and that's how Harry was born with a syndrome. —Alicia F., 17, Illinois.

My dog once chewed up the handle of my brother's rolling backpack. We were standing in the school carpool line one day when a girl walked up to me and asked, "Did your brother chew that up?" —Nora G., 13, Virginia

I've been asked if he was taking medicine to make his Down syndrome go away, or if someone could catch Down syndrome. —Katie J., 19, Illinois

"Are you twins?" —Lydia Q., 13, Massachusetts

"What's his name?" And then I say, "Why don't you ask him?" —Emily J., 14, Colorado

He could have the girlfriend he has wanted forever. —Cassie W., 13, Colorado

If you had one wish for your brother or sister, what would it be?

Normality. —Allison S., 17, Connecticut

I wrote a poem and dedicated it to Nathaniel and Sophia for this question. I'm kind of an amateur poet, and I think sometimes poems answers questions better than prose does:

Wherever you may on life's winding paths tread

May you never know fear or dread.

I wish you could know

That wherever you go

For your happiness I long.

May those you walk among

Embrace you and love you

As I do.

—Alethea R., 13, Minnesota

I would wish that Vickie would understand that no matter what happens, no matter what disability she has, she will always be my big sister and I will always love her. She is the best big sister anyone could have and she is also my best friend! —Michelle O., 14, Virginia

I wish that David would have someone fall in love with him and he would fall in love with her too. And they would live happily ever after. —Katie J., 19, Illinois

For my brother to meet Justin Timberlake. He idolizes him. It would be great to see him so happy. I mean he gets happy over getting a toy he wants, I would want to see his reaction when he met Justin. —Alisa A., 18, Oregon

For his behaviors to start changing for the better. Or to have him meet Michael Jordan. —Katelyn C., 16, Virginia

That he would be healthy, happy, and supported financially for the rest of his life. —Alicia F., 17, Illinois

That he's always as happy as he is now and able to live a full life and find a woman who is perfect for him, get married, and maybe have kids someday. And to know he has some great purpose. —Rebekah C., 17, California

I just hope that my sib has a successful life. That he makes goals, and then achieves them. I have faith in him and I know he will. —Nicole P., 15, Pennsylvania

I wish that my brother never lets anyone stop him from doing what he wants to do. I wish that people treat him like a typical person and not look at him as simply a disability. —Michelle D., 16, New Jersey

To be happy—which I think she is most of the time. —Megan D., 14, Michigan

I wish that Monica could talk because then she could say if she is in pain, happy, or sad. —Martha P., 13, Connecticut

It would be that she is always taken care of, no matter what. —Matt M., 15, Illinois

That she didn't have Down syndrome. —Lydia Q., 13, Massachusetts

That he could have speech, however poor it might be. Sometimes I feel like communicating with my brother is a guessing game, and I'm never sure if I understand what he wants or has said. Speech would open up his world like nothing else--and I could get to know my own brother even better. —Maggie W., 17, Wisconsin

That my brother could walk. He's not able to do a lot of things that he wishes he could do because he is in a wheelchair. —Emily P., 13, Indiana

I wish that my little brother would be a regular kid his own age instead of an autistic boy. I think if he were normal so many more opportunities would be available to him. —Daniel C., 17, Illinois

Just happiness and financial security. —Jemma J., 18, Berkshire

I want him to wake up some mornings and not feel that he has any limitations. Nora G., 13, Virginia

For Alex to be able to live his dreams. He has so many ideas and goals that he wants to pursue—I just want him to be happy and achieve his goals. —Stephanie B., 16, Maryland

That Matthew could talk and tell me what he did during the day, what his dreams are, stuff like that. —Britny G., 16, Missouri

For her to grow up and be happy with what she does with her life. And if that's collecting grocery carts in the parking lot of the nearby Fry's, then by God, I hope she loves it and has fun doing it. —Stephie N., 15, Arizona

My brother loves ball games. I wish he could play in the NBA. Kat F., 16, Washington State

If would wish that she always be happy with what she has. I think that the feeling of being unsatisfied is terrible and I would hate for her ever to feel like that. —Ariella M., 16, N.S.W.

To understand that life is not bad, even though some times bad things happen, even to a good life. —Lauren V., 14, Connecticut

To get rid of her arthritis so she can be taller. —Nancy R., 13, California

To have all the bonfires, golf cart rides, and anything else he wants all the time, and to always be safe. —Kathryn C., 14, Illinois

Reader's wish . . .

I wish she just knew how much I loved her because I don't think she knows. —Margaret C., 14, Illinois

For her to have some place to stay when my parents are no longer able to take care for her. I would wish that this environment would help her learn and stay on the right track. —Emily N., 17, Oregon

That he would be able to live a near-normal life, on a diet that is not special, not have seizures, not have behavior problems, but still be my sweet little brother that I love. —Cassandra W., 15, Iowa

For him to always be taken care of and never picked on or called names. —Leslie C., 16, Washington State

What's the one question we should have asked but didn't? (And what's your answer?!)

Where do you see your sib in 10 years? I see Jeremy happy and with a small part time job. He loves working with people and he is especially excited when his paycheck comes. At 28, he is no doubt living large. If he can afford it, he'll definitely have that built-in movie theatre he's been dreaming about. —Lindsay D., 17, North Carolina

Did you have any fun at all doing this? LOL. And the answer is most definitely YES! —Lindsay K., 15, California.

Do you ever feel really scared or want to cry when you think about you sib's disorder? Yes, I do. Every night almost I think about it and cry myself to sleep. —Leah K., 13, Iowa

Does life ever just suck? The answer is yes because it seems like people don't understand. —Margaret C., 14, Illinois

If you play an instrument, what is it? I play clarinet in a school band and piano at home. —Mandi D., 13, Wisconsin

Do you go to the same school as your sib? If so what is it like? Yes, my brother and I go to the same school. Being in the same school is mostly nice, and I keep an eye out for him a lot. But he embarrasses me in front of all of my friends, he likes to mimic me and annoy me until I get mad. Most of the teachers at my school baby him, and I hate that! —Emily P., 13, Indiana

What is your favorite book? The Wizard of Oz —Alicia F., 17, Illinois.

If you could be a superhero, what would your name be, and what would your powers be? Answer: I would be Captain Optimism, and I'd make everyone happy, all the time!! —Stephanie B., 16, Maryland

What are your favorite sports? NFL Football, Cheerleading, Soccer, Baseball, Basketball, Hockey. —Katelyn C., 16, Virginia

How do you feel when you hear people making fun of you bro/sis? It makes me soooo mad!! I can't stand it!! Especially when it is right in front of my sib. They just disgust me! I just want to give them a piece of my mind! —Michelle M., 15, New Jersey

Do you enjoy answering all these questions? Yes! It is allowing me to take time to reflect on my life and think of ways to help others. —Carly H., 17, Georgia

How do you cope with being a sib? I cope by using words and pictures. Whether it's drawing, or journaling, or talking to someone, I try to vent in a way that won't hurt myself or others around me, and only in ways that I won't regret later. —Alli J., 15, Ohio

What is the most heartbreaking thing you have ever heard your sib say? "I'm trying to help myself but I can't." —Kate F., 13, Wisconsin.

What would you want to tell the siblings or family members of a disabled baby about what they are going to face? It may seem like the end of the world right now, but it's not. You have been blessed with a wonderful miracle that will change your life for the best. You will soon see things much differently and you will experience a love you have never felt before. Try to stay strong during hard times. Talk to family members about your worries or fears; the chances are that they have the same worries and fears, and talking helps so much. Make a support web—with family members, friends, people from your spiritual group—or find a support group like SibKids or a group for parents or grandparents. Never be afraid to speak about anything on your mind. These people really understand what you're going through and all the hardships and joys you're having raising your new baby. Never take a day with them for granted. Love them as much as you can. And never ever, ever give up. —Rebekah C., 17, California

What is your favorite book series? Invasion cycle by J. Robert King or The Dark Tower series by Stephen King. —Calen P., 14, Michigan

Reader, what about you?

What is your favorite food? My favorite food is red peppers. Red peppers are sweet but not too sweet, crunchy but not too crunchy, and juicy but not too juicy. —Monica R., 15, Massachusetts

What flavor/type of ice cream would you want to make? I would make a pizza flavored ice cream. It would be tomato sauce and creamy cheese with bits of pepperoni in the mix. I'd call it Pizza Pizzazz Puree. —Brooke W., 13, Virginia

Do you have any pets? I have two longhaired dachshunds, Joy and Rooney, and they are a huge love for my brother. They are the best dogs. —Cassie W., 13, Colorado

What is your favorite snack? Easy Mac! —Melisandre P., 14, Kansas

What's your favorite game of all time? The Sims—with all the expansion packs. Anything can happen and it's always a surprise. —Kathryn C., 14, Illinois

Who's your favorite band? Simple Plan. —Ashley S., 13, Minnesota

How capable are your parents to get help or help your sib? My Mom is an occupational therapist so she helps my sister a lot. Both my parents are very patient and I am constantly amazed at the things they can help her do. —Erin G., 14, Alberta

What motto do you live by? I live by "Everything happens for a reason." Think about it. It's true. —Emily N., 17, Oregon

Who's your hero, and why? My dad's my hero. He's raised 2 kids by himself for over 15 years. He's a good guy and he never gave up. He does a lot for us. —Leslie C., 16, Washington state

What's something that makes you smile every day? My dog, Lauren V., 14, Connecticut

What is one thing you never want to do? Grow up. —Megan D., 18, Texas

"Don't worry, be happy!" —Carly H., 17, Georgia

Leave us with a good quote—or lyric:

"Everyone is unique ...just like everyone else." —Emily N., 17, Oregon

"I have been blessed /And I feel like I've found my way /I thank God for all I've been given /At the end of every day /I have been blessed with so much more than I deserve /To be here with the ones that love me /To love them so much it hurts /I have been blessed." --Martina McBride, song "Blessed," written by Hilary Lindsey, Troy Verges, and Brett James (did I give enough credit?). —Alethea R., 13, Minnesota

"Life is truly a ride. We're all strapped in, and no one can stop it. As you make each passage from youth to adulthood to maturity sometimes, you just hang onto the bar in front of you. But the ride is the thing. I think the most you can hope for at the end of the ride is that your hair's messed up, you're out of breath, and you didn't throw up." --Jerry Seinfeld. —Michelle D., 16, New Jersey

"Hey Dad, Look at me, think back and talk to me, did I grow up according to plan? And now I try hard to make it, I just want to make you proud; I'm never going to be good enough for you. And nothing's alright cuz we lost it all and nothing lasts forever I'm sorry I can't be perfect. Now it's just too late and we can't go back I'm sorry I can't be perfect!" --"Perfect" by Simple Plan. —Ashley S., 13, Minnesota

"Ladies and Gentlemen take my advice; pull down your pants and slide on the ice" --from the TV comedy series M*A*S*H. — Daniel C., 17, Illinois

"Be the change you wish to see in the world." --Gandhi. —Emily D., 18, Virginia

"Don't cry because it's over, smile because it happened." This quote has helped me through some hard times. —Amelia C., 18, Minnesota

"Life is hard. After all, it kills you." --Katherine Hepburn. —Kat F., 16, Washington State

"A silver lining sometimes isn't enough to make some wrongs seem right." --Creed, "Children Don't Stop Dancing." —Kate F., 13, Wisconsin.

"Everybody poops." —Caitlin M., 14, Maryland

"No one talks to him about how he lives; he thinks that the choices he makes are just his. Doesn't know he's a leader with the way he behaves, and others will follow the choices he's made. He lives on the edge; he's old enough to decide. His brother who wants to be him is just nine; he can do what he wants, because it's his right, the choices he makes change a nine-year-old's life. Heroes are made when you make a choice, you could be a hero, heroes do what's right, you could be a hero, you might save a life, you could be a hero. You could join the fight for what's right, for what's right, for what's right." --"Hero" by Superchic[k]. —Alli J., 15, Ohio

"Don't let anyone look down on you because you are young, but set an example for the believers in speech, in life, in love and in purity." --1 Timothy 4:12 NIV. —Christiana R., 13, Wisconsin

"Any act of exclusion is an act against all of humanity." --Fr. Neil McGarrity; Glasgow, Scotland. —Stephie N., 15, Arizona

"It's all good." ☺ —Michelle O., 14, Virginia

"Shake off that nervous twitch and feel your strength/Stand astride the width and walk the length/Step into joy. Walk into light. /Stand tall and be yourself." --"Fly By Night" by Ian Anderson. —Nicole P., 15, Pennsylvania

"Hey, my friend, it seems your eyes are troubled... care to share your time with me? Would you say you're feeling low, and so a good idea would be to get it off your mind... see, you and me have a better time than most can dream, have it better than the best, so can pull on through... whatever tears at us, whatever holds us down, and if nothing can be done, we'll make the best of what's around." -- "Best of What's Around," by the Dave Matthews Band. —Stephanie B., 16, Maryland

"You always dress in yellow, When you wanna dress in gold, Instead of listnin' to your heart, You do just what you're told. You keep waiting where you are for what you'll never know, So let's just get into your car and go, baby, go!" --"Why Not" by Hilary Duff. —Lauren V., 14, Connecticut

"We all wear masks...metaphorically speaking." --From "The MASK" with Jim Carey. —Erin G., 14, Alberta

"God is with us always thru the good and bad!!!! —Mandi D., 13, Wisconsin

"One day you'll come to me and ask me what's more important: You or my life. I'll say my life and you'll walk away never knowing that you are my life..." —Kaleigh H., 16, New Hampshire

"I believe in Karma what you give is what you get returned / I believe you can't appreciate real love until you've been burned / I believe the grass is no more greener on the other side / I believe you don't know what you've got until you say goodbye." --"Affirmation" by Savage Garden. —Amanda M., 19, Washington State

"We all take different paths in life, but no matter where we go, we take a little of each other everywhere." -- Tim McGraw. —Amy McK., 16, Tennessee

"Life isn't measured by the number of breaths we take, but by the number of moments that take our breath away." —Lauren O., 16, Georgia

"I never felt too good but in this world who would /I was always thinkin' somethin' wasn't right /But then you came along and helped me sing a song and /now I feel OK I hope it can stay this way." --From "Good Thing" by Reel Big Fish. —Monica R., 15, Massachusetts

"Lean on me when you're not strong and I'll be your friend. I'll help you carry on." —Bill Withers. —Megan D., 14, Michigan

We could learn a lot from crayons: some are sharp, some are pretty, some are dull, some have weird names and all are different colors; but they all have to learn to live in the same box. --Author Unknown. —Kelsea R., 15, New Hampshire

Reader's favorite quote or lyric?

A woman came up to Gandhi and asked him to tell her son to stop eating sugar. Gandhi responded by telling her, "Come back in three days and I will." She came back in three days and he told her son to stop eating sugar. Afterwards, she asked Gandhi why he needed three days before he could answer. He said, "I had to stop eating sugar myself." —Ty H., 17, Washington State

"You know the world is off tilt when the best rapper is a white guy, the best golfer is a black guy, the tallest basketball player is Chinese, and Germany doesn't want to go to war." --Charles Barkley. —Megan D., 18, Texas

"The most pathetic person in the world is someone who has sight but has no vision." —Helen Keller. —Laura P., 15, Virginia

"If you're going through hell, keep going." -- Winston Churchill. And: "My momma always said life is like a box of chocolates; you never know what you're gonna get."--from Forest Gump. —Catherine C., 13, California

"Everything has beauty, but not everyone sees it." – Confucius. Also, "I'm not giving up, No, going to stand up and shout it!" --"Workin' It Out" by Hilary Duff —Teresa H., 13, Minnesota

"Yea, though I walk through the valley of the shadow of death, I shall fear no evil for thou art with me. Your staff and rod uphold me." --Psalm 23. —Leah K., 13, Iowa

"Believe that life is worth living and your belief will help create the fact." --James Truslow Adams. —Rebekah C., 17, California

We take love where we find it. But sometimes it takes a stronger heart to walk away. --Unknown. (This was the hardest question 'cause I have many favorite quotes and lyrics.) —Kathryn C., 14, Illinois

"Great is your mercy towards me. Your loving kindness towards me. Your tender mercy I see. Day after day." --From "Great Is Your Mercy" by Donnie McClurkin. —Elizabeth T., 19, Oklahoma

"Not everything that can be counted counts, and not everything that counts can be counted." --Albert Einstein. Also, "The only normal people are the ones that you don't know very well." --Joe Ancis). —Ariella, 16, N.S.W.

"Love makes the world go 'round." --The PowerPuff Girls. —Nora G., 13, Virginia

"Don't laugh at me, don't call me names, don't get your pleasure from my pain. In God's eyes, we're all the same. Some day we'll all have perfect wings. Don't laugh at me." --Mark Willis, "Don't Laugh at Me." —Britny G., 16, Missouri

Question: "If Heaven exists, when you get to the pearly gates, what would you like to hear God say?" Johnny Depp: "Wow." —On "Inside The Actor's Studio." —Allison S., 17, Connecticut

"Those who matter don't mind and those who mind don't matter." --Dr. Seuss. —Alicia F., 17, Illinois.

152 ★ Leave us with a good quote or lyric:

"No Regrets." —Matt M., 15, Illinois

"The future stands not there like a statue to be uncovered, but lies like clay in our hands to be shaped." -Florene Stewart Poyadue. —Emma F., 15, Michigan

"If we wrapped up against the cold, we wouldn't feel other things, like the bright tingle of the stars, or the music of the Aurora, or the best of all the silky feeling of moonlight on our skin. It is worth being cold for that." — Philip Pullman, "The Golden Compass." —Maggie W., 17, Wisconsin

"Be not afraid of going slowly; be afraid only of standing still." -- Chinese Proverb. —Lindsay D., 17, North Carolina

"Live and let live." —Dave S., 14, Michigan

"Love like you've never loved before, dance like no one's watching, and live like you're going to die tomorrow!" — Melisandre P., 14, Kansas

"Violence is not the answer!" —Martha P., 13, Connecticut

"Life's a dance...you learn as you go." — Cassie W., 13, Colorado

"The time is always right to do what is right." --Martin Luther King, Jr. —Leslie C., 16, Washington State

"The hottest places in hell are reserved for those, who in times of great moral crisis remain indifferent." --"The Inferno" by Dante. —Miri L., 16, Illinois

"Hearts will never be practical until they can be made unbreakable." --The Wizard of Oz. --Katelyn C., 16, Virginia.

"When you find the person you want to spend the rest of your life with, you want the rest of your life to start right away."--From "When Harry Met Sally." —Katie J., 19, Illinois

"Worrying does not empty tomorrow of its troubles, it empties today of its strength." --Corrie Ten Boom. —Emily I., 15, Washington State

"Life is like a shit sandwich and it's always lunch time." —Cassey C., 15, Southland, N.Z.

"Honesty is the best part of any art form. If you don't have that, you're kidding yourself and your listener." --Billie Joe Armstrong. —Ali N., 18, Massachusetts

"I have a dream or two of my own-- we all should." --Coretta Scott King. —Nancy R., 13, California

"Wrinkles should merely indicate where smiles have been." -Mark Twain. —Emily J., 14, Colorado

About the Editor:

Don Meyer is the director of the Sibling Support Project of The Arc of the United States. Don is probably best known for creating Sibshops, lively programs just for young brothers and sisters of kids with special needs. There are over 200 Sibshops in eight countries. Don also created SibKids and SibNet, no-cost listservs for young and adult brothers and sisters, which allow hundreds of siblings from around the world to connect with their peers.

As a sought-after speaker, Don has conducted hundreds of workshops on siblings, fathers, and grandparents of children with special needs and trainings on the Sibshop model throughout the United States, Canada, Ireland, England, Italy, New Zealand, and Japan.

Don is the senior author and editor of four other books: **SIBSHOPS, UNCOMMON FATHERS, LIVING WITH A BROTHER OR SISTER WITH SPECIAL NEEDS**, and **VIEWS FROM OUR SHOES**.

Don is married to Terry De Leonardis, a special education preschool teacher and consultant. They are the proud parents of four children: Gina, Angela, Tony, and Rosie. With a wonderful family and the greatest job in the world, Don considers himself one lucky guy.

To learn more about Sibshops, SibKids, SibNet, workshops, and the other activities of the Sibling Support Project, visit:

www.thearc.org/siblingsupport

or simply google "Sibling Support Project."